THOUGHTS

... for the Adept - 1

Sermons of Yogi Ashwini

Published by

Dhyan Foundation
A-80, South Extension Part II, New Delhi - 49
+91-11-26253374, +91-99999567895
info@dhyanfoundation.com
www.dhyanfoundation.com

Printed in India by

Guide Offset Printers

Print Date: April 2014

₹ 450

ISBN 978-93-82890-01-0

THOUGHTS
... for the Adept - 1

Sermons of Yogi Ashwini

FOREWORD

Creation consists of many aspects, some are perceivable by the five senses and for some, higher senses are required which require opening of the third eye. Today's men being ruled by desire have little inclination to go beyond the realm of five senses and their objects. Through these sermons I have tried to expand the realm of desires of people so that the quest to access the final frontier sets in and the journey of the spirit takes a new dimension.

I have picked up concepts and critically discussed the cause and effect of higher senses and what lies beyond the realm of five senses. The book is for the people who have a little background of *yog* and for those who want to know beyond the realm of five senses.

- Yogi Ashwini

CONTENTS

Foreword v
GURU 1
Accessing your Guru 11
Shakti of an Individual and Guru Shakti 19
Yog: Priority, not an Option 31
Importance of Kriya 35
Anubhav 43
Pitfalls and Progression in Sadhna 49
Complexities of Ashtang Yog 59
Satya 69
Brahmacharya 77
Tattva Gyan and Atma Gyan 83
Leading a Spiritual Life? 91
Dhyan 95
The Purpose of Dhyan and Mantras 105
Performing a Havan 113
The Process to Achieve Sri 123
Pradakshina Kriya 133
Siddhasan and a Straight Spine, Pre-requisites for Yog 137
Bhakti Yog 143
A Thousand Names of Lord Shiv 147
Sakshatkar of Shiv 151
Everyday has its Shakti 157
Devs and Devis in your Spine 163
The Beginning of Creation 171
Yog and Yugs 179
Human Desires and the Four Vedas 187
On Makar Sankranti... 195
Glossary 207
Some Characters and Places 216
About the Author 220
More Books by the Author 222

SERMON 1

GURU

“ When a being finds a Guru, there are certain indications for it. The first indication is that there occur certain changes in your body- it starts looking the way you always desired. Secondly, any imbalance or disease in the body, disappears. You cease to fall ill. And the third indicator is that you start experiencing the energies that run this creation. ”

1

Many people ask me if they can have more than one *Guru*. Let us first understand what a *Guru* is. *Guru* is not a human, nor a body, *Guru* is energy. When you look at your *Guru*, you see the *swaroop* of that energy. You will not see his/her physical form but something else. It is this energy that is called *Guru*. So you cannot have multiple *Gurus*, because eventually it is just one energy.

Meeting the *Guru* is dependent on your *karmas.* Even if the soul yearns, but you do not have the *karmas*, you cannot meet your *Guru*. People go on searching for a *Guru* at various places and get many kinds of experiences and yet the one experience that is meant for them, does not happen because they do not have the *karmas*. If the *karmas* allow, and that moment comes when you find your *Guru*, you will not see it written on his/her face that "I am a *Guru*". It doesn't happen that way. When a being finds a *Guru*, there are certain indications for it. The first indication is that there occur certain changes in your body — it starts looking the way you always desired. Secondly, any imbalance or disease in the body, disappears. You cease to fall ill. And the third indicator is that you start experiencing the energies that run this creation.

There are different *shrenis* of *Guru*. You get a *Guru* as per your individual capacity. It happens at times that in a family there already is a *Guru* whom everybody is expected to follow. But sometimes such a person may be born to the family who may not have the *karmas* for the said *Guru*. His/her *karmas* may be higher or lower with respect to that *Guru* and hence he/she may not be able to relate to this *Guru*. In that case, he/she must be allowed to go his/her own way. If you stop him/her at that time, you will be spoiling your own *karmas*. That person will not get his/her experiences from where you are getting yours because his/her energy level is different.

There is no competition among the *Gurus*. *Adi Guru* is only one and it is Him that you see in every *Guru*, irrespective of their physical form. You'll see the same radiance, the same light, the same *mantras* and the same energy. When that time comes to go from one *Guru* to another then you don't decide it on your own, that decision is taken by your *Guru*. The *Guru,* understanding that this energy has a different route, sends you in the direction that is appropriate for you. And when he does that then you must walk that path only, not any other.

You must be absolutely sure when you make someone your *Guru*, and never rush into making one. Once you call someone a *Guru*, if you have that feeling (*Guru bhaav*) towards that energy and if after that you disrespect him/her or change your path — then you will never get a *Guru* again in this lifetime. Then the energy of the *Guru* leaves you, even if you continue walking with him. If you have disrespected the *Guru*, it means that you do not have the capacity to have a *Guru*. In that case, you do not need a *Guru*, you should continue with the experiences that you have taken birth for.

A *Guru-shishya* relationship is always one to one, you have to make a *Guru* on an individual level. *Guru* is never made in masses. A *Guru* has certain tasks to complete and if he is unable to complete those tasks then he cannot become a *Guru*. In addition to those tasks, the *Guru* has certain responsibilities. One of the major responsibilities of the *Guru* is to monitor the *shishya*, not monthly, daily or hourly, but every moment. Let me give you a small example for this. There's a member of the Foundation who is in Germany. I'd given him some *mantras* for the *chakras*. The *beej mantra for Mooladhar chakra* is "*Lam*". Now, this person is always in a hurry since his job is very demanding so he heard "*Lam*" as "*Nam*". And for 4-5 days he kept chanting "*Nam, Nam, Nam*". He didn't tell me. But I felt that something wrong is happening somewhere. After a couple of days, he called up and told me that he wanted to ask something because he had seen me in his dream the day before in which I told him that he was doing the wrong chant. So, if there is *Guru bhaav* in you and if you are doing something wrong, then you will be informed of it. And at that time you have to listen to it, no matter how strongly you feel that what you are doing is right, but if you are told, then you have to leave it.

If you have a *Guru*, and if you have *Guru bhaav* in you, then the *Guru* monitors you every second, every moment. There is not a moment of your life which your *Guru* is not aware of. At times, I get amused when people walk up to me and make up stories when the truth is something else. It is foolishness to think that the *Guru* is unaware, for the one who is unaware of the events of your life is also unaware of the subtler worlds, and is not your *Guru*. Never think of your *Guru* as a human or a body, that is when you make a mistake. Till the time you do not have the capacity to think of the *Guru* as being beyond a human body, you must not be in a hurry to make a *Guru*. But once you do, then you must not make such errors, else it shall affect your entire lifetime.

Guru is not the body and he is always in a body. It doesn't happen that the *Guru* is outside the body or has left the body. When a *Guru* leaves the body, then he takes some other body. It is necessary for a *Guru* to be in a body but a *Guru* is not merely a body.

The *kshamta* of a *Guru* is decided by *vairagya* or detachment. When you meet your *Guru* for the first time, then you feel a sense of detachment. And that detachment is felt within oneself as well as in the ones you see outside. Despite having everything around, being in complete *vaibhav,* there is a feeling of detachment. You feel that there is something different and then when you peep within yourself, you see the state of detachment. Whatever happens after that, are all indications. If nothing happens, then he/she is not your *Guru*.

Let me share an experience with you. There is a member of the Foundation in Karnataka. He is into construction business and he was facing many losses. He had a *Guru* who is no more in his body. Whenever he wrote to me (he writes really long mails), 20-25 lines would be in praise of his *Guru*, and the rest would describe the problems he is in. One after the other, his problems would solve, and he would come with another one. When this continued for six months, I finally wrote a mail to him and asked, "This question that you've asked me, did you ask your *Guru*? Did he not give you a solution for this?" As soon as he read this, he realised his folly. I wrote back to him that if he had a *Guru*, then what was the need for him to look elsewhere? So, then he wrote a very nice mail to me, "You have opened my eyes." It's been quite a while since then, but his problems are still continuing and he still sends me long mails describing them. So he 'thought' that I have opened his eyes, but they are still shut.

It is necessary to understand that if there is a *Guru*, then you do not need to go anywhere else. A *Guru* is not the body and the experiences that have to happen will only happen from there. *Guru* has to be in the body because what is outside the body is energy and in order to channelise it, a body is needed. So, a *Guru*, and that too in the body, is very essential to enter *yog*. If you are going somewhere, walking a particular path and you are getting the indications, then continue to walk that path, do not change it. If someone changes paths in between, then he is not able to reach anywhere, because there is no competition in the *Gurus*.

At times people ask me, "If my *Guru* stops me from coming to you then should I not come here?" To them I say, "In that case, you must not come here." Because what the *Guru* says is a *mantra* for you. *Dhyaan moolam Guru murti; puja moolam Guru padam; mantra moolam Guru vakyam, moksha moolam Guru kripa*.

The words of a *Guru* are *mantra* for you. If your *Guru* tells you something, you should not go back home and open books on it. Nothing happens from reading books, it is only your experience which counts. Your experience and *Guru* alone can remove the stones from your path. So, if there is progress somewhere, then don't leave that path. When you leave a *Guru* and go elsewhere without his permission, it amounts to disrespect to the *Guru*.

Let me tell you a story. Once there was a man who was very eager to find a *Guru*. He went to many places searching for the same. Finally, he met a saint in the Himalayas who was sitting in seclusion. He went and told him, "*Mahatmaji,* I want to make you my *Guru*." That *mahatma* was sitting in complete seclusion. He wasn't in a state to take that human as his *shishya.* Sometimes, it so happens that you reach a state of *vairagya* where you have to leave the person who is not able to walk with you. A person who cannot walk with you, whose state of *vairagya* doesn't match yours, you leave that person because it is not good for him to walk with you. Similar was the state of this *Guru* (*mahatma*). Since this gentleman did not have that state of detachment to match the *mahatma's*, the *mahatma* suggested to him to go to a temple in Banaras. "It is the temple of the Goddess. When you go there, you'll find your *Guru*. And when you see him, you'll recognise his energy. But after that, don't leave him, come what may." The gentleman obeyed and went to Banaras. While he was crossing a temple, he felt as though the earth beneath him was trembling. He felt a very strong surge of energy within himself. So he looked around and saw a *vairagi*, sitting near a temple chanting some *mantras*. He was in a very bad state, his clothes were torn.

This man saw him and thought to himself, "Oh, what a poor man he is. This cannot be my *Guru*. But I can feel some energy... the *mahatma* had asked me to come here but I can't see anything." He kept watching the *vairagi* who, after completing his chants, joined the row to receive *langar*. The *vairagi* was in such a bad state that other people sitting in the row asked him to leave, since they did not want to sit with him. He obliged them, got up and walked to a nearby dustbin; put his hand in it, ate whatever he got from there and started walking. Now the gentleman thought, "Probably the *mahatma* was referring to this man only, I must not leave him." He followed the *vairagi* into the jungle.

The *vairagi* asked him, "Why are you following me?"

The gentleman replied, "I wish to make you my *Guru*."

The *vairagi* then enquired, "What do you see in me that is like a *Guru*, what do you expect to get from me? Leave me, I do not have anything."

The man refused to leave saying, "A *mahatma* in the Himalayas had told me that I would feel some energy. When I first saw you, I felt that energy. I experienced something inside me that was real. So, I am certain that you are the one my *Guru* had told me about."

The *vairagi* replied, "No. I am not the one." And he again resumed walking. This man kept following him inside the jungle.

The *vairagi* again looked back and warned, "If you don't leave I'll break your head with a stone."

Though scared, the man continued following him. As they went a little further, it became dark. The *vairagi* picked up a stone and asked, "Are you leaving or should I break your head?"

So then this man said, "No, you look very dangerous. You can't be the one. It must be someone else." And he returned.

He came back and sat outside the temple for a week but found none. He did not get that experience again. He again went back from Banaras to Himalayas, to that *mahatma,* and said, "You lied to me. I went there and did not find anything. I just wasted my time." The *mahatma* asked, "You did not find anything?" The man answered, "No, I did not find anything. I sat there for a week." The *mahatma* replied, "That cannot be. Did you not find a *vairagi* there and go after him?" He said, "Yes, I did find him. And I did go after him. But he wasn't my *Guru*. He was about to break my head with a stone."

If there is Guru bhaav in you and if you are doing something wrong, then you will be informed of it. And at that time you have to listen to it, no matter how strongly you feel that what you are doing is right.

The *mahatma* replied, "You got scared and left him, despite my asking you not to. Then what respect did you give to my words? You set out looking for a *Guru*, but do you have the capacity to look for a *Guru*? If a stone scares you off, then what *Guru* can you find? He was indeed your *Guru*."

When you see a *Guru*, you do not see the appearance like beautiful hair, flowing beard or attractive robes nor do you get carried away by words and promises, because the *Guru* does not make promises, as you are the one who needs something from him, he needs nothing from you. You only feel the energy, and the radiance and attraction, which a *Guru* ought to have. If there is an experience of energy and if there are indications, then you know that he is your *Guru*. The one thing that you must never forget is that the *Guru* doesn't need you, you need the *Guru*. And after sometime when you start doing *yog sadhnas,* then the *Guru* needs you. But initially the *Guru* doesn't need anything from you, only later he needs *Guru seva*... And what *is Guru seva*? To walk on the path that the *Guru* has shown. Why? Because that is the path of his *Guru*. It is the path of his *Guru* that he lets you know of and if you walk that path, then it is the service of his *Guru* that is being carried out. No monetary transactions should happen between you and the *Guru*, he should not be selling you courses, and you buying them with the hope of salvation, because money is *maya* and a monetary transaction is tying you to that *maya*. A *Guru* releases you from the bonadages of *maya*, he does not tie you in it.

When you reach the state of making a *Guru*, then you do not keep any physical, emotional or financial relationship with the *Guru*. As soon as you make any physical relationship with your *Guru*, you start considering him/her as a normal person, because you can only have physical relationships with normal people. Isn't that so? You cannot make Lord *Krishna* your business partner, can you? Only if you have the state of *Radha*, if you have that kind of *vairagya* in you... only then can you understand *Krishna* as *Krishna* and only then *Krishna* can be a lover for you. Only one or two in lakhs have that state of *vairagya*. Know your state.

It is not difficult for the *Guru*. He has that state of *vairagya*. You cannot do it because somewhere you will start taking your *Guru* to be a normal person. And the moment you make the mistake of considering him a normal person, your birth becomes useless. And you are bound to make this mistake if you form a relationship. There was only one *Radha*, and there was only one *Parvati* who won *Shiv* as her consort.

Another mistake that people often make, is judging their *Guru*. In *Gita*, Lord *Krishna* has said that, "Judgement lies only in my hands, not yours". You cannot judge anyone. Never even attempt to judge the *Guru* because your *buddhi* does not have the capacity to understand the *Guru*. If it had, then would there have been any difference between you and your *Guru*?

A *Guru* gives you some tasks to do (*swadhyay*). The task given to you could be as simple as to get a bottle of juice from a shop. But were you able to go to that shop and get that bottle of juice? This task tells you whether or not you have the state for that *Guru*. Ninety per cent of people fail in this seemingly simple task. And if your *Guru* has given you a task and if you can complete it, then *moksha* is not very far from you. A *Guru* never gives work for himself; behind every task he gives, there is a purpose.

Let me give you a small example. Whenever I travel, an oven is always taken along to heat the food we get from outside to a very high temperature, before being given to me. Once I was traveling with dedicated group of Foundation members. These people made a small mistake of which even they were not aware of. The flow of their thought faltered for a moment. I saw it, but for them to notice it there had to be a sign. I hadn't eaten anything since morning. So they got something from the market, placed it in the oven, and started heating it. After sometime, there was a foul smell. When they checked, they saw that because they had placed the food in plastic containers, the plastic had melted into the food, making it inedible, and I had to sleep hungry.

I'll give you another example. There is a Foundation member, who is a pure vegetarian. Once, she was going to Europe, so I asked her to bring tinned fish. She was horrified at the idea and said that she wouldn't be able to get it. She asked me if she could get me cheese instead. I said, "Ok, get cheese. Doesn't matter." So she got me cheese from her trip. I asked her to read the label. The ingredients had cow's rennet. Rennet is extracted from the stomach of the cow after slaughtering it. So I asked her, "You could not get me fish but you've got me a dead cow?" I could not eat it and it had to be thrown away.

So, whenever the *Guru* gives you a task, there's always an aim behind it. The aim is to tell you where you are going wrong. It is just an indication for you.

Once you start getting the indications of the *Guru*, then there are tests. *Gurus* do not collect too many disciples, because when there is a *shishya,* then you have to carry his entire weight and walk. And you cannot carry everyone, just like that. You must have heard of a proverb, 'Don't change horses in the middle of a stream.' If in the middle of the stream, you start doubting the strength of the horse and if you jump onto another horse, you will drown. If you've sat once, then just see what happens, have some patience. If you have had some experiences earlier, which showed you the right way, then you are at the right place. Don't use your own *buddhi,* else you'll make mistakes.

Guru is not a body. It's an energy and you see it very clearly. When you sit with your eyes closed and do *dhyan* on the form of the *Guru*, then you do not see his physical form, you see the energy form. If someone asks you who your *Guru* is, and if you have one, then just ask the person to close his eyes and look at you and if he has the capacity, then he will be able to see the form of your *Guru* within you.

At times, people come to a *Guru* with a very strong thought/desire. Whenever you come to an evolved soul, do not ever make the mistake of asking for anything. If you'll ask me for something from your limited *buddhi*, that 'problem' you will surely get. Consider it a problem only, because when you ask for something from your limited *buddhi,* then it indeed is a problem. Once you get it, then you'll ask to get rid of it. Your *Guru* knows this. That is why, you do not ask for anything physical from your *Guru*. When you meet your *Guru*, then whatever is good for you, starts happening automatically. So you do not need to ask for, or say anything. It happens on its own. Whenever you ask for something and you get it, it is immediately followed by a test. If you fail the test, the connection breaks.

Making a *Guru* is a *sadhna*. One should never be in a hurry to make a *Guru*. Understand everything, test everything, all the aspects and then take the decision. But when you do, stay fixed on the thought of making the *Guru*, then, you must not take your eyes off, even for a moment. For this you need 100 per cent focus. When you give 100 per cent then you get 100 per cent. If you are not giving 100 per cent then you get 0 per cent. It is difficult, but in a *Guru-shishya* relationship, it is necessary. Because then even though the bodies are two, the soul is still one. And your background doesn't matter. Whether you are *vaishya, shudra, Kshatriya* or *brahmin*, it doesn't matter. You will not be differentiated on the basis of your income or the beauty of your body. Only your *karmas* will decide, nothing else matters. If you give your 100 per cent then no matter how you look and what your capacity is, you will get it.

This is the *mahima* and the *Shakti* of the *Guru* and when you have a *Guru* then nothing can touch you. Just remember,

Dhyan moolam Guru murti — Your *dhyan* should not be anywhere else but on the *Guru*.

Puja moolam Guru padam — There is certain energy at the feet. It radiates from there.

Mantra moolam Guru vakyam — If the *Guru* has asked you to get fish and if you are a vegetarian, you should still get it.

Moksha moolam Guru kripa — *Moksha* is not possible without the grace of the *Guru*.

Guru's grace is solely dependent on *Guru seva*. Service to the *Guru* is walking on the path shown by the *Guru*. And be very clear that if you've been asked to reach somewhere at 12 o'clock, and if you have an urgent board meeting at the same time, something that cannot be missed, then it will either be cancelled or it was not required for you to go there at all. Don't ever think that there's any physical energy that is stronger than this *atmic* energy. That can't be. Just try this sometime. But that is, when you have been asked by your *Guru*, not when you have assumed him to say so. I've heard many people say, "We thought you'll say this." There are so many people, who do so many things, without asking me, simply because they 'think' I'll stop them from doing it. If you are scared of asking me something, or you are doing it even after knowing that I have asked you not to, then, I would suggest, you don't do it. Rest is your birth and your *karma*.

It is necessary for a Guru to be in a body but a Guru is not merely a body.

Original/unedited pictures of manifestations in *havan* performed by *sadhaks* at *Dhyan Ashram*.

OM

A *havan* is a medium to interact with gods and goddesses. The practice involves making oblations to fire alongwith specific chants. The fire having the ability of transformation can transform the physical into the subtle and the *mantras* have the ability to manifest the ability and power of *devs* in the physical world and also have the power and ability to control nature and normal human physical lives.

SERMON 2

ACCESSING YOUR GURU

" *The capacity of the Guru is limitless for the shishya, he is willing to give it all away, but you should have the desire and capacity to receive it as well. Most people shy away, they come to me with tiny containers... I want to pour it all, but there is no space to pour!* "

2

In the 20 years of teaching *yog*, I have interacted with lots of spiritual aspirants — some come looking for solutions to their problems, some are seeking peace and happiness. Some want to add to their knowledge and some just want to try something new. Most of these people remain dissatisfied and leave the path. The experience of *yog* evades them because one can only get what they are looking for and none of the above is a search for *yog*.

Yog begins and ends at the feet of your *Guru*. *Guru* is the channel through which the *gyan* and experience of *yog* flows into the *shishya*. And to get a *Guru*, you need to have the intent for the *Guru*. That is, whoever you are going to, you must want to access him completely, whatever he is, his positives as well as negatives, only then can you reach somewhere because his positives and negatives are not for you to judge and if you are judging your *Guru*, you might as well read a book. The path of *yog* first leads to the *Guru* and then your *Guru* carries you on the journey that lies ahead. So before going to anyone for *yog*, be sure that you want to be that, only then can you get any experience from him.

What is experience? When I ask people if they have had any experience of *yog*, they tell me, they saw certain shapes and colours when they sat with their eyes closed... Even the mentally unsound see shapes and colours; the experience of *yog* is something else. Mentally sound and unsound, those with eyes and without, those with exceptional hearing abilities and those who are deaf, all those who are connected, experience the same things.

There is person at Dhyan Foundation who went for jet skiing with his friends, his ski turned over and he was stranded in the middle of the ocean with no one around to rescue him. He just remembered his *Guru* and out of nowhere a boat emerged and took him to the shore. In those ten minutes of being stranded in the ocean he got his experience... there was a complete transformation in him, he who could not see beyond himself and his social life, suddenly immersed himself into charity and service.

There is yet another person in the Foundation, who regularly lectures a huge crowd on *Bhagwad Gita*. His friend, who is well into his 70s, recently developed a serious ailment. He came to me, nervous and in a state of frenzy, asking me to help save his friend. I asked him, why just your friend? Why not thousands of others, who too are suffering? After all, *Gita* teaches *nishkaam karma* that is, helping whoever comes your way in a detached manner. He had no answer, he just asked me to help his friend live ten more years. Here was a man who preaches to the world the path of detachment, a slight problem in his own house, and he was in a state of complete mess, *Gita* forgotten. I wonder what would be happening to his students! This event explained to me the reason for the present state of the world, for here the teachers themselves have no faith in what they teach.

Yog is the process of *Guru* and *gyan* and it is beyond the understanding of the brain. In a matter of seconds a complete nobody can get so much *gyan* that he starts teaching me only and someone who had attained so many heights, reaches rock bottom. Till this process begins inside you, you will keep wandering in circles looking for solutions to your problems.

There were four kids who came to me to learn chess. They were fourth-class students who wanted to appear for an open tournament (where classes upto 12th were participating). The game of chess requires at least six to eight months of training and they had just three weeks. Nevertheless, they had complete faith in me and for those three weeks they came to my house every single day. At the end of the training, I accompanied them for the tournament. I would go with them every single day, excepting one day when I reached late. That very day, the instructor replaced one of the better players in their team with an extra, who was the son of a bureaucrat... No prize for guessing that the instructor had got a call from the top. The final result was 2-2 but the 4th class kids got half a mark less than their senior team, thanks to the 'call'. The 'call-business' is the most unfortunate thing in our country...

Imagine if 4th class students could match the capacity of their senior teams in just a matter of three weeks, there is no limit to what you can achieve if you have the focus. The capacity of the *Guru* is limitless for the *shishya*, he is willing to give it all away, but you should have the desire and capacity to receive it as well. Most people shy away, they come to me with tiny containers... I want to pour it all, but there is no space to pour! Their desire itself is so small —

some want to look good, some want to cure a disease, some others want to mend relationships and rest want to expand their business. That bureaucrat was only concerned that his son should sit there and play chess once; he had such a small desire, which got fulfilled. Wish he had asked for something more...

There was an *asur* called *Mali,* who did severe penance for Lord *Shiv* for many thousand years and was finally able to access him. But when he did, he asked him to be his bodyguard — that is what he wanted, to have Lord *Shiv* to guard his body. It pumped up his ego, but he did not realise that the body is perishable and can only be guarded till it exists, what after that? Despite accessing the ultimate force, he chose to make him his bodyguard. The thought pattern of an average person is no different from that *asur*...

Accessing your Guru means, you think of something and your Guru does it for you. No matter what that is. A Guru is ready to do anything for the shishya, but you need to have that connection, dedication and attraction that he cannot refuse you.

You want to access the infinite energy of nuclear power, but only to light a bulb.

You can choose to access the *Guru* in a particular aspect, but then you will only be able to reach till that aspect, and if that is a physical trait (which it most likely is, because with your limited five senses, you cannot think beyond the physical), just remember that the physical is temporary and destructible, it will perish sooner or later. There are two elderly people in the Foundation, who have been diagnosed with brain tumor. One wanted to open a big law firm and the other wanted a big farm. But within a period of a half an hour, when the doctor looked at the MRI and said 'brain tumor', their desire changed. No matter what your desire, the minute circumstances change even slightly, that desire will change indicating perishable nature of desire linked to the perishable body, both redundant. Therefore, it is best not to think with your limited *buddhi* and access your *Guru* in totality.

Accessing your *Guru* means, you think of something and your *Guru* does it for you. No matter what that is. A *Guru* is ready to do anything for the *shishya*, but you need to have that connection, dedication and attraction that he cannot refuse you, even if it is something as frivolous as guarding your body. There are only two ways to access your *Guru*, *bhakti* — that nothing else exists for you or *shakti* — if you tie your *Guru* with *shakti*, he will get tied. You need to decide which category you fall in and then walk just that path.

But both *bhakti* and *shakti* lead to ego, you need to be careful of that. Whenever you get something you try to show it off... Recently a lady got married and she came to visit me. Throughout the conversation, she had her hand waving. When she left, I asked the people around if there was something wrong with her hand. The reply came, "Did you not notice the diamond on her ring?"

So whatever you get, whether it is *Guru*'s *shakti* or *bhakti*, you will try to put it on display and show others how much ability you have. That is the time to exercise control and focus on just your path otherwise you will get carried away. The *shakti* of *bhakti* and your own *shakti*, both are there only to light up the path for you, so that you pick up some speed and instead of five seconds you reach in one second. The path is just one.

People tell me they want to do *yog* but when I ask them if they are following the five *yams*, they start looking here and there. You are at A and you have to reach B, the path is very small, all you need is to access your *Guru*. You can go straight and reach in five seconds or you can take zigzag routes of curing illness, mending relationships, to learn and understand etc — for even 100 years and still not make it. And you will take birth again on the route you had left and again keep wandering and again you will not reach your destination. I never asked for solutions from my teachers or my *Guru*, I never judged them, nor assessed them. I simply tried to access them completely in every aspect that they taught me. I know what I want and I want it completely, not even partially, because I just want that, nothing else. Unless you have this intensity, you will just keep going in circles searching for solution to your problems.

All your problems, big or small, are a result of your *karmas*. Your *Guru* has the capacity to remove those problems, but then you are taking your *Guru* as a means to solve your physical problems and wasting the phenomenal force that you have access to. Till how long will your *Guru* remain in the body to stop your *karmas* from fructifying? The moment he leaves his body, all the collected *karmas* would start playing out and all the problems will land on your head together, because you cannot escape your *karma*. I knew a lady who was very kind, she spent her entire life doing charity and service, and yet in the last five years of her life she was in extreme pain... all kinds of diseases had taken shelter in her body. One might wonder why such a charitable lady had to go through so much pain. Well, the lady had a very strong desire, 'Let this be my last birth, grant me *moksha* after this life'. For this to happen, you have to clear out all the *karmas* from this life as well as previous births, which is what happened in case of that lady. There was a reason why our ancestors took to *vanprastha ashram* at the age of 50. They possessed far more comforts and luxuries, but they left it because they knew that they have to pay back for their *karmas* to be eligible for *moksha*. If in the last stages you say that 'I want *moksha*' and if your voice is heard by some *shakti*, then all the *karmas* that you were yet to go through will all fructify one after the other, just like that lady. She was going through that pain, because her *karmic* account was getting cleared. You cannot stop it, because that is what she had asked for.

Understand that when your bank balance is increasing, you are buying bigger cars and houses, your businesses are expanding… those are not your requirements; you are simply collecting more negative *karmas* for yourself. It is foolish to think that your *Guru* will stop them; a *Guru* can stop them but only for some time, till the time that *Guru* is in his body. But what will happen once that time passes away? When your *Guru* stops a problem from coming to you, that is an indication or sign for you to begin improving your *karmas* because once you do that only then your negative *karmas* will start getting balanced out and then you will not go through the pains or payback as you have already paid back with service and charity.

And always wish for your *Guru* only. Whoever, wherever your *Guru* is, wish for every aspect of your *Guru*, the whole of your *Guru*. Only then your *karmas* will play out or balance out and you will be able to reach somewhere. Whoever your *Guru*, you cannot go ahead of him, so at least attain him completely. People come to me talking of big-big things — *dev, devis, mantras* and weird practices that they do — half of which even I don't understand. I just tell them that they should continue doing what they are doing, they can get nothing from me as they are at a level much higher than mine — they chant *mantras*, which I have not even heard. In fact, I have hardly traversed any journey till now; so only those who want to cover the journey that I have completed so far can come with me. If you have gone far ahead of me, then why look backwards? But if you are behind me, then at least first reach up to me…

Original/unedited pictures of manifestations in *havan* performed by *sadhaks* at *Dhyan Ashram*.

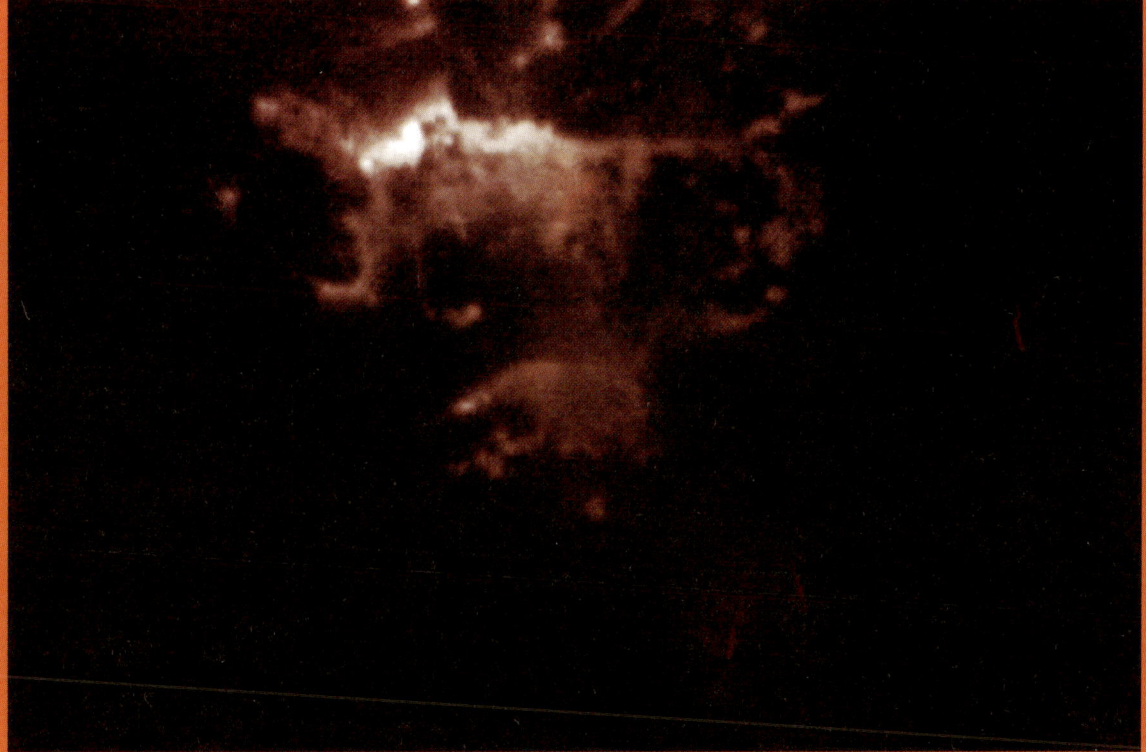

WILD BOAR (VARAHA)

Agnihotra is special kind of *havan* performed at the time of sunrise and sunset, the prime chant being "*idan na mam*" (all this is not mine, indicating detachment). It is essential for everyone to perform *agnihotra* as it gives you fearlessness, longevity and ability to control the elements. Exactly at the time of sunset and sunrise, a specific shade of the sun's *prana* is awaited and as it appears the *havan* starts. The entire *havan* is normally completed in a minute or two.

Original/unedited pictures of manifestations in *havan* performed by *sadhaks* at *Dhyan Ashram*.

LORD SHIV WITH HIS TRIDENT

A *havan* performed under the *sanidhya* of a *Guru*, with purity of thought, ingredients and the correct chants, has the effect of completely changing the environment – the weather changes, air becomes fragrant, birds perch on the trees around, there is peace and stillness within and outside. These are all indications of the invocations being heard and responded to by the *devs*.

SERMON 3

SHAKTI OF AN INDIVIDUAL AND GURU SHAKTI

" *Guru is a shakti and this shakti is meant to be given only, it is not for the Guru. Only when this shakti is given to someone can a Guru go forward. Till the time he/she does not give, he/she cannot go forward.* "

3

If you talk to any stranger in a bus, on the road, in the office or the market, and ask them about what is going on in their lives – their office, house, friends-circle, etc, you will be surprised to know that whatever they have to say will not be very different from what is going on in your own office, house or friend-circle. The only difference would be that some would have more money, some less, beyond that each person you find will be going through the same things.

By this, one thing is very clear, that in this physical world, the physical dimension, every individual's focus and thought is more or less the same, there is not much of a difference; that means, everyone basically wants the same things, and because everyone's focus is on the same thing, we get similar things as per our capacity. The difference is only that of capacity.

I get mails about problems from all over the world from Bangladesh to Canada, from the one who is earning 5000 monthly to the one who earns five crore, and irrespective of their background, I find that everyone has the same basic problems. Somebody's spouse is not happy, somebody's kids do not listen, somebody has job difficulty, somebody has a disease, somebody is emotionally unstable that's all. Everyone can be categorised into these five problems, there is no sixth category. There is one more category but which comes in *yog*, that says, "I am doing *yog* just like the person sitting next to me is doing but experience alludes me, whereas s/he has experiences of the subtler world. Why is it so?" Or, "Why do you spend more time with that person and not with me. You meet person X daily but not me. Why?" So, the simple answer to this is that every person wants to buy a car; some can afford to buy a Mercedes while some cannot think of even a Maruti. But what is interesting in this is that the problems of both of them are exactly the same; the situation in their house is just the same, just one or more of these five (plus one) problems. People all over the world fit into these categories only, except of course, the rarest of rare cases (two among 1000), who are *sadhaks* and come to me only for *yog* and *sadhna*, the rest of the 998 fit in these five categories only.

The interesting thing is that all of these people, whose problems are of these basic five categories, want to do *yog* and nobody considers him/herself to be less than the other and they all complain that they are not getting the experience when they are so good and doing so much. Another interesting thing is that those two out of 1000, who come to me only for *yog* and *sadhna*, never say things like "You spend more time with them or you spend less time with me." Whatever might be their status or position, even if you make them stand outside for one hour, they do not complain. If you do not call them to any function, they do not complain. If they come to meet me, and I do not talk to them or if they are made to go back from the gate only, still they do not complain. They do not complain if they are told they are wasting their time, they do not complain if they are made to pick used utensils after a *langar*. They never complain, whatever you keep saying. The rest, who come for solutions to their problems, have a problem in everything. In fact, there are some who keep testing and judging me only. They will notice everything about me and make enquiries about my diet and lifestyle. The two out of 1000 never do such things. The rest of the majority, question everything I say or ask them to do. "Why like this and why not like this? Till yesterday you were saying something about that person, then why did you treat him like this today?" All the time their question to me is "how come like this?" They never get an answer, though even if they did get the answer, they will just not understand because their problems fit in those five categories only. They are not among those one or two from thousand. No matter how much force or *shakti* they have, they still do not fit in that category of 'two in 1000' and a very simple person who does not have anything, no capacity, fits in the 'two in 1000'.

I find it extremely interesting that 998 out of 1000 have the same basic problems at the same basic level and except their own selves, they see everybody around. And only two fit into the category of being *sadhaks* and are not concerned about anyone else. They never ask me what I am eating, what I am wearing, where I am going, who I am talking to, who I am not talking to, they never enquire about me. If you make any enquiry about me, from wherever you do it, I come to know about it. It is better that you ask me directly because I do not lie and if you think I will lie, then what are you doing here? It is only those two people who can reach somewhere in *yog,* the rest, no matter how much *shakti* or force they have, no matter how much capacity they have, whatever I may give them, they will destroy it in one second.

Let me give a small example, I have a student in Karnataka, she had many miscarriages and abortions and was very depressed as she was not able to get a child. She began doing *yog* and within three months, she became pregnant and when I could see that the soul had taken the body inside her womb, which happens in the third or fourth month, after that every second week, I used to get a mail from her saying "I am in a lot of tension today." I would ask her, "Why are you in tension now?" "I had a fight with my boss; my boss said this to me and now you give me a solution for it; I am crying continuously since the last two days." I would always tell her to not make this mistake, because a pregnant woman, in fact, not just a pregnant woman but any person who takes any kind of emotional stress or holds any kind of negative emotion within, creates a disease inside. Emotional congestion is one of the major reasons for diseases to set in the body. Of course, if you eat something wrong, then that is different matter, but otherwise it is only jealousy, envy and what we call as pent-up emotions, that lead to disease in the body. I would repeatedly warn her to be careful with a baby in her womb, but she did not change her ways till the eighth month. The baby was born, but it had congenital defect... after wanting and waiting for five to six years, this is how it happened.

This is what I mean when I say that whatever I might try to give you, if you do not have the state for it, then, even after taking it, you will throw it away because you do not have the capacity for that thing, because you are searching for a solution to those five problems only. You have managed to come to me, to come this far and started the *Sanatan Kriya* but you still do not have the confidence in me to follow what I ask you to do. Life is like a battle and your *Guru* is the horse, which you have mounted. It is foolish to distress the horse amidst action. I tell everyone who comes to me the same thing, that do as I say and then if still nothing happens, you come and talk to me. If you do not want to follow it, then why come and waste your time? You waste your force as well as mine and what is the ultimate result? Nothing.

So when you do *yog* and when you are going to a *Guru* and calling him a *Guru* then you have to listen to him completely — 100 per cent and not 99 per cent. You cannot say that "I did everything but just left one thing." If you have the capacity to listen to everything, only then come to me, otherwise I have no interest in having a huge following. In fact, on the contrary, my responsibility only increases every time a new person comes to me. So if you have the capacity to listen completely to what I say, then it is 100 per cent my responsibility and not yours. I will see what happens to you. But if you have to do as per your mind only, even after coming to me, then it is your responsibility, your problem and not mine. When you have a *Guru* then 'might, if, but' is not there. When you go to a *Guru* then you surrender completely, there is 100 per cent togetherness, no difference remains after that. If you do not have that capacity, then there is no point in wasting time with me, nothing will happen. You will come for six months or one year, do *yog*, nothing will happen and you will go somewhere else. What is the use? I will get a bad name. So it is better to come to me only when you have the strength to follow me completely.

If you are following what I am saying 100per cent, but even after that any *anisht* happens, then it is my responsibility. It cannot happen, it is not possible. The *Guru-shishya parampara*, which our *Guru*s have given and the *gyan* of the *vedas* are not random things that you understand them as whatever you feel like and do it the way that suits you... It is *poorna gyan*, a complete science and I have studied this science in great depth for a few decades, every aspect of it. I know the power, ability and capacity of this science, so do not waste it just like that. If you fit in any of the five categories of problems, if you have come because of them, then keep one thing in mind that you will not be able to do *yog* till you rise above them.

In fact, I am thinking of keeping a separate computer in my house with a software in which I will put these five problems so that I don't have to reply to the 1000 to 1500 mails that I get daily. The computer will access my mail and the software will send the answer on its own. This is what is happening these days; the astrologers today do this only. The software will give the answer to the problem because there are only five problems. The astrologers make 12 programs for the 12 *rashis*, for me only five would be enough. You can see my mailbox sometime, 1500 mails will be there and just five problems and the sixth problem I have told you is "why do you talk to them and why not me?" But the basic problems are just five, the difference being only that some have a Maruti and some a Mercedes, yet they all want the same things. What is this difference between two physical beings, when their problems are the same?

Look at the sun; it has all the planets revolving around it. Why? Because it has that force in it, that *shakti.* In every individual there is a specific *shakti,* specific force, that creates the ability to attract and the ability of manifestation but it is only a *shakti.* In *yog,* a person is not assessed by his/her social status, beauty or money. The only thing, which is looked at is how much force is there inside a person. Where there is sun and its *shakti,* there all the planets revolve around it.

Usually one considers *Guru* to be *sthool*, a physical body, but this body is nothing, it is

The way to access that shakti and to increase your capacity is ek tattva nirantar abhyas- one pointed constant focus.

made of five elements and when the time comes these five elements will go back to the respective five elements in the creation. These elements will not be like this forever but that *shakti* or force will remain the same always or rather it will only increase. So you have to make yourself *sthir* on that *shakti* or force. And that *shakti* or force is there in every individual. Like I just said, a person may be given anything but does s/he have the *shakti* or the force to carry it, to keep it? Without the *shakti,* you just cannot carry it.

Every person who is sitting here, who has been with me for even one year, you do not even know that in one year what all have you got from me and what you have done with it... When you become *sthir* in *yog,* I will show you your journey with me, from the day it started. I will not explain with words but I will show it to you practically. In fact, a few of you have been made to see what all you got from me since the day you started your journey and what all you did with it and how much time you wasted in throwing away all that you got, just because of your personal jealousies and frivolous desires: "Why more time with them, why not with me?"

How much *sthirta* and how much force is there inside you, determines what you can accept, what can come inside you and when it comes to you, how you can assimilate it and what you can do with it. All this is told by the *shakti* inside you. And when that *shakti* comes inside you, you can do anything with it. You can even force a *Yog Guru* for anything, with your *shakti.* There have been individuals who have had so much force that as soon as I gave them something, they had the *darshan* of entire creation and every *shakti* that runs the creation, every *beej mantra*, every *dev and devi.* Then there are those who, irrespective of what was put inside them, even after one or two years, their first question would be: "I have become a little fat. Please tell me some way to become thin." "I am facing loss in my business; please tell me how to recover from it." "My stomach is paining; please give me some remedy for it." "Will my girlfriend/boyfriend marry me? Will we have a happy, perfect life?" A person who has been with me since 10 years came to me recently and said that the doctors have told him that he has some problem and now we will have to 'show' the doctors how the problem disappears without medicines, so I should do something and 'show' them. Even after 10 years the mental state is "Do this and show." Although he did show it to the doctors but the question arises that till when will we keep doing all this? There has to be a limit. For how long will you continue like this? One day the breath will end. It can be now or after a year, but it will definitely happen. You will again take a birth and you will have to start once again.

Just ask yourself that this *shakti*, this force, which is there inside you right now, what are you doing with it? That force is so much that you can attract anything with it; you can even attract the entire *shakti* of the *Guru*, because

Guru is not the physical body. *Guru* is a *shakti* and this *shakti* is meant to be given only, it is not for the *Guru*. Only when this *shakti* is given to someone can a *Guru* go forward. Till the time he/she does not give, he/she cannot go forward. But whom to give, when nobody has the capacity to carry it?

You can imagine the state of *Gobind*, when the time came for him to give the *shakti* forward, he could not find a single person whom he could make a *Guru* for the future and so he had to put everything in the *Granth, b*ecause he had to pass it on, he had to leave the body. So he put everything in the *Granth* and left his body. Similar was the case with *Ramakrishna Paramhansa*, he had so much *shakti* but no one to transfer it to. When the time for him to leave the body came, his most capable disciple was *Vivekanand* and he was sitting there with him. *Ramakrishna Paramhansa* looked at him and only told him one thing, "Even now you are sitting here and thinking that only if he comes to know that I still have doubt, then I will be convinced he is my *Guru*." So *Vivekanand* in spite of having access to such a *shakti* and sitting with him when the time for the *Guru* to leave his body had come, even then he was thinking that, "If he comes to know what I am thinking, then I will be convinced." He just did not accept it; though he was given the *darshan* of the entire creation, still, he was not ready to believe. Why? Because whatever *Ramakrishna* gave, *Vivekanand* did not have the *shakti* to carry it. This is a perfect example of how difficult it is to make a *Guru* and how intellect becomes your biggest impediment. So *Ramkrishna Paramhansa* left without a *shishya*, what else could he do?

If someone has that *shakti* to carry it and if others do not, then they should not get jealous due to it. Because that *shakti* can pull the *Guru* even to America or to jungles of Africa and you will just sit and think 'He ran away with that person." There is little that the *Guru* can do because his/her body too is destructible. The body is not the *Guru's shakti* and what is the *Guru's shakti* is the *shakti* of the entire creation, that is the *shakti of Lord Shiv. Shiv* has kept that *shakti* for you all only. Have you ever heard of *Shiv* using his *shakti* to do something for himself?

There was a *rakshas* by the name of *Bhasmasur.* He did *tapa* and asked *Shiv* for a *vardan* that on whoever's head he keeps his hand should turn into ash *(bhasm). Shiv* gave him the *vardan.* After getting it, the first thing the *rakshas* did was to run after *Shiv* thinking that 'let me try if it works on *Shiv*.' So *Shiv* is such a *shakti*, whatever he has, it is to give to others, even if it is a *Bhasmasur*. Two to three '*Bhasmasurs*' have even come to me, but *Shiv* did not let *Bhasmasur* keep his hand on his head and neither did I. When you give a *shakti* to someone, it is bound to show its effect. Once you have told someone the way to use that *shakti*, then whoever you have given it to, if s/he uses it, it's effect will be felt by one and all, irrespective of who it is. If the *shakti* is there, then the effect will be there.

If anybody has the capacity to take that *shakti* from me, then take it. The day that thing goes from me, that day I will be granted *moksha*, before that I will not get it. I will have to search for another body like this, which is a little difficult to get. I do not think I will get it again. So before leaving this one, I will need someone who has that capacity, to whom I can give that *shakti*, otherwise I will be wandering just like you see *Ramakrishna* wandering. Among you all only, there are those who have had the *darshan* of *Ramakrishna Paramhansa* while he was wandering. Whom to give that *shakti* to? One only finds people like *Bhasmasur*. But even a *Bhasmasur* does *tapa*, and with his *tapa* compels you to give him that *shakti*, then after that he decides to put his hand on your head, then it is his problem, not yours.

I would suggest do not waste your time in jealousies. I am very much accessible; you have got complete access to my force, my *shakti*. I cannot do anything in this, it depends on how much force, *shakti* you have. You can take my complete *shakti* because what am I supposed to do with it? I don't need it; I don't have any physical aspirations anymore. I have no aspiration, which requires a lot of physical force. Everything is going good. I will get *moksha* only when somebody takes that *shakti*. Instead of getting jealous of a person, try to understand what is there in that person, why is it that, "in every *havan* he is called but it has been six months since I was called."

Guru has been given the highest place and importance in our shaastras. Even when Vishnu took avtar, he made a Guru first.

Yog is a subject of experience, of *shakti* and even if you do have that *shakti*, it is not necessary that you are taking it on the right path. No doubt you have the *shakti*, but the question is that what are you doing with it? Have you thought about it? You get up in the morning for yourself and you go to bed in the evening for yourself. The *shakti*, the force that you have got or you are getting, what have you done with it till now? Are you getting so lost in that force that you start to drink and dance? What is its use then? The *Guru* is equally tense that again he will have to do so much *sadhna* and hard work to get that force and again he might get one more *Bhasmasur*.

Ravan and Bhasmasur were *sadhaks* of *Shiv* and *Shiv* gave *shakti* to both of them, but after that what did they do with it? *Shiv* gave the same *shakti* to *Ram* and *Krishna*. All of them had the capacity and did *tapa*, so they got it and those who were jealous of them, kept watching and wondering why they were given what they were. *Anusuiya* had so much *shakti* that she called all the three *devs* — *Brahma*, *Vishnu*, *Mahesh* — down and put all of them in one body — the body of *Dattatreya*. She had the *shakti* of *Sati* and the *shakti* of *Sati* is phenomenal.

It is only when you go above your jealousies and the basic five problems that you can do *yog*. If you remain busy in all these things, then you cannot do *yog*. *Guru* does not give the *shakti,* you should have the capacity to take it. It is a misconception that you sit with your hands folded and eyes closed and something will drop in your hands. You have to work for it, create that attraction, that *shakti,* within you and compel the *Guru* to give it to you. *Vishwamitra* created a parallel *brahmand* (universe). Did he ask anyone for it? He created it with his *shakti*. Forget what the *Guru* will give, look at how much capacity you have, how *sthir you* are, how much *shakti* you have... how much confidence do you have?

There is a stage in the beginning when a person is in the state of doubt, which is very important to have, even questioning at that stage is very important. But once that initial doubting stage is crossed and then again, if that doubting stage comes, then that is a problem. Having one doubt is allowed and that is important also, everyone should have it. And when you have that one doubt, then do a thorough investigation, look for anything and everything and once you are over with your investigations and have the experience of the subtle world, which your *Guru* has given you, then don't waste your time with further investigation and looking for further experiences because if you doubt the second time, then you cannot reach anywhere in *yog*.

It is very important that if you see that *shakti* in someone, then stop getting jealous of him/her. What will you achieve by getting jealous? Enhance yourself. And this is a continuous process — if someone has the *shakti* and is close to me today, it is not necessary that he/she will remain that way tomorrow also because even the size of his/her *katora* is limited. If by doing *yog* he/she is simultaneously increasing the size of *katora* then that is different. But even if his/her *katora* is bigger than yours and it remains that way, then after a point the flow will stop, at least you are increasing the size of yours. Focus on yourself individually; see how big you can make your *katora* because there is no scarcity of experiences and *shaktis* in this creation and the *shakti* of the *Guru* is limitless.

The way to access that *shakti* and to increase your capacity is ***ek tattva nirantar abhyas*** — one pointed constant focus, that is it, nothing else. If you have the thought pattern that "Today morning I went to that temple, in the evening I have to go to another and in the afternoon let me go and meet X *panditji* who has come." Or, "I have to meet you tomorrow; today an astrologer has come so let me confirm with him what you had told me earlier whether what you said is right or not." In that case I would suggest that you make him your *Guru*, why are you wasting your time with me? You are making fun of him in front of me and then you are confirming my word with him, tell me what is my value because that means I am worse than him. Then where is your confidence in me?

There should be *ek tattva nirantar* abhyas, your eyes should not even blink, 100 per cent, one-pointed focus. What you have seen, what you understand, and believe as your *Guru*, the entire focus should be on that, "I just have to achieve this, whatever might happen." Only then something happens or else nothing happens. When *Draupadi's cheerharan* was happening, from the beginning, her focus was one. Although the greatest of *sadhaks* and biggest of *yodhas* were sitting there, but nobody could do anything, only that *ek tattva* saved her. When you do *nirantar abhyas* on that *ek tattva*, then everything in the creation will be in your hands.

I understand that you have many desires. But to fulfill those you go out looking for *upays* with people who are busy making a fool of the world. The people you approach might be having thousand problems in their own houses for which they have no solutions, how will they solve your problems? What you follow, so shall you become. A *Yog Guru* never gives '*upay*' for anything, a *Yog Guru* only has *shakti* and everything in the creation is run by that *shakti* only, including your body. A person who has a Mercedes has that *shakti,* that force, that is why he has been able to attract the Mercedes. If someone has beauty, s/he has attracted that beauty by his/her force. If someone has money, he/she has attracted that by his/her force. If you make your connection with that force, your desires are automatically fulfilled.

Do not try to understand that force with your brain... It took me a few decades to understand; how can you understand it so early? It is very difficult. In fact, this is not something, which has to be understood. Everything is *sanchalit* through that *shakti* and there is no need to even tell anything to your *Guru* about your wants or problems. Just indicating once is enough, after that, have the patience and see what happens. Your impatience is an indication of *asthirta* inside you, it is a weakness and a sign of lack of confidence in yourself and your *Guru* figure.

When your shakti, your capacity, your *kshamta*, increases, then what you desire, comes walking to you. Do not go looking for *upays* to a *Yog Guru*. In fact there is no such thing as an *upay* or solution. These are only ways to make a fool of you. Never forget that he who is himself tied by bondages of *maya*, who is taking a fee from you to solve your problems, he cannot open your bondages and opening these bondages of *maya* is what *yog* is. When the bondages of *maya* open, then automatically all the *shaktis* of creation come inside you and you can do whatever you want to with them. *Yog* is that *shakti* but it has been made into a joke, 'tell this cure or that solution'. Do not ask these things from me, if there is a *Yog Guru*, then his one look is enough, nothing more than that is required, after that if you have the capacity, see what happens.

How you choose your *ek tattva,* is your subject, your *karmas* will tell you. I cannot recommend that follow me or follow him or follow her; that is not my subject. People ask me if that *ek tattva* could be God – it is the best thing to focus on the *param shakti* but in that case it becomes difficult to dissolve the ego and he/she is not able to reach anywhere. If you focus on the *param shakti*, that means your ego is so high, that you are taking the *Guru* as a physical body, a human. *Guru* has been given the highest place and importance in our *shaastras*. Even when *Vishnu* took *avtar*, he made a *Guru* first. The capacity of *Guru* is above all these *shaktis* for you (and not otherwise, otherwise it is a lot lower than these *shaktis*) because the *Guru* takes you to these *shaktis*. But if your ego is so high that you consider *Guru* as physical, then you cannot do anything. *Guru* is never taken as a physical body; *Guru* is a *shakti,* which you have to achieve, come what may. Like *Eklavya* wanted to achieve it anyhow and he did it, by whichever means possible. You too have to attain it, that's it.

Yog is no myth or an illusion, nothing in our *vedas* and *shaastras* is a myth. I am a scientific person; I know what I am talking about. I have not found a single piece of *gyan* as myth. All the things are 100 per cent there, which if you do *yog* properly, I will not only tell you, I will show it to you, you will see and hear from your own eyes and ears.

How much sthirta and how much force is there inside you, determines what you can accept, what can come inside you and when it comes to you, how you can assimilate it and what you can do with it. All this is told by the shakti inside you.

Original/unedited pictures of manifestations in *havan* performed by *sadhaks* at *Dhyan Ashram*.

TRIDENT

At the beginning of a *havan*, a *sankalp* is made which indicates the purpose for which the *havan* is conducted. Then the *aahvan* (invocation) of specific *devs* and *devis* is done requesting them to bless the *havan*. When conducted in a proper manner, these *devs* and *devis* reveal their form in the *havan-agni* at the time of *purna-ahuti*, indicating the success of *havan*.

SERMON 4

YOG: PRIORITY, NOT AN OPTION

" *Yog is not a subject of the intellect, there is nothing to understand in it. It is a subject of dhyan and it is the ultimate subject. It encompasses all the other subjects and commands top priority, above them all.* "

4

There are so many things in our lives, some more important to us than others... We prioritise various things/aspects as per their relative importance in our lives. Priority means first preference. Whatever you give first preference in life, gives you first preference in return and vice versa. For example, while with a group of friends, you bump into an old childhood friend and instead of greeting you first, he decides to greet the rest of the group. How would you feel? After that, will you still give preference to that person? No, he will no longer be your priority; instead, you will wait for the time when you can do the same to him. This holds true for everything, including the subject of *yog*. Only when you give the subject priority, will the subject give you priority, otherwise, nothing will happen.

There are some students who stay up all night, a day before the exam to prepare for it and there are those who start months before thinking of nothing else but their target. In fact, at times, they cut down on their television, outings, etc and immerse themselves in studies. So, for a simple class exam, they leave/stop everything and work so hard... and it shows in their results.

Yog is the ultimate subject, there is nothing beyond it. It is the subject that will eventually not just tell you who you are, but also show it to you. It will also tell you how to go beyond what you are. Yet, people tend to look at other things before *yog* — "Do I need to go for something more important today?" "Today I have no other work to do, so I can go for *dhyan*." This is the case with majority of the people; only when they have nowhere else to go, do they come for *dhyan* sessions. If that is the kind of priority that you give to the subject, it will do the same to you, it will never give you priority and you will end up wasting your time. So if that is your thought pattern, it is better to sit back at home and watch television, because nothing is going to happen till the time the subject is the priority for you.

People tell me that they are unable to understand *yog* and come here because 'maybe' hearing me would help them understand the subject and they 'might' want to venture into it. Let me tell you, *yog* is not a subject of the intellect, there is nothing to understand in it. It is a subject of *dhyan* and it is the ultimate subject. It encompasses all the other subjects and commands top priority, above them all. It's a desire, which will only be if you have sufficient positive *karmas,* if there is any lack of good *karmas* in your life then *yog* will never be your priority... It will only be an exit route from the maladies of your daily life, which are further dependent on your *karmas.* To make *yog* your first priority you have to increase your good *karmas.* There is no other way or '*upay*' and I can assure you there is nothing higher or more fulfilling than *yog*. It is the ultimate subject.

I will give you an example of how all other subjects come under *yog*. There is a student of mine who is an engineer now. He never missed his *dhyan* and would sit for it at the time for it, no matter where he was or what he was doing. Some years back, when he was preparing for his engineering exams abroad, he had a dream where he saw the entire question paper of the exam, which was to happen the next morning. When he woke up, he thought there was something wrong because half the questions that he saw were out of course. But then, he had complete faith in me and did not dismiss it since he had seen it right after his *dhyan*. He prepared for all those out-of-course questions and went for the examination next morning. He topped the University exams.

How did this happen? As I said, all other subjects fall under this ultimate subject. If you have any thoughts in your mind regarding anything physical, even that thought falls under this subject. And if you are in this subject then all the subjects are in your hands, and you can do anything, anywhere. Whatever one might want, where ever one wants to go, if a being gives top priority to this subject then that thing will just manifest in front of him/her.

You too can experiment with this by being completely dedicated to the subject, have full confidence in it and with that confidence do *yog* and *dhyan* and then if you wish for anything and if it doesn't happen, then tell me. This is *parvishay*, it has all subjects under it — just like the *partattva,* which has all the *tattva*s under it. Do not take it lightly, give it priority. I have travelled a lot and studied in detail most of the arts and the philosophies of the East and the West, and experimented too, but I have not seen any subject beyond this. It is a phenomenal subject, so give it first priority, then whatever has to happen will happen automatically because it's a subject of experience and not the intellect.

Infact, the very first day you come to me, from

that day onwards you should start seeing, hearing or sensing something. It should not even take a second day. If the experience happens, it means you are with me, you are in the subject, if it does not, then there is some break in the connection, i.e., you are not giving the subject its due priority. Give *yog* first priority and then see what happens...

To make yog your first priority you have to increase your good karmas. There is no other way or 'upay' and I can assure you there is nothing higher or more fulfilling than yog.

SERMON 5

IMPORTANCE OF KRIYA

"Sanatan Kriya is the process of removing the veils that have curtained your senses. When you do the kriya, you establish a connection with the Guru tattva. It is like inserting the plug into socket, after that the current will flow. But the problem is that you do not want to put the plug, so despite having the sense, you are unable to experience it."

5

What is the point of playing the best music in the world to a person whose ears are plugged? What is the point of showing the best scenery in the world to someone who refuses to open his eyes? What is the point of offering the finest delicacies of the world to someone who does not have the appetite for them?

Yog is the final frontier, a very serious subject. If you are not ready to do the practices as told to you, there is no point of taking up *yog*. You will only be wasting your time. You will neither get the experience, nor the glow because your higher senses will not awaken. Even if those senses are forcibly activated for sometime by putting some energy in you and you are forcibly made to experience, it is not going to last forever. After sometime you will turn around and talk to me about the same old things: business, relationship or health. If that is what you are looking for, it is best to go to a consultant. Why waste your time and spoil your *karmas* by coming here? What is the use of seeing, listening or understanding, when your higher senses are not active?

There are two kinds of people. First is the kind in whom this sense is completely missing. Such people cannot come to me, they may accidentally land up once or twice, but after that they will go away. Most of you belong to the second category. You have the sense, but it is curtained with veils of *maya*. For you to experience the truth, these veils have to be removed.

Sanatan Kriya is the process of removing these veils. The practices that you have been given, individually or collectively, are a process to remove the veils that have curtained your senses. When you do the *kriya*, you establish a connection with the *Guru tattva*. It is like inserting the plug into socket, after that the current will flow. But the problem is that you do not want to put the plug, so despite having the sense, you are unable to experience it. You only perceive the creation by your five senses — see, touch, smell, hear and taste. You do not know anything beyond because you are veiled by the five senses, *maya*. At times, I forcibly remove that curtain, you are made to experience what lies beyond. You see it, appreciate it, but after sometime the curtain is back because of your inherent desires. *Yog* is *ek tattva nirantar abhyas*. There are five basics to*yog* — one *asan* (you do not change your *asan*), one *mantra*, one *Guru,* one *isht* and a single intent (that of evolution). If your intent is evolution, if your intent is of your *Guru,* you can never digress from the path.

In fact, there are only two reasons that make a person digress from his path – ego and attraction.

Ego is the biggest roadblock for a *sadhak*. A gentleman from the Foundation is well versed in the *Gita*. Once, he was arguing with me quoting from the *Gita*, how contrary to what I say, *Gita* never mentions that one should not suppress the senses. I have never read the *Gita*, so I said okay. Few days later in a recording from the *Bhagwad Gita*, we accidently came across a *shloka* where *Krishna* was telling *Arjun* that one must not suppress the senses, because that amounts to violence. One has to rise above the senses, holding the hand of *Guru*. Listening to that *shloka*, the gentleman was speechless. You must understand that *gyan* never comes from reading books or listening to lectures, it comes from somewhere else... Divine gives his messages in mysterious ways. Ego is the greatest veil, which never allows you to see the truth. It makes you believe that you know everything. The one who understands and accepts what is lacking in him, where he is going wrong, can very easily go ahead but the one who keeps denying till the very end, nothing can be done for such a person.

Most of you come here with the thought that 'maybe there is something that I might miss... so let me go and sit there. After all, it's just a matter of two hours.' You only know the attraction of the five senses, of the physical, nothing beyond it. Beyond it, there is a big '**maybe**'. No matter how many times and in how many different ways you are told, warned and at times, even threatened, you still do what you have to because you are not able to see, hear, touch, taste or smell anything beyond that physical. Every interpretation of yours is at that physical plane only.

Here you miss a very important point — the one who is a *Yog Guru*, who is the custodian of the *Guru tattva*, he tests you at every stage. When you are given something or something is taken away from you, at both the times you are being tested. Something has to be given to you on a regular basis as per your capacity, so that you may progress. However, it is only given to a *supatra*. *Gita* says that *gyan* must not be given to the one who will not value it; the one who commits this folly will get a *pishach yoni*. For it will be like handing a loaded gun to a monkey. The monkey will first shoot himself only and the blame will come on you. So you can imagine what risk I am taking!

You must have noticed that when you meet me initially, you find it very nice, whatever you want starts dropping in your hands and you feel happy. But at the same time I always warn you. I can sense the pain you are about to experience and I warn you because I know that you will not be able to bear it because you see, think, assess and understand everything with your five senses. I keep warning all of you but only one to two per cent of people listen to me. Then, when you experience the pain, you come looking for solutions. But there are no solutions to these things. The only solution is your *karma* and your memory, which you have lost. You have forgotten the *dharana* (or intent) with which you had come to me initially. You are completely immersed in the physical and your ego has skyrocketed. The subject of *yog* is not that easy.

To move from avidya to vidya, Guru tattva is required and it is important that both you and your Guru are in the body because to go beyond the senses and the body, body is needed.

The *kriya*, which you have been asked to practice, is so that the curtains are removed and you see the reality. Till the time you do not see and experience that reality on your own, you will not reach anywhere. You will go on wasting your time and birth under the effect of the five senses and the ego. And these senses will not last forever, they too will be lost as you reach the crematorium but by then it will be too late. Your next birth will be no different from this one; you will be stuck and troubled in the same way. You might think, 'So what? One birth went past, I will try in the next one', but the truth is, that we have reached a stage of *Kaliyug* beyond which the *Guru* will not take birth. If you are not able to rise over the senses when I am here and explaining it to you, how do you expect to do that at a time when there will be no *Guru*?

Shankaracharya had said 2000 years back, "*Dharma* has been destroyed. Nobody will understand *dharma* in this *yug*. But still, I will try throughout this lifetime." He had a lifespan of 40 years, he tried all through, but who understood? No one. *Rishi Patanjali* said the same thing that *Kaliyug* has started and no one will understand the *yogsutras*. But since the *Guru tattva* has to do its *karya*, so he gave *yogsutras* and went. How many people understand them? In *Gita*, *Krishna* said not to speak of *gyan* in front of those who do not value it. All these *Yog Gurus* tried as per their capacity — *Patanjali* gave *yogsutras*, *Krishna* gave *Gita* and even *Shankaracharya* made four *shishyas*. *Gurus* never stop trying, they might take your tests but that is only to make you rise above, for your transformation. If you try to see that change by picking up *Patanjali Yogsutras* or *Gita* or *Saundarya Lahiri* (by *Shankaracharya*), you are mistaken. *Brahma* gave the four *vedas*. Can you understand *Brahma* by reading them? In the same way, by reading any of these texts can you understand *Patanjali* or *Krishna* or *Shankaracharya*? All of them gave the *gyan*, but what came of it? The condition is right in front of you. These are pure energies, accessing them leads to opening of higher senses and divine interactions. The *Guru* has the ability to channelise all this into you, but is your body ready for it? If it is, then it is immaterial whether the *Guru* gives it to you or you compel the *Guru* to give it to you by your own force. The purpose is the force, not the knowledge — any which ways you have to get it.

A *Guru's karyakshetra* is *gyan*. If you have the capacity and the connection, then that *gyan* will certainly flow into you. Otherwise, you have been sitting here listening to me for the last ten years, you will continue for another year or two (beyond that you will not get the opportunity) and after that you will remember neither the words, nor their meanings. A *Guru*'s task is to give *gyan*, it is on you how much you receive. If you can, then wake up now! Otherwise, it does not matter, you have passed so many lifetimes, you will pass a few more.

When you are with your *Guru*, your life starts heading in the direction that you desire. The question is: what is your desire? How many look for a spot to do *dhyan* at the time of *sandhya*? Majority is looking for a liquor bottle and a place to enjoy that bottle because that is their desire. You pick up a pig from a garbage dump, shampoo and blow-dry it and put it in a clean room, but as soon as it finds the door open it will rush back to that garbage dump. I have a beautiful white dog. We used to shampoo him daily and keep him indoors but he would just keep crying. The minute we opened the door, he would rush to the mud and come back all dirty. Now we have stopped bathing him. I can make you take a 'bath' once, twice, thrice — but if after that also you want to dive into the mud, what is the point of me wasting time and energy? Even if I force something in you, you will dissipate it. I will lose it and you will gain nothing, so it is pointless.

Your desires tell your worth. Some have a desire to become a dacoit, some doctor, some engineer, some lawyer and some politician — each of them has their own role and importance. I'll give you an example. Few years back, the workers who pick up garbage went on a strike in Delhi. For most of you these workers are a non-entity, but because of their strike, Delhi became a stockpile of garbage and the authorities had to bow to their demands in just two days! Every person has a way of his own and by that way he has the capacity to do anything. You cannot say, 'I have a desire for alcohol and I can do nothing about it.' Even if you have such a desire and if you trouble me daily for it, then your habit will go in two months. But if you don't have time to come to me or listen to what I am telling you, then that desire will not let you go ahead and you will keep hiding from reality behind that liquor bottle. Even a worker has the capacity to become a CEO. The question is, what is the intensity of his desire? If you develop a desire for something inside you, then irrespective of your present state, you will be able to attain it. But if you take the five senses as basis and if you assess your *Guru* also with these five senses only, then you will only be wasting your time. Don't waste your time. If an awakening has to come inside you, it will come now. If it doesn't, it never will, you will continue going round and round.

Do not try assessing the subject of *yog* with your limited brains and five senses, that 'this will happen' or 'this should happen', wait for your experience. What you are, that is your beginning. You like eating and drinking, sexual activity, good house, good car, good music — that is normal. You are a normal human being — you have five senses and certain desires. Every soul has a desire and to fulfill that desire it takes a body and to rise above that desire it holds the hand of the *Guru*. The problem arises when people start doing *yog* for *bhog*. *Yog* is for rising above the *bhog*. The body and the five senses are for *bhog*, there is no prohibition on that. I have never stopped anyone from fulfilling their desires. Your body is for desires but *yog* is to rise above the desires. *Yogah chitta vritti nirodh*. Even *Gita* talks of control of senses. What that control is, the *Guru* will tell and you have to experience that control, not understand it with your brains. Just like indulging in senses is an experience, similarly control of senses too is an experience. But for this, you need a *Guru*.

People ask me how to free themselves from the worldly ties. When I ask them why do they want to do that, the answer usually is, 'to be happy'. Think about it. You had tied yourself into those bondages — marriage, kids, business — to be happy. Now you want to break free from them to be happy. You don't know what you want, you are confused and that is because, you do not have a *Guru*.

I usually carry a *gada* (mace) with me. Once I had gone to meet someone and on seeing the mace, the person commented, "You are the biggest fraud." On asking why, the reply was, "You are fooling people into thinking you are strong by flaunting this toy object." I told that person to just try lifting one end of it and I was supporting the rest of it. With just that much weight, the person lost balance and was about to fall and exclaimed, "This is very heavy!" The problem is that people do not have the sense to distinguish real from unreal; *vidya* from *avidya*, because they don't have a *Guru*. You find everything fraud because you yourself are fraud. You only see your own reflection in a *Yog Guru*.

You want to open the bondages that you once willingly tied. That is the *avidya* in you. Those who are in 20s want to tie these bondages and those who are above 40, want to open them. It is just a question of 20 years, for some even less. After that, everyone wants to open the bondages that they tied with so much desire because they are stuck in *avidya*, which is *sthool* and controlled by the five senses. All these bondages will open at the cremation ground because when you leave your body, you will forget everyone and everything. But at that time, you cannot move from *avidya* to *vidya*. As soon as you leave the body, you are tied to the attraction of your *vasnas* and take up a similar body.

To move from *avidya* to *vidya*, *Guru tattva* is required and it is important that both you and your *Guru* are in the body because to go beyond the senses and the body, body is needed. Only then you will get the *vidya* and then, you will not want to open bondages because then there will be no bondages. Bondages exist because you think they exist. Just like that pig is tied to the mud. If it understands that it is filthy, then its bondage with mud will open. Similarly, all your bondages are a question of one nerve, which when pressed you will forget everything. If you happen to visit a neurological ward, you will find the relatives of patients crying that he/she no longer recognises them, just because of that nerve-press. It is just a matter of time that your body will be taken to the cremation grounds and put to fire. What bondage will you remember then? This is *Maya*, which is in every speck and it will not leave you. This is *avidya*, which is holding you, that is why you require the *Guru tattva* to make you rise above it.

The one who is an MLA today, he is troubled because he wants to become an MP, an MP is troubled because he wants to become a CM, a CM is troubled because he wants become a PM and PM does not know what he wants to become but even then he is troubled because his *buddhi* is limited and he sees everyday his chair is going away and fears losing it. Even if you are at the top of the ladder, you are troubled because there is no top of the ladder. That top too is physical. The difference is only of *avidya* and *vidya*, and that is the difference between *bandhan* and *bandhan mukt*.

Every soul has a desire and
to fulfill that desire it takes a body
and to rise above that desire
it holds the hand of the Guru.

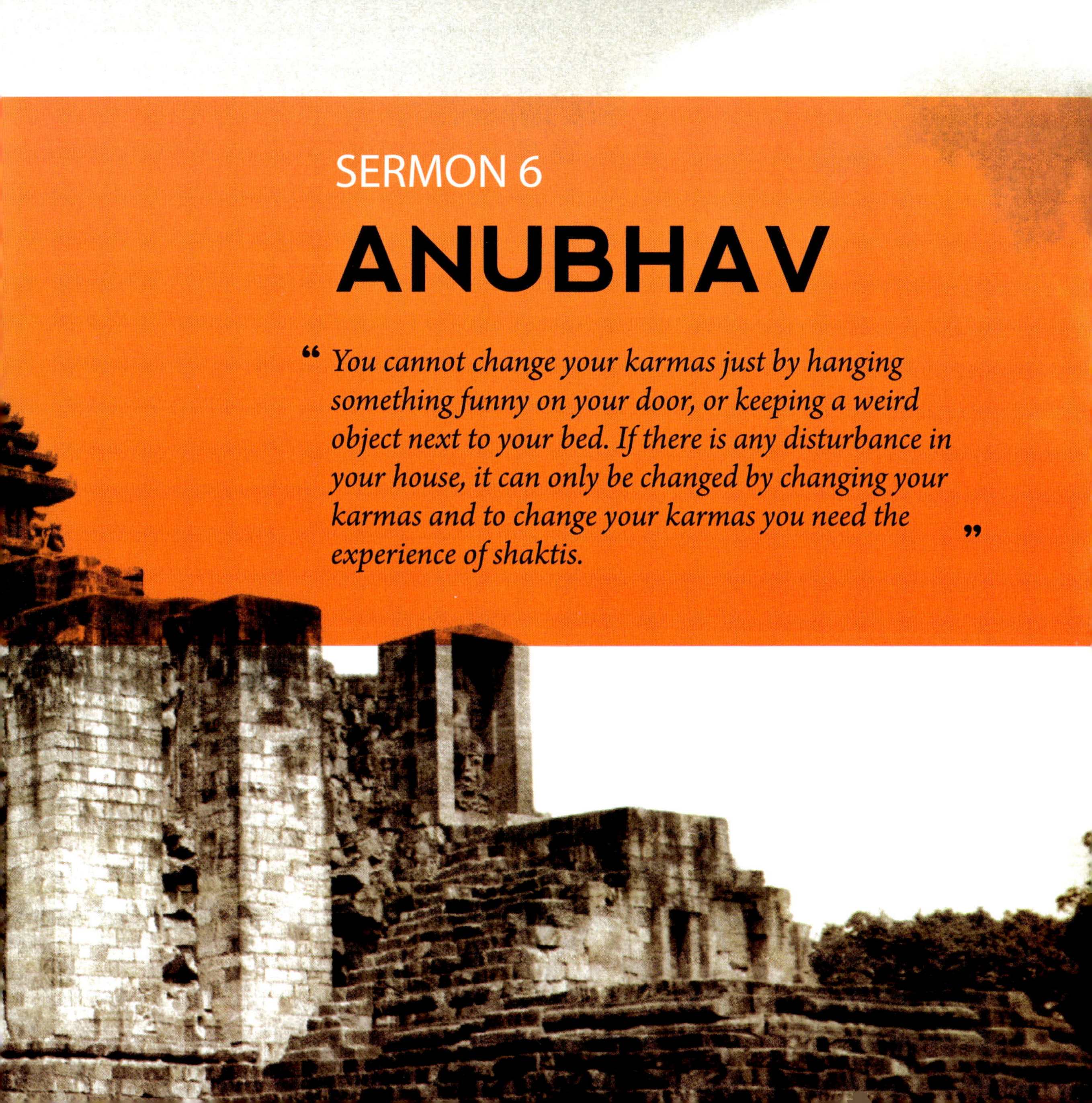

SERMON 6

ANUBHAV

“You cannot change your karmas just by hanging something funny on your door, or keeping a weird object next to your bed. If there is any disturbance in your house, it can only be changed by changing your karmas and to change your karmas you need the experience of shaktis.”

6

The *rishis* and *munis* have described the various *shaktis* that run this creation. All these *shaktis*, all the *akritis* and all the *darshans* are right in front of you, but to access them, you need to be in *yog*.

Yog is transformation. The physical body or the *sthool* is made up of the five *tattvas* — *prithvi, jal, agni, vayu* and *akash*. Even your brain, which leads you to believe that you have reached places, is just these five elements. As you tread on the path of *yog*, under the *sanidhya* of your *Guru*, even though the physical body remains same, there occurs a change in you. What that change is, cannot be described; and till the time there is no change, all the talks of *atma, paramatma, chakras,* etc are of no use.

When you cut open this body, you neither see the *atma,* nor the *chakras*. In fact, you see nothing, which is above the five elements that constitute your physical body. But the *chakras* are definitely there. There are *sadhaks* at *Dhyan Ashram*, who have seen and experienced these *chakras* through *yog*. Some of them can also see and read the aura (and all of them are highly educated and intelligent men and women). These, however, do not exist in the physical state. You cannot see the *sukshma* even if you cut open the body. There are no machines, which can photograph these *chakras*, as machines are made by men using the five senses. These *chakras* are beyond the five senses and need higher senses to be experienced. Yet, all over the world, lectures are given and highly educated men teach you about all this... It is a very dangerous thing to do; the world of energy is extremely potent and must not be played around with.

Once, a student of mine had gone to attend a programme at the reputed California School of Ayurveda. The Head of Department there is a doctor who also teaches *Ayurveda*. One day, I got a panic call from this student saying, "All that they are teaching is diametrically opposite of what you say." I told her to ask them, why they are teaching the opposite way. She replied, that when she tries to explain to them, the response she gets is, "Do you know more than us? Are you the only one who knows things? There could be a difference of opinion... Your opinion is different from ours and you are also right and we are also right." This is a very dangerous thought.

The particular discussion was about the five *mahapranas* that control the body. These *vayus* move in a particular direction only. *Prana* and *Udana* go upwards, *Samana* moves sideways, *Apana* goes down and *Vayana* is in the whole body. According to the Head of Department there, *Udana vayu* goes towards the sides. If *Udana vayu* goes towards the sides then what will make the brain function? He also held the view that *Prana vayu* is directed downwards. I personally wrote a mail to the doctor saying, "There is a *shloka* in *Shiv Samhita 'Prana Apana Manipoorak sthitpragya'*, which means when the directions of *Prana* and *Apana* reverse to become *sthir* at the *Manipoorak,* it is then that the awakening of *yog* starts. Unless the directions of *Prana and Apana* are reversed, awakening of *yog* cannot begin, as they have to become still at *Manipoorak*. *Prana vayu* corresponds to the area of the chest, so if *Prana vayu* is getting reversed and becoming *sthir* at *Manipoorak* (around the navel), then it is surely going upwards in its normal functioning." I am yet to receive a reply from the University.

This is the present state of affairs where everyone is educated and knows a lot, and yet, no one understands that *yog* is not the subject of the seven to eight pe rcent brain; it is a subject of experience. The seven to eight per cent brain is enough to experience and enjoy the physical body and related pleasures of the five senses. However, when you do *dhyan* under the *sanidhya* of *Guru*, this seven to eight per cent activity or the five senses are stilled for some time. That is why, for some time, you feel peaceful and your body feels relaxed, because the senses are put to rest for that duration. That is also the reason why all over the world, meditation is seen as a relaxation technique. However, when you start *dhyan* with me, you will realise that the state of *dhyan* starts to come only after two hours of sitting still. Just try sitting without moving for two hours, you will be assured that *dhyan* is not for relaxation. What relaxes is only the seven to eight percent of the brain, and as a result, certain higher centres of brain get activated, which take you to subtler dimensions of creation and make you experience the other world. Day-dreaming, while remaining in the five senses is only relaxation, which has nothing to do with your evolution and interaction with the gods.

The discussions of *atma-paramatma* are

redundant for you till the time you have experienced them. What you experience is *yog* for you. If there is no experience and only words, then it is just the intellectual mind, which is showing you different things, nothing more than that. Intellectual knowledge is different from *gyan*. When you read something somewhere, what you are reading is someone else's experience. It is pointless to have a debate or discussion on that. Till you get the experience, the intellectual knowledge alone can serve no practical purpose. In fact, when you have a lot of intellectual knowledge, it means that seven to eight per cent of your brain is highly active, and it will take that much more time to make it *shant*.

Yog is a subject of your personal experience. Once you get the experience, all your questions dissipate on their own because you can see and feel things right in front of you. Just do a simple exercise. Close your eyes and get both your hands near your body, around the region of the navel, with your palms facing each other. Be aware of the space between the two palms. Just keep your hands and body relaxed, and get your palms closer together and then apart, and so on. See, if you feel anything between your palms.

The *yogsutras* describe five particular sensations that might be felt by you — heat, cold, attraction, repulsion or a tingle. The sensation you get indicates your state. The *shakti* that you connect with, whatever is its characteristic, that is the feeling you get between the palms. The science of healing is based on this only. However, you cannot learn healing by attending a course. The science cannot be sold; it has to be developed through self experience. And the experience happens only when you are completely focused on this science. And once you have experienced it, you can receive and give (not buy and sell) this science, and there is no counter-effect.

These days many shops have opened that offer you the grade of a 'master' or 'grand master', when you learn the 'techniques', by paying a fee. When you attend such courses, you merely learn the technique, without experiencing the energies or developing an understanding of them. It is important to understand that there is NO technique in *yog*. There is only experience of *shakti*, and with that experience, you also get its *tattva darshan.*

There is a very minute difference between the different *shaktis* that run this creation. You may compare the situation to the shade card of a painter that will have 1000 shades of just colour pink. Every *shakti* is a specific colour and, in fact, the colour or shade that you like is because you are in contact with or relate to that specific *shakti.* When you get deeper into *yog*, you are shown the colours of every *shakti*, and made to experience the subtlety of difference that distinguishes one from the other. Only after you experience and understand these variations can you start with healing. Only then you can become a 'master' or a 'grand master', not before that. And as per the ancient sciences, the term is '*Guru*', not master or grandmaster… there is a marked difference between a master and a *Guru*.

A *Guru* takes entire responsibility of a *shishya* and monitors him not yearly, monthly or hourly, he monitors the *shishya,* by the moment, which a master or a grand master cannot do. Once you experience the *shakti* and get the *shaktipath*, from there on, you are monitored every second. A *Guru* is the one who has the experience of all these *shaktis*, he is a *tattva gyani*. He has *vaak shakti*, when a *Guru* says something for somebody, it happens; when a *Guru* makes someone his *shishya*, then that person stops falling ill. If there is any *anisht* that is about to happen with him/her, then it is stopped before coming, and it is stopped by taking help from these *shaktis* only.

What you felt between the palms is an experience of basic level. This experience gradually changes to colours and then into *shaktis* and then *sanchalan* of those *shaktis* becomes your personal experience. And when these *shaktis* start functioning inside you, then your *shreni* becomes the *shreni* of a *Guru*. The subject of *yog* is a composite whole of all these *shaktis,* and the growth in this subject does not depend upon your beauty, position or power; growth in *yog* is measured by your own experience. The experiences of *yog* cannot be bought with money, power or influence. For this you have to come in the *sanidhya* of a *Guru*, and do hard work, only then can you experience the realm of *shakti*.

Today, so many different arts and yoga courses have come up in the market. It is like going to a multi-brand store with various brands being sold over different counters, enough to confuse a person not for this lifetime, but many lifetimes. It is important to understand here that *yog* is not a course, it is a *sadhna*. Once, I read a newspaper article about why one should hang windchimes in middle and not on the side of the door… Such things beat all logic. People say whatever comes to their mind first; just make it sound a little different. Once it is different, it is something new, an innovation that is ready to be marketed and sold! What is forgotten in this buying and selling is that the basic purpose of the science of spirituality is to free you from the bondages of *maya*, and not to tie you in them. You have to un-tie the shackles of *maya* that are not letting you experience those *shaktis*, and unless you do that, you cannot experience or know what *yog* is.

One enters the dimension of *yog* without knowing where one is headed to or what one wants. Majority who enter, meet clever businessmen selling them courses and realise after a few years, that they wasted this lifetime and achieved nothing. You cannot change your *karmas* just by hanging something funny on your door, or keeping a weird object next to your bed. If there is any disturbance in your house, it can only be changed by changing your *karmas* and to change your *karmas* you need the experience of *shaktis*.

Entire creation, everything you see around you, is nothing but *shakti,* a vibration. Your body is a specific frequency of that vibration. Within your body the various parts and organs again are a different frequency of that vibration. The manifestation of the frequency is what the physical creation is. The difference between you, me or any other entity, is the difference in frequency of vibration, and the only way to know that difference is by experiencing that vibration. This is called *anubhav or gyan*. All you have to do is to tune into that vibration to access it. You cannot learn about that vibration in a book; or over an intellectual discussion. Only when you experience that vibration can you say that, 'yes, it exists for me'.

The science of *yog* unlocks the door to access the various frequencies and vibrations that govern this creation. If our *rishis* and *munis* could see the *chakras* and experience them, you too will see them and experience them; not 99 per cent but 100 per cent they will be visible to you. If any kind of imbalance is about to set in the body, then those *chakras* will tell you about it, beforehand. And these *chakras* are neither inside the body nor outside it. Where they are, what they are, how they look and how they behave will all be revealed to you such that you will be able to send and receive all the frequencies that exist. But for that, you have to take the plunge and experience *yog* through a *Guru*, not a grandmaster/master; and earn it by your hard work, not by buying or selling.

These days many shops have opened that offer you the grade of a 'master' or 'grand master', when you learn the 'techniques', by paying a fee.
When you attend such courses,
you merely learn the technique,
without experiencing the energies or developing an understanding of them.
It is important to understand that there is NO technique in yog.
There is only experience of shakti,
and with that experience,
you also get its tattva darshan.

SERMON 7

PITFALLS AND PROGRESSION IN SADHNA

"It is said that you go through 84 lakh yonis to get human birth, which is actually the journey of the spirit. The experiences of the spirit start from the kingdom of the lowest beings and as it evolves, it goes through one yoni after another and reaches the dimension of a human."

7

There are many who ask me what are the pitfalls for a *sadhak*. For this one needs to first know who a *sadhak* is. And to understand who a *sadhak* is, one needs to know what a dimension is...

Let us take these concepts one by one, starting with dimensions. When you look at creation around you, you will find that everything exists in a compartment, and yet it mixes and merges with other things. Take, for example, the world of insects that exists below the ground. These insects are a complete world in themselves, engrossed in their chores without a worry about the rest of the world. If you disturb a row of ants, they scatter for a bit but quickly form a row again and resume their tasks, unaffected by what is happening around them, unconcerned about whether they die or live, just like a computerised program. Even among insects, there exist different species that are similar in their actions and behaviours and yet distinct from each other. These insects may be busy and limited in their own respective dimensions, but they still are a part of a greater whole. They cannot live in isolation from that whole. They live as they do and as a part of creation. In fact, nothing can exist in isolation. Isolation is an indication of leaving creation and going beyond creation. As far as the different insect kingdoms are concerned, the variations are minuscule between different species and beings, there is very little for them to do and they continue doing what they have to do. If you compare two ants, they will bear striking resemblance in their nature and behaviour, much in contrast to two human beings who can be poles apart.

Moving up a level, on the surface of earth, one finds the plant kingdom, which is yet another dimension and again, limited. Plants behave, more or less, in a similar, predictable way. How does one distinguish between a plant and an animal? It is the stimulus and response mechanism. The same stimulus evokes a very different response in a plant as compared to an animal or a human being. Plants and insects are limited to the dimension they are in; they are bound by their basic character, and cannot go over it, even if they want. They have to remain there, at that level, and are not bound by the Law of *Karma*. The movement from one dimension to the next, for them, is automatic. If you kill an ant, it will not be born as an ant again. It might become a cockroach, that is, automatic evolution, from one kingdom to the next. Their evolution is fixed and out of the ambit of *karma*, they are in their present state for a stipulated period of time and as that time period finishes, they move to the next state.

Moving to the animal kingdom, let us say, a dog. A dog is more or less bound, so is a cow. As you come up from the insect kingdom to the plant kingdom, it is more or less one, but when you come into the animal kingdom, every species is an evolution. *Asan*, as mentioned in *Ashtang yog*, is a posture in which you are still and comfortable and as you perfect an *asan*, you transcend the animal *yoni* that the *asan* represents. For example, *Mayur asan* does not cure your stomach ailments, instead takes you through the *yoni* of a *mayur* (peacock). It is an experience, which cannot be explained in words, one has to go through it to understand what I am talking about. So the *asan* has to be maintained and held for long periods, and must not be confused with acrobatics or gym class. *Asans* should be simply understood as the movement through a *yoni*, movement through a dimension, movement through those traits and the traits you possess determine the dimension you are in. Once you go beyond the animal *yonis,* you come to the human dimension. In the animal kingdom too, the Law of *Karma* does not hold. If a lion eats a deer, it does not mean that it will become a dog in the next birth as it is bound by its instincts. The *karmas* of animals are defined and their evolution is natural. There are no pitfalls for them. Whatever they may do, they cannot go beyond the limitations of their *yoni* and will act accordingly to their basic nature only and finish their birth. So evolution for them is natural, they just go through one stage to the next. It is said that you go through 84 lakh *yonis* to get human birth, which is actually the journey of the spirit. The experiences of the spirit start from the kingdom of the lowest beings and as it evolves, it goes through one *yoni* after another and reaches the dimension of a human. There is evolution, there is *sadhna*, there is a dimension, which is transgressed, but there is no pitfall in the lower dimensions. The pitfall is applicable only to the human kind.

Moving up these levels, one enters the dimension of a human being. There is a lot of variation and conflict of character in this *yoni,* no two humans are alike. In this dimension, you go through what you desire and pay for what you have experienced, because you are bound by the Law of *Karma*. And there is no escaping this law for a human being, for it is a law of creation.

Let us observe different strata of human beings, starting with the labourers digging pits, constructing buildings, tilling farms — those who are engaged in work from morning to night. You may put them all in one compartment since they are quite similar, but there exist a lot of differences in their individual traits, which keep them stuck and evolution is not automatic, they need to work to go beyond their present state. Next we can compartmentalise the office-going people, who have a fixed routine and job. They share a similar nine to five routine with a one-hour lunch, a similar thought pattern and outlook towards life and their living patterns too are more or less comparable. Even their preferences in terms of what they like to watch on TV, read, talk about, eat and drink, will be similar. It's a kind of a compartment, within which there exist individual differences. To move out of this compartment, again a conscious effort has to be made to break the monotony; otherwise there is no evolution for them. They will remain there, and even though they may go on for a million lifetimes and be born again and again, they will remain there, because they are bound by the Law of *Karma.* The Law of *Karma* has to be transgressed, they have to go beyond, only then their dimension will change. Next, moving a little higher up, are the people who control everything. For them there exists no lifestyle, no time limitation — just creativity, ideas, anything, anytime. These people are very similar to each other, though there may be a huge gap in their characteristics and so they too can be put in one compartment. They too need to break their *karmic* bondages to move out of their compartment.

A pitfall is essentially a way of tying you down and breaking the continuity of your sadhna, which means, keeping your eyes away from the sadhya, which could be even for a millisecond.

Then comes the dimension of saints (not the ones you see on TV, but the real saints). You will find them to be very different from the rest, even though they are human beings. When you look at them, you are plagued with questions like — why do they sit in a certain way or why do they speak so little or why do they not wear clothes or how come they are so content etc. However, even this dimension requires the saints to break the bondages of *karma* and go beyond it. And once you go beyond this stage, then the human dimension ceases and you go to the next *lok.*

In *yog*, there are various dimensions — *Bhulok* (where and what we are*), Bhuvahlok, Svahlok (Swarglok), Mahalok, Janalok, Tapalok* and *Satyalok. E*ach of these *loks* is a dimension, a complete existence, a compartment, yet each one is characterised by different kinds of thoughts. So while the general pattern will be the same, there will be a difference in thought. For example, in the case of charity, how do you differentiate if someone is in a higher compartment or in a lower compartment? Most people who do charity ensure that half the world knows about it or they do it on a public forum where they can be seen. There are some others who will just do it and not care whether the person needs charity or not. "You want something, here, you can have it." The same act of charity, the same human *yoni,* the same human trait, yet difference in dimension. The person in the higher dimension is not going to bother; the person in a lower dimension will ensure that everybody knows about the charity he has done, because for a person in higher dimension, it is nature, like the act of breathing, and for a person in lower dimension, it is showing off, something extraordinary.

For a human being to move from one dimension to another, *sadhna* has to be done. For an animal or a plant, *sadhna* is automatic, it's in-built, it will happen on its own as without it, there is no evolution. There are no pitfalls for an animal but a human, faces certain pitfalls on the path of *sadhna*. Whatever level you are at in the human dimension, you have to give that up, in order to go beyond it. Unless you leave what you have, you cannot go beyond. Going to temples, *gurudwaras, masjids* and pilgrimages or doing *paaths* in your house, or burning fire and calling it a *'havan' alone,* will not get you anywhere, you will continue to remain in the same dimension. It may satisfy your ego a little, but nothing more will happen. Pilgrimage has a purpose, but you can only understand it once you reach a certain stage. So even if you do a thousand pilgrimages, till the time you do not let go of all that you have collected in the physical, you will remain where you are for as many lifetimes and there will be no evolution.

Sadhna is the process of setting a *sadhya* (an energy that you want to achieve) and achieving that *sadhya*. Once you achieve it, your *sadhna* is complete in that dimension, at that level, and you are ready to go beyond it. In an animal or insect kingdom it is natural, but in human kingdom, you are given so many choices and attractions, that they limit your evolution. These attractions are called pitfalls. If you trip or face a loss, it is not a pitfall, it is in fact a payback for your *karma.* A pitfall is you getting a million dollars suddenly and depositing them in the bank happily, or your power and status increasing manifold because of which you forget your *karma, dharma* and *sadhna,* and get engrossed in the unreal world. When a pitfall comes your way, it means you are now ready to move to the next dimension of evolution. You have achieved your *sadhya* and completed your *sadhna* at one level. At one level, because, this is an unending journey, there is no limit, and the *sadhna* is unending. It goes from one compartment to the next and so on till you reach the *Satyalok* and you will be disappointed to know that even that ends after 3 lakh 84 thousand human years, after which you start again in some other dimension.

After reaching *Satyalok*, you start from there again. You once again have a *sadhya,* do *sadhna,* achieve it and again you go beyond. The purpose is not to keep going beyond by *sadhna* and achieving more and more and then starting all over again; but it is to go beyond all of this and this is possible only through *yog*. Have you ever thought why did you start this journey? It is because you wanted an experience. Even not wanting something is a desire, "I don't want this." Even that should not be there. It is ok to want things, but you should be over that experience. It is something like, you want to eat a *gulab jamun* but it does not matter to you when you eat it and when you will get the next one. So you might want to have it, but it does not have an effect on you. It's when a thing stops having an effect on you that you have crossed it, not before that. Till you want an experience, the journey continues and the day you are over all experiences, the journey will end. You will go back to where you came from and you will experience it sitting right here. You don't have to go to the Himalayas to experience it, sitting right here with your family, you will experience it. A lot of people tell me, "It's not possible for us because we have children and so many other duties", but all these people at Dhyan Foundation are also busy people, with children and families, and their experiences are proof enough that experience happens while being in the environment, with a family; that is what detachment is. And that is also the most difficult path — being here and yet achieving it. Leaving and running away is very easy and a selfish thing to do. Being here and yet being in *sadhna* is what is a little difficult, but so is *yog. Yog* does not tell you to run away or eat only *ghiya-roti* or get up at four in the morning, *yog* says that do everything and what is not good for you will leave you automatically, you don't have to leave anything. And what is *yog*? *Yog* is *chitta vritti nirodh.* Once you are able to establish your *vrittis* and the various modifications (*Patanjali* says there are five kinds of modifications) and go over them, then you are beyond everything, otherwise you keep moving from high to low to high and so on. So, pitfall is nothing to be worried about, it is not something that will harm you or hurt you. However, if you are very weak internally, if your *sadhna* is weak, and if you don't have a *Guru,* then the pitfalls can be negative — where you hurt yourself, suffer an accident or a financial loss. A pitfall is essentially a way of tying you down and breaking the continuity of your *sadhna*, which means, keeping your eyes away from the *sadhya,* which could be even for a millisecond. Once you take your eyes off, it is over. You have been attracted by the force of *maya*, and that is what a pitfall is for. A pitfall should always be taken progressively and the reason for the pitfall should be overcome and you should emerge victorious.

The purpose of the human life is to go beyond, from one dimension to the next, experiencing the pleasures of the physical world and not getting stuck in them by taking them to be the purpose of life; and this journey is taken through evolution, which is by giving away what you have and not by making pilgrimages or reading scriptures. By scriptures and pilgrimages, I mean, the physical act — the verbal repetition of the scriptures or doing *artis* in front of an idol without having a clue of the energy, simply as a moral duty. I am differentiating the physical from the etheric, accessing the ether can take you from one dimension to the next but to be able to do that you have to reach that state of accessing it, and that will only come by giving away what you have. Everything that you take for yourself, including the breath you inhale or the food you ingest, is a negative *karma* because, the breath you take in for yourself belongs to the whole creation, the potato or chicken you eat is also taken from the resources of creation. It is the level of consciousness of the thing you take in, that decides to what degree it is negative. Look at the Divine, look at Lord *Shiv*, what does he take for himself? He has no pleasures for himself, he just gives. That is evolution. When you evolve, it is felt and experienced by those around you. You do not need to give healing energies to people for them to know that you have evolved, whatever has to happen, happens automatically as they come in your vicinity. Anybody who comes in contact with you gets benefited then and there.

For every practitioner of *yog*, for every human being who wants to go beyond, who wants to evolve, *sadhna* is a must and for *sadhna,* there has to be a *sadhya*. *Sadhya* is simply a target that you have to reach. By reaching I don't mean to go to a temple on the other shore of the ocean and come back. That is not *sadhna*, nor is it reaching your *sadhya*. *Sadhya* is energy, you have to tune into the energy of the *sadhya*, only then can you access the *sadhya*. For that you have to understand what your *sadhya* is all about, merge with it and completely absorb all its qualities and compel it to give you what you want completely by becoming one with it and taking everything and then going beyond. Running after something is physical, go beyond the physical. Only then will you be able to reach somewhere. Beware of the pitfalls, when something good happens or when something bad happens, they are both indications for you. Good means that you are on a strong footing and you have reached somewhere, so now be careful; bad means you have hardly any ability or consciousness inside you, so bad things are happening again and again. Something good or bad is given to you to tie you down here, to divert your mind off your *sadhya,* to distract you to get you stuck in the play of *maya* so you cannot go beyond. Don't ever divert your mind, don't ever break your *sadhna*, don't dilute it with anything else because once it is broken, it will never come back. You would only need a miracle after that and miracles are very rare. The day, the minute, the second, you dilute it — it is finished and you start all over again. This is the play of *maya*.

A dimension is the compartment you are in, *sadhna* is the route to move beyond that compartment and a pitfall is the attraction or the negativity that prevents you from going beyond that compartment and the seven *loks*. The purpose is to go beyond the dimension you are in, and that will happen with the simple technique of giving whatever you have, through evolution, evolution of the spirit. The *yoni* of a human being does not evolve, nor does an ant, a human remains a human and an ant remains an ant, it is the spirit that goes through the experience of both and evolves. Once you go into *sadhna* and if you go a little deeper into *dhyan* and are able to transgress your body, then you can even experience the sun if you want to and feel like the sun. You will know exactly what is happening in the sun. Understand you are not this body; this is just an experience that you are going through. A plant or an animal or even human does not have a soul, these are just experiences through which the soul goes, it is not contained in anything. It might go through ten different insects in a matter of minutes, but it just goes through, it is not bound to it. When you are in *dhyan*, and go out of your body, you can just go into an ant, or into a cockroach. It's an experience you go through but you won't remain there because you have transgressed that dimension long back. To head to a dimension beyond your present level of existence, all you need is to find a *Guru*. There are certain laws that govern this creation and a *Guru* gives you the experience of these laws by giving his energy to you. When you access your *Guru*'s energy, you experience your *Guru*'s level of evolution. Ideally, by your sheer force or focus, the *Guru* should be compelled to give all his years of *sadhna* so that all his experiences become yours and this is achievable. *Guru seva,* which is walking your *Guru*'s path, is the strongest *karma* for evolution. The Law of *Karma* says — what you give comes back to you. If you want knowledge, you give knowledge to people and more knowledge will flow into you. If you want good health, serve the poor and the sick, and good health will flow into you.

Once you come under the *sanidhya* of a *Guru*, your *karmas* start improving from day one and you start evolving automatically. But this is something, which you have to experience, like the charity example I shared with you. You give charity, but the day you do not remember how much you gave is when you know that you have reached somewhere. If you are giving and counting, then you know it is a drama. It is a self-indicator, which every human being has inside, and *Guru* just shows you where you are. How far you reach from there depends on your desire. In *yog*, there is no such thing as age, whether you are just born or you are 100 years old, in *yog* there is only one thing and that is *Guru*. When you have the *sanidhya* of a *Guru*, then *yog* happens on its own. *Guru* knows what *anubhutis* you need at the moment and so the *kriyas* (practices), *karyas* and *karmas* (tasks and actions) are given in accordance with those *anubhutis.*

You cannot understand what or why the *Guru* does, the problem is that you try to understand it with your mind, obviously you will falter. I'll share a small experience. In one of my lectures, I found a person sitting with hands on his head. So I sent somebody to find out why he was sitting like that. The man revealed that he was actually calculating that he had spent 3 lakh rupees in the last two years to do various courses and was wondering why he spent so much for such a simple thing. So understand this — your mind limits you, and when the mind limits you, you do not know what is beyond that. It is something like, if I tell you of a colour, which you have never seen and if I tell you it's a very beautiful colour, you will not be able to understand what I am saying because you don't have the experience of that colour. The *Guru* takes you through the experience and once you are taken through that experience, then you know the beauty of it and once you have experienced it, then you want to go beyond it. Till then it is an intellectual exercise for you, just a play of mind — it is knowledge, not *gyan*. And **your mind is simply your natural state of consciousness** (***jagriti ki avastha***), it is unlimited and from this you can go anywhere. A human has so much ability that he can do anything, reach anywhere. In the *Bhulok,* you are only using seven to eight per cent of the mind, which is enough for the five basic senses, beyond this you don't require. When you get ready for the next *lok,* say *Bhuvahlok,* the mind is similar but it is not in this form and shape, its attractions are different. Right now, you have five senses in the *Bhulok*. In *Bhuvahlok,* there is only one. Also there are seven *chakras* in *Bhulok* but in *Bhuvahlok* there is only one big *chakra*, one energy. Thoughts are there, but not of this kind. Thoughts are always there, till you cross *Satyalok*. Every *lok* has its speciality, its own attraction and its own dimension. But you cannot think of *Satyalok*, sitting in *Bhulok,* because your senses are not awakened. For instance, an ant cannot think about a human life unless it connects in consciousness to a human being, which is an impossibility. But, for a human to connect with the higher forces and make them submissive and to go beyond is very much a possibility, but pitfalls are a plenty.

The person in the higher dimension is not going to bother; the person in a lower dimension will ensure that everybody knows about the charity he has done, because for a person in higher dimension, it is nature, like the act of breathing, and for a person in lower dimension, it is showing off, something extraordinary.

Original/unedited pictures of manifestations in *havan* performed by *sadhaks* at *Dhyan Ashram*.

LORD SHIV

Puranas abound with descriptions of *havans* performed by *rishis*, *munis*, *tapasvis* and *sadhaks*. *Ram* and *Lakshman* went with *Vishvamitra* to protect one such *havan*. Another famous *havan* was conducted by *Janmajeya* to exterminate *Takshak* and the entire clan of *nagas* to avenge the killing of his father *Parikshit*. At the completion of all such *havans*, *devs* and *devis* would appear to bless the *havan*. These are not things of the past, even today, divine manifestations are reported at the time of *purna-ahuti* in genuine *havans*.

SERMON 8

COMPLEXITIES OF ASHTANG YOG

" *The state of asan is when you are 'still' in a posture for a long time and are peaceful, your pulse does not shoot up, rather it falls, as does the body temperature. It indicates that you have complete control on the body.* "

8

It is disappointing to see what all is being discussed in the name of *yog* on the television these days. It is not *yog*. It is grave misinformation projected by the media about the science of *yog*. It is a crime… All of you, especially the ones who want to go forth in *yog*, it is very important for you to understand this. People start doing *yog* blindly, thinking what they are about to get. You need to understand what you are going to get, otherwise you will end up wasting your time. I have done that for many years. Since you have come to me I don't want you to waste your time.

When a human being takes birth, he has three options available to him. He can do any one of the three things.

The first is to run after the thing that attracts him. Just sit and think — what was it that attracted you when you were six months old? What were you stuck at when you turned six? And what is it that you want now that you are 60? If even at 60 the attraction is for something physical and at six also it was for the physical then it clearly shows that you are in the same *yoni* that you had started with; you have not moved forward even by an inch. Your body has changed, your form has changed but you are still the same, there is no change. And if you are the same at 60 as you were at six, then it is certain that you will be the same even when you leave this body. And when you take up the next body, it will be one level lower than the level you are at right now.

When you take birth, the first option available to you is to chase the physical attractions and keep running in circles. After the circle gets completed, you spiral down to a lower circle and once that completes, you move to an even lower circle and so on. This explains the deplorable condition of human beings and the environment in present times.

People who come to the *ashram* tell me that there is a marked difference in the environment inside and outside the *ashram*; that they experience tirelessness, peace and stillness here. I rarely move out of the *ashram*... Once when I was going for a session, I saw that the road, which was constructed only two months back, had potholes in it. Few hundred meters down the road there lay the corpse of a dog; none of the passers-by were bothered. Next, we were met with clouds of dust as some construction work was in progress. Then suddenly a signboard in front of us read 'cannot go beyond this'. If only the board was placed some two kilometers back, many would have been saved the inconvenience of coming till there and turning back... As we turned back and plied on another road, the first site was that of a herd of cows feeding on plastic and waste from a garbage dump. Few meters ahead there was yet another garbage dump where people were busy burning the waste material and releasing toxins in the air. Moving further, there were truck-drivers and owners of SUVs busy swearing at each other, it was difficult to tell one from the other. Next was a *mandir,* which had opened recently in the heart of a market, next to a beauty parlour. I thought to myself, what beauty would a parlour give in this environ and what *moksha* would a *mandir* provide... I wondered what would be the condition and state of mind of the people who live outside in this environment only. Then it struck me, why people are unable to understand what I say, despite my repeating several times. While living in such an environment, it is not possible to understand what I say. People keep running after physical attractions, spiraling down with every new birth, which is what has brought us to the present state of affairs. What is next after this, I can see, perhaps you cannot, but it is not right to disclose it right now, it will unnecessarily create fear in you.

The people who choose the first option complete a circle in one birth and spiral down in the next and so on. The ones who take the second option are the ones who take pleasure in causing harm to others. They are unable to complete even one circle in one birth and constantly spiral down. Everyone causes harm to the others in chasing their own desires and attractions, since the resources are limited. But the ones who feel happy on harming someone else — "See, I taught him a lesson. Look, how troubled he is. It will be so much fun now" — they belong to the second category. These are the people who torture and torment animals because it is pleasurable to them. They go down continuously at a very fast speed. They will reach *narklok* in this birth only; they will not have to wait for long.

The third category is the people who can see what is happening around them. Whether 18 or 12 or 60 — irrespective of their age, they see what is happening and where they are headed and they look for a way to get out of it. Again the people who look for a way out are of two kinds. First, is what the majority sitting here belongs to — those who 'think' they are looking for a way out but the minute the slightest of attractions come their way, they slip and fall in the pit. So they think they are looking for a way out but actually they are not interested in going anywhere, they just want to show-off that they are coming out of this and how good they are. Second, are those who actually believe that they are stuck here; they look for a way out and actually walk that path. The percentage of people in this category is minimal. Let us understand why...

If you look at *Patanjali Yogsutras,* you will realise that it is in fact very complicated. It is not as easy as what is shown on the television these days — breathe fast and cure cancer or stand on your head and reach the seventh, eighth or 19th dimension. Just understand how complicated it is — *yam, niyam, asan, pranayam, pratyahar, dharana, dhyan, samadhi.* Let's start with the five *yams — satya, asteya, aparigrah, ahimsa, brahmacharya. Satya* means no matter what happens, do not lie; always, under all circumstances speak the truth. *Asteya* and *aparigrah* emphasise not to take what belongs to others and not to hoard what is yours. You will appreciate how difficult it is to not snatch from others and to not collect, the dominant thought in every individual being how to safeguard his/her future. *Ahimsa* is to not harm anyone. Who in today's date is willing to follow *ahimsa*? Till we harm another person, we are not at peace. "He did this to me at office. I will show him his place." *Himsa* goes deep down in our veins. *Brahmacharya* is celibacy. I tire out telling people to abstain but they are just unable to sustain it. So you see, you have not even started *Ashtang yog*, you are stuck at the five *yams* only. (I am trying to make you understand why the percentage of people is so less.)

Next come *niyams — shauch, santosh, swadhyay, tapas, ishwar pranidhan.*

Shauch means cleanliness. Cleanliness is not taking a bath. Even if you take a bath in the water that runs in the taps these days, you will not get cleansed. It might leave you dirtier than before. Whatever you come in contact with, whatever you ingest, your thought pattern becomes like that. With the chemical laced water, foods and cosmetics that you consume, you too are becoming chemical — artificial. Whatever goes inside you, whatever is its nature; that becomes your nature on the inside and the outside. Today, waste from septic tanks is emptied into agricultural fields. When you consume the vegetables grown in those fields, you become like that waste. That is why the condition of human beings is like this; that is why it is so difficult for them to understand all this. Until that filth is cleaned, that energy cannot flow into you. It is not possible. I have been telling for the past six months that anyone who wants to do business of pure and organic products should let me know. I will sell it the world over and I want nothing out of your profits. Till now, there is just one lady who has come back to me with the idea of providing organic vegetables — just one from the so many of you. You are the people who want to do good for others and yet you are unwilling to take this up even when you are provided a ready market. You are anxious of what might happen. This is your own thought pattern. You can well imagine what will be in the heads of those who are in the market for profits.

Recently, a wholesaler of food products was telling me that a certain organic food company purchased the rice from his shop (which is not organic) and sold it in the market as organic at three times the price. Imagine what risk you are putting yourself at by consuming anything that is available in the market these days. The soaps, shampoos, and cosmetics that you apply on your skin are known to contain toxins like SLS, SLES etc. Even the products from brands which claim to be organic and herbal are not free from chemicals. In today's time there are very few entities providing genuine and pure organic products, Quinta Essentia Skin Organics being one of them.

Our body is 75 per cent water. So most of what we are is the water that we consume. At *Dhyan Ashram* we did a small experiment on this. We have our own bores through which we obtain water for bathing. It goes through a six stage purification process, the final being reverse osmosis. After this process, 70 per cent water goes in waste and only 30 per cent remains. This is the state of water in Delhi. We do not use this water for drinking, because we know what the condition of water is outside. One day I decided to drink it and see what happens. People told me not to do this but I wanted to see what happens. Then I thought let it get filtered one last time, so we put that 30 per cent remaining water into the RO system, which left us with a mere 10-15 per cent of it and I drank that. Within minutes of drinking that water I had a severe stomach pain. Normally I don't feel pain but my stomach was aching so much that I realised what pain is. So you can imagine the levels of contamination around you, if even water through a seven-step filtration process leads to stomach infection. This is the importance of *shauch* or cleanliness. I was trying to understand why *Ashtang yog* is made so complicated — I got my answer. These days I am experimenting with every stage of it.

Swadhyaya is the next *niyam*. It means self-study. How many people sit and think about their self? Everyone. But here we are not talking about thinking of ways to enhance your looks, bank-balances and/or lifespan. How many think about where they are headed? How much have they improved in the last six months? No one. Everybody thinks they are fine. They think that sitting with eyes closed for 15 minutes shoves them of all responsibilities and they can continue doing whatever wrong things they were up to before that. All of this is because there is so much filth inside you. Who among all those sitting here is satisfied with his/her life — *santosh* or the third *niyam*? None. And you people have come here after crossing a filtration system. Whatever the condition in Delhi or the world, you are the people who have survived the stage one of RO. Whether you have this much or that much, if you are not satisfied with that, it simply indicates the *asthirta* in you. If you are *asthir*, you cannot do *yog*.

Shauch-santosh-swadhyay, then *tapas*. How many of you sit for *dhyan* in a room without fan or cooler or air-conditioner? Only twelve hands... Those who raised hands are the ones who are moving towards *tapas*. When I used to do *dhyan* initially, even in the peak of summers I would close the room from all sides and sit in silence. By the time I would get up, there would be water everywhere... that is the heat of *tapas*. The fifth *niyam* is *ishwar pranidhan*. That is, to take time out to think of somebody who is sitting up there, who is superior to you and is observing every thought and act you indulge in. Normally I say there is no one. But *ishwar pranidhan* means that there is someone and even though you should be scared of your own self, if not that then at least be scared of the one who is up there. Think of Him on a regular basis. These are the *yams* and *niyams* — *satya, asteya, aparigrah, ahimsa, brahmacharya, shauch, santosh, swadhyay, tapas, ishwar pranidhan.*

The reason why a normal person is not able to understand what I say is because my vani is a kind of energy, and to catch/receive that energy, the receptor should be of that frequency only. This can happen only when the person is doing Ashtang yog, otherwise it is not possible.

You will now be able to appreciate the complexity of *Ashtang yog*. Next is the stage of *asan. Asan* is not *XYZ's Veerbhadra asan* stage one, two and three. That is body-building. *Asan* according to *yogsutras* is '*sukham sthiram asanam*'. That is, a posture in which you are comfortable and still. Now if you are still while lying down, that does not make it an *asan*. An *asan* is a *yoni*. *Mayur asan* is the *yoni* of a peacock, *Shashank asan* of a rabbit, *Shirsh asan* is the *yoni* of *Sahastrar chakra*, and so on. These days one hears of terms like *Sukh asan*. There is nothing called *such* in creation, so forget such innovative terminology. When you are able to maintain an *asan* (not lying down) for 10 to 15 minutes then that is the *sthiti* of an *asan*. Recently, a journalist came to us. He wanted the demonstration of certain *asans*. As the *sadhaks* performed the *asans*, I noticed that the journalist did not take any pictures. One minute passed. Two, three, four, five... I asked him what was it that he was trying to do. He replied, "I had gone to another organization where they did not even hold an *asan* for 30 seconds.

They started shivering within 30 seconds and exclaimed *Jai Gurudev!'"* Then I asked him if he had enquired about the reason for the same. He said he did and the reply that he got was "Our *Guruji* has told us that when we do this, we get so much *shakti* in our body that it is unable to hold it and starts shivering." This is a very serious matter... because a journalist who was doing a show on *yog* actually bought that explanation. I then asked him if he found any difference in what these people are doing and what they did. He said, "There is a marked difference. These people have good bodies and a natural glow." I said, "Do you understand what is happening?" He nodded at that time but as he left he was still thinking that 'these people must not be having strength because of which they did not shiver even after five minutes.' It is serious. This is what is happening these days. The state of *asan* is when you are 'still' in a posture for a long time and are peaceful, your pulse does not shoot up, rather it falls, as does the body temperature. It indicates that you have complete control on the body.

Next is the state of *pranayam*. Your body is run not by the *sthool* (physical) but by *sukshma* (energy) called *prana.* This energy controls your breathing process. When *pranayam* is performed, the body starts getting cool, calm and still. If you were doing a task in 10 breaths previously, you will do the same in five. And there comes a state, when your breath process ceases completely and the energy is in your control at that time, which is the state of *pranayam*.

Pratyahar is the withdrawal of the senses. You are no longer ruled by the senses. If your sense is telling you that you are hungry then you do not desperately forage for food, or if a sexual urge rises you do not give in to it helplessly. You have complete control (*saiyam*) over the five senses, that is, your senses function as per your wish. After coming to this state you can eat and indulge sexually in any way because you are in full control of yourself, but not before this. The *yogsutras* explain this with the example of a tortoise. Just like a tortoise pulls his legs inside but he still has legs, in the same way a *yogi* pulls his senses inside but he still has senses. He can use them as per his discretion without getting *vichlit* (out of control). Next comes *dharana*, where you decide that 'you want to do *yog*'. Then you are able to enter *dhyan* and *samadhi*.

It is a long journey. For now you need to understand that the reason why a normal person is not able to understand what I say is because my *vani* is a kind of energy, and to catch/receive that energy, the receptor should be of that frequency only. This can happen only when the person is doing *Ashtang yog,* otherwise it is not possible. Like the other day, a couple had come to meet me and the husband said with folded hands, "Just keep our child out of *yog*." This couple has been coming for *dhyan* sessions for quite some time now. This just goes on to prove that until you do *Ashtang yog*, you will not understand that *vani*, you will just think of it as a problem which is making your child useless — 'He doesn't do any work since he does not earn any money'. Just think this is the condition of people who have been hearing my lectures for so many years. One can only imagine the plight of others who jump like monkeys on TV channels and think that they have reached somewhere, and of those who throng in thousands and lakhs to attend their *shivirs* to learn all kinds of *vidyas*.

Recently, somebody came to me after suffering a business loss. I asked him, "But you had learnt *Shri Vidya*?" He replied, "That is what I want to talk to you about." I asked him, "Did I teach you?" He said, "No. I must have learnt it wrong, now you teach me correctly." I told him that I could not teach him something I myself have not completed as yet. To this he exclaimed, "You haven't finished it? What are you talking! I know of at least 500 people who know *Shri Vidya*." I said, "Just go to the one who taught it to you." He told me that the gentleman is not approachable anymore. People who teach such vidyas are the reason why are culture is mocked upon. They are the *asurs* of present times. *Asurs* in olden times roamed in jungles and filled their stomach by hunting and killing, *asurs* of present times do not get satisfied even after destroying lives of millions, still they want more and for that they introduce some newer *vidyas* to sell.

Some time back a very renowned *Guru* was selling a *shakti* oil in our neighboring country. He would call someone from the audience and apply the oil on his arm, then ask someone else to forcefully bend the oil-applied arm, and when the person would be unable to bend it, there would be a roar of *'Jai Gurudev'* from his students. That is how they sold all the bottles of *shakti* oil. But alas! *Shakti* oil is not in stock now... too bad if yours did not work! I am not joking, this is what is happening these days. This is the cause of downfall of this culture. Nobody is ready to do *Ashtang yog*. When I talk about *Ashtang yog*, some say 'it is too long' and others want to get their child out of it — 'Our child should drink, party and have fun, that is better as we don't know where he will reach after doing *yog*.' But even kids are at fault because at home they say 'we are doing *Ashtang yog*' but outside they are doing some other *yog* only. So when they are doing their own *yog*, how will *lakshan* of *Ashtang yog* come in them? As a result, they spoil my name, their name and the name of *yog* and the parents come to me with such requests. Until a person follows *Ashtang yog* properly, he will not understand what I say, no matter how many years he has been with me, because he will not have that frequency. Till the time you do not receive my *vani* of *Ashtang yog*, till then *sanchalan* of that energy will not happen. It is just not possible because your body is like a machine, it requires cleanliness. It requires clean food. Clean thought process. Purity. These are the conditions given for it — *yam, niyam, asan, pranayam, pratyahar, dharana, dhyan*. When all these conditions are fulfilled, then you will understand my *vani*, not before that. And if you are unable to understand my *vani* then you should take it as a warning sign. It clearly means that you belong to the category that is going round and round in circles. You don't belong to that category that is looking for a way out of that cycle because if you are looking for a way out then you should be able to understand what I am talking about and that can happen only if you are doing *Ashtang yog* properly as told to you. Otherwise you will not be able to understand it.

There is no *shakti* in creation that you cannot access but for that at least do what you are asked to do. You do not do that and so nothing happens but you show off on the outside that you have reached a state... Why collect bad *karmas* by spoiling my name? It would be better if you tell at home that you are going for a party. That is better than lying and keeping your family and yourself in dark, it is better to speak the truth openly. Start from *satya* only, at least start somewhere. You are not able to complete *yams* only and if your *yams* are not complete then how will your *Ashtang yog* get completed?

I have been telling you that my state is becoming such that the distance between you and me will start increasing rapidly. And in this coming year that distance between you and me will increase very fast, if you are not following *Ashtang yog* completely. So if you want to stay with me, start following *Ashtang yog* properly. Nobody gets harmed by following *Ashtang yog*. On the contrary, many *siddhis* and many *dwars* get opened.

Just like a tortoise pulls his legs inside but he still has legs, in the same way a yogi pulls his senses inside but he still has senses. He can use them as per his discretion without getting vichlit (out of control).

SERMON 9

SATYA

> *"Only those who practice can walk the path of yog, rest simply waste their life and birth, having no experience till the very end. When you are driving a car and you are asked to put the first gear, but you put the reverse instead, would you reach your destination?"*

9

The first *yam* as mentioned in *Patanjali Yogsutras* is *satya* or truth. One may wonder why... It seems so easy to escape an adverse situation with a lie. Just observe your day's routine. How many times do you lie in a day to get out of situations, big or small? When I ask the spiritual aspirants who come to me whether they practice the *yam* of *satya*, the answer I usually get is, 'I try not to lie'. 'Trying' or 'working towards' something is equivalent to not doing it; you either do it or you don't, anything in between is redundant.

Yog is a very practical subject. There is no theory, only practice. Only those who practice can walk the path of *yog*, rest simply waste their life and birth, having no experience till the very end. When you are driving a car and you are asked to put the first gear, but you put the reverse instead, would you reach your destination?

Switch on the television these days. You will find hundred men trying to market and sell *yog* in 100 different ways. Some offer miracle cures, some claim to predict your future, some others have *mantras* and *yantras* to solve your problems and the rest are narrating *kathas* with tears in their eyes. Who among these appears to be speaking the truth to you?

I had recently been invited to a meet of over 200 '*yoga*' *Gurus*. All the *Gurus* were sitting in the first three rows while the media people occupied the following rows. A particular *Guru* called one gentleman from the media, who wields a lot of influence in the 'spiritual circle', to sit with him in the first row. This media person has, on many occasions, interacted with me as well and during all such interactions, he has educated me on the *siddhis* and greatness of various spiritual heads and the closeness he shares with them. Recently, somebody in his family fell seriously ill. Despite knowing everyone from top to bottom, he made frantic calls and wrote numerous e-mails to Dhyan Foundation to help save that person... It seemed quite strange that somebody who canvasses the *siddhis* of various '*yoga' Gurus* all through the day; could not put his trust in any of them when it came to saving a family member. Deep down, he knew it was all a lie. Imagine, 200 *Gurus*, and not even one out of them he thought could help him out, he chose healing through *yog* at *Dhyan Ashram* over them all... this is the truth of the world today.

Patanjali Yogsutras clearly prohibit lying. The*yogsutras* are extremely scientific and technical. Every *sutra* is linked with the next one, the *gyan* of one flows into the next... if you miss one then you miss the rest that follow it.

Why is it that truth, has been emphasised upon in the *yogsutras*? What happens when you lie?

Somebody told me that a lie is spoken for personal benefit and so, is wrong. Everything you do, from morning till night, is for personal benefit only. Even when you do charity, it is in the hope that some good will come to you. So what is wrong in lying? Somebody else told me that that lie takes you away from your soul. You are already quite far away from your soul... Had you been any closer, you would not be reading this text, but would be sitting in silence somewhere. You would have only been seen if your *Guru* had entrusted a specific responsibility on you.

Physical manifested world is all *asatya*/ falsehood. So anybody lying or taking the help of falsehood would forever get stuck in this physical world. To realise the truth and to go beyond the physical world and to access the energies which control it, one has to resort to truth. It is difficult, but it is the only way.

Satyanand Paramhansa, the founder of Bihar School of Yoga, at the age of 40-45 left all that he had established and lived in silence for the next 40 years of his life. Once he had gone to lecture in a foreign country. The morning after the lecture, he packed his bags and came back to India, as soon as he got permission from his *Guru*. He could have gone to the Bihar School in Munger, which he had himself constructed by laying bricks for the building, but he chose to go straight to silence. He was a practical person and never imposed any kind of restrictions or lifestyle regimes on any of the practitioners. He simply told them to make a *Guru* and do whatever they like. Most of you run after name, fame and wealth throughout your life and this gentleman had it all, but chose to abandon it to settle in silence... Here lies the *gyan* of truth and lie.

Something, which directly benefits you and harms somebody else, is a lie. Something, which benefits somebody else and does not affect you, even though a lie, is not a lie.

What is truth?

Your body, the flowers and trees, sun, moon, water… all of them are changing all the time. What you looked like 10 years back, or even a year back, is not same as what you are this instant. The body is constantly moving towards destruction. A new set of cells replaces the cells in your body every seven years. Even what you see as death, has happened many times before; it is just that you are only able to understand it when the body is taken to *shamshan*. Just think about it… today your hair are grey, ten years back they were black. So are you the same person who had black hair? The *prana* that governs your body is undergoing a change with every passing thought of yours. In fact, it is because the *prana* is changing that the body too is undergoing a change. What then is truth — how things were a moment back or how they will be the next instant? What is changing is *nashwar*; that which is not there at all, because it is there this moment but it will not be in the next. What is not there, what you are only assuming there to be, how can that be the truth? In fact, the biggest illusion is that change only. Name one thing in this creation that is truth.

At the time of *Raja Janak*, *shaastrarths* (meets, where meaning of *shaastras* were pondered upon) were held. Learned scholars (*pandits*) would get together and debate on truths of creation. Those who were defeated would behead themselves, take *jal-samadhi*, observe penance, etc — their fate decided by the king. So, even *shaastra,* which takes one from mortality to immortality, were reduced to *shastra (weapons);* that take one towards *nashvarta (*destruction*)*. Even the most learned *pandits* missed out on the essence or *gyan* of *shaastra,* and turned them into untruth.

A gentleman once told me God is truth… When you do *yog*, you experience these energies, but till the time you have experienced them, they are non-existent for you. Having an experience is important, that is the only way to progress in *yog*. So I asked this person if he had seen God or knew what he looks like, or where he exists. The reply came, 'God is in every speck of creation.' I then asked him if there was God in the microphone from where I was speaking. He said, 'maybe'. Another gentleman came to his rescue and said, 'We have grown up hearing that whatever we have is God-given, so we assume God is everywhere.' Mind the words 'maybe' and 'assume' in the two replies. Both of these indicate that it is the mind speaking, not experience. When you have experienced something, you do not doubt upon it. A single doubt is enough to keep you away from your path. The greatest of philosophers have fallen in this trap…

Adi Shankaracharya was once looking for someone to do a commentary on his work, *'Saundarya Lahiri'.* He decided to approach the learned *vedic* scholar *Bhattacharya*, for the purpose. When he went to meet him, he found *Bhattacharya* immolating himself, one of his eyes was badly injured. *Shankaracharya* showed him the book, upon reading which *Bhattacharya* complimented saying *'ati uttam'* (brilliant) (his body was already on fire). *Shankaracharya* asked him for the commentary, to which *Bhattacharya* replied, that he had no time left and his body would turn to ashes within few minutes. He recommended his *shishya, Mandan Mishra*, for the task of writing the commentary. *Shankaracharya* then asked him the reason for putting his body through all this, and also how he injured his eye. *Bhattacharya* explained that when Buddhism started going against *vedic* teachings, he decided to learn Buddhist teachings under a Buddhist *Guru* incognito, and debate with the followers upon the authority of *vedas*. When his *Guru* got to know of his lie, he ordered the rest of the monks to throw him off the cliff. As he was being thrown down, *Bhattacharya* said, 'IF the *vedas* are true, then nothing will happen to me.' Just like those gentlemen who had used 'maybe' and 'assume', *Bhattacharya* used the word 'if'. Result? While he was saved, he lost an eye. Had he said, '*Vedas* are there, nothing will happen to me, throw me', he would not have injured himself. Regarding why he was immolating himself, *Bhattacharya* replied that he was doing penance for *Guru Droh.* Even though he did what he did for the *vedas*, in the process he went against the one whom he looked upon as his *Guru*.

Satya is *satya*. There are no 'ifs' and 'maybes' in it. Never make the mistake of doubting upon it, wait for your experience, so that you can say without doubt, that God is in every speck because that is the only truth, and *yog* and *Sanatan Kriya* take you towards this. There is only one *satya* in this creation, but in order to awaken that within you, it is imperative to do *yog* in totality, as only then you will have the experience of it. And when you have the experience, then that means you are doing *yog*. And only then you can experience *satya*.

Satya is a *shakti*, which is not there even in the '*kan kan'* (every speck) because even that '*kan kan'* is *nashwar*. Every speck of creation is a lie, so is your body, and the idol that you worship. All of it is false, perishable and constantly changing. *Satya* is that which is *shashwat* (eternal). It is an experience and *yogsutras* say, that you will have that experience only when you practice *satya*. You just cannot lie because to attain the truth you have to follow the path of truth, there is no scope for doubt or lie.

The destruction of our culture began because of this very reason. When Mahmud Ghaznavi attacked the *Somnath* temple to plunder it, the residents came up on the roofs. The General thought they would attack his army, instead the residents just asked them to leave, and said that if they don't, their God will kill them. The invaders concluded that it was a city of mad people; and they were not entirely wrong. The plunderers killed the entire population of the city — men, women and children alike... And that temple was looted 17 times. Just take a look at the history of invasions in this country, they came, they plundered and they spared no one, all were killed. What was the reason? The reason is the 'if', 'may be' and all kinds of *vahams* (superstitions) that took shelter in the minds of people — 'God is in this idol, in this picture, in this *maala*.' All the time there were debates on where God is? God is not sitting hidden in an idol that will take out a sword and kill those who attack a temple. That is why so many invaders looted so much from here so easily because we started searching for God in something, which is itself *nashwar*, somewhere it can never exist. How can something which is eternal be in something which is destructible? It cannot be.

People died but the culture survived; because the culture is truth, it is the interpretation of the people that was false. Hence, the present state of affairs is such that truth is being represented by falsehood through people who themselves do not believe in truth. One who practices truth is complicated to understand and does not sell. The ones, who sell *yog*, use gimmicks of innovation, which are away from reality, are a lie. Only a minority can practice or preach the truth. *Yog* is for the truth-speaking minority because only a minority deserves to go beyond. The majority would want to continue here, enjoying the falsehood of the physical worlds.

Till the time you consider yourself a body, till the time you 'think' (and not believe) God is in every speck, till the time you consider what is false as true, till that time you will remain in lie. That is why the *shloka* — *Asato ma sadgamaya, tamso ma jyotirgamaya, mrityor ma amritam gamaya*. That is, how it will happen. First, go from *asatya* to *satya*, then from darkness to light and only then you can go from death to immortality, or the ultimate truth. And to get the *darshan* of *satya* in *asatya*, one has to speak the truth. No matter how many books you read, how many discussions and debates you have, till the time there is lie or doubt inside you, till the time you are taking physical that is *nashvar* to be *satya*, till that time you cannot attain truth.

Understand it this way, *satya* is like an *indri* (sense). A human being has a total of 16 *indris*, of which only five are awakened in you, which are enough to enjoy the physical creation, the *Bhulok*, that which is manifest at the basic level of existence. Even the unmanifest has *shrenis* (levels) such as *Bhuvahlok*, *Swahlok*, *Mahalok*, *Janalok*, *Tapalok* and *Satyalok*. All these are *loks*, every progressive *lok* being higher than the previous one. For an ordinary person, all of them are unmanifest, because he/she exists at the level of five senses. But for someone who is a little ahead in *yog, Bhuvahlok* and *Svahlok,* is also manifest. So how will you define, which *shreni* of *prana* (all these *loks* are *shrenis* of *prana* only) is *satya* and which is *asatya*? Defining it is not possible. How will you understand something, which cannot even be understood by the sixth or the seventh sense? How can you understand something, the sense for which is lacking in you? Besides, what will happen even if I do put it in words? There are plenty of books available, which detail all the *siddhis*, *sadhnas*, and *beej mantras*. In fact, a simple internet search will give you all the matter. Do that search and let me know if you are able to attain even one *siddhi* by reading about it. You will have to practice it and get it from a *Guru* who has already achieved it because only he can initiate the process of activation of *shakti* in the *mantra*.

I have researched for more than two decades and the conclusion that I have come to is, that this journey is your own journey and it is not possible without a *Guru*. The job of the *Guru* is to bring the *shishya* on the path and tell him to walk it; he will automatically reach his destination. If your *Guru* has the capacity and he has shown that path to you, and if you are walking on that path and then if you don't reach anywhere, then that is the *karma* of your *Guru*, you do not have to worry about it. And a *Guru* is capable of putting the *shishya* on the right path; the only thing is *shishya* has to listen to the *Guru*. When you meet your *Guru* and are in his/her vicinity, then the energy/aura of the *Guru* has an effect on you. Some of your *karmas* change and you get some benefits in your life. But if you make these small benefits — cure of some disease, problem, or relationship issue — as main focus of your life, then what you are doing is similar to plucking a grass straw upon entering a garden full of different varieties of flowers. All those flowers are for you only, but you get nervous, pluck a straw and go back. Then what can anybody do about it?

Whatever you collect in the physical — a beautiful body, wealth, status, etc — is *nashvar.* It will only be for a very short duration and after that it will crumble in front of your own eyes. Always remember, whenever you collect more than what you require, you are taking someone else's share and you will have to pay back for it, in this birth or the next. There is no restriction on enjoying, you can enjoy as much as you want to— eat, drink, travel... but what is prohibited in *yogsutras* is, collection. Because you can never get satisfied with physical, no matter how much you have, you will always want more. This is what is *maya*, this is what is lie, this is where you get fooled. You will collect everything and give it to someone who drops into your life suddenly one day. After that you will go to the *shamshan* and that person will enjoy all that you kept so safely with you, saved it from everything and everyone. You will see that, but you will not be able to do anything, as you will not have a body. But you will surely see that and feel helpless, I can guarantee you that much. And I do not lie...

Something, which directly benefits you and harms somebody else, is a lie. Something, which benefits somebody else and does not affect you, even though a lie, is not a lie.

SERMON 10

BRAHMACHARYA

" *The higher your state of evolution, the greater is your ability to manifest your thoughts and the lesser time you take to accomplish what you set out to achieve. It is the state of evolution that distinguishes a successful person from a normal person.* "

10

If you trace the birth of any religion that exists today, you will observe that it was always preceded by its leaders — be it *Mahavir*, *Gautam Buddha* or *Guru Gobind Singh* — going into a long period of isolation. It is then that their thought manifested and they achieved what they had set out to achieve. All the religions are just a manifestation of the thought of one person, who was able to achieve it, by isolating himself for sometime and connecting with the ultimate reality with one-pointed focus. And then, as per the capacity of the person, the ultimate reality revealed itself, the level of revelations was reflected in their works. These were the *rishis* of *Kaliyug*... You can well imagine the capacity and ability of the *rishis* of *Satyug,* who gave us the *vedas.*

Even today, if you go to the higher reaches, you will be able to find the families that trace back to the *rishis* of yore. If you ask them where their fathers were from, they will point half a kilometer up in the mountains. If you ask them where their grandfathers were from, they will point a little higher than that. Then if you ask them where their forefathers are actually from, they will point towards a far-off mountain peak. The peaks that they point towards are unlivable even today, despite the rise in temperatures, due to global warming. The *rishis* stayed there in the times when it used to be freezing...

Why? What was the need for them to settle in such inhospitable environs when they could have stayed in any part of this beautiful country and enjoyed all the pleasures? They were not foolish, *rishis* of the yore were very powerful beings. Then why were they living in isolation?

There is a story in the *Ayurveda* in this regard. It so happened, that some *rishis* came down from the higher reaches, and decided to settle closer to the habitation of common people. After a few years, they observed that their bodies were aging even though their lifestyle had not changed. They were doing their practices, chanting the *mantras*, performing the *havans* and yet, their bodies had started to age. Their power of manifestation was reducing. They wondered why all this was happening. Then it occurred to them that their interaction with commoners had increased. They were eating food brought by commoners and having social and physical interactions with them. That is, they were getting into normal physical pleasures. Pleasures are of two kinds — the normal physical pleasures of the body and the pleasures of the higher senses — the pleasure of *dhyan*, the pleasure of *yog*. So, from the pleasure of *yog,* which is a balance, they had come down to the pleasures of the physical.

In earlier times when saints used to make a visit, (I am not talking about the 'saints' who appear on television but the real saints, who have the abilities) from ancient times, everyone would come out of their houses to make offerings to them. These offerings led to collection. For example, people would cook spicy and delicious food and the *rishis* would eat it. Women would go to their *ashrams* to serve them. Though the *rishis* did not change their ways, such a treatment from people gave a boost to their ego . Also, the food that was offered to them had strong taste that stimulated the basic senses. Some of them, just by looking at the womenfolk, got sexual thoughts, again leading to contamination. Once they identified these three reasons, and their effect on their bodies, they retreated back to higher altitudes.

If you meet a true Himalayan master even in this day and age, you will notice that he would speak very less and whatever he would say in the four to five seconds when he makes a direct eye-contact with you, it will come true. It is because of his state of evolution. The higher your state of evolution, the greater is your ability to manifest your thoughts and the lesser time you take to accomplish what you set out to achieve. It is the state of evolution that distinguishes a successful person from a normal person. The ones, who are rich and influential in the present times, are the ones who have performed strong penance and lived by the principles of *Ashtang yog* in their previous lives to collect a strong *karmic* balance, which they are en-cashing upon right now. If you have a lot of money, you did not get it just like that. You have been an evolved soul doing good deeds and you have en-cashed those good deeds for all this physical pleasure. When you have a lot of money, you have a choice to either spend it on liquor or give it to charity. Similarly, the one who is in a position of power or ability, has a lot of *karmic* money. Such a person can achieve anything he wants with his focus and internal stability. Now it is his choice, whether he uses his power to aid the creation or to cause further disturbance.

What is that energy or force that lies with a successful person making him achieve all that he does, and that lacks in an ordinary man? That is the force of celibacy. One might argue that people who are successful usually have multiple partners; how then is celibacy relevant?

The body works on the force of the *Kundalini* and the *Kundalini* is a semi-dormant force that rests at your *Mool chakra* and sends out pulses of energy. The strength of these pulses determines whether they get consumed at the lower *chakras* or are able to penetrate and reach the higher *chakras*. To activate your higher senses and thought manifestation power, it is imperative to pull this energy till the *Agya/Sahastrar.* To achieve this one needs to follow the five *yams* as given in *Patanjali Yogsutras — satya, asteya, aparigraha, ahimsa and brahmacharya* or celibacy.

It is a misconception among people that if sperm is not released, problems develop in the body. *Swami Vivekanand*, many claimed, had died early because he was a celibate. However, this is not how it happens. When sperms accumulate in the sack, they neither rot nor become redundant but are released into the bloodstream and are pulled back from there the next time you get sexually excited. If you celibate, they remain in the bloodstream and the stronger is the sperm count in your blood, the healthier you will be. Old age and disease will not be able to touch you and you will develop more *karmic* strength. By *karmic* strength, I do not mean that having sex is bad. Sex is not bad, what is bad is the waste or release of this phenomenal force out of your body. It is a very strong pleasure and the immediate effect is opposite of that, a big drain on the body. Like the modern physicists now say, every action has an equal and opposite reaction.

People who are very successful are seen to have multiple partners since they have earned the force of celibacy within them with the austere practices that they carried out in their previous births. When you release this force in a sexual act to get this extreme pleasure, there's a very strong opposite reaction. And that reaction is that the energy, which you could have used for a higher purpose, gets released back into the atmosphere, into the elements and goes waste.

Celibacy does not merely mean abstaining from the physical act, it means that even the thought of it becomes redundant, naturally (not forcefully or artificially). A celibate will have a different look, which could be identified even by a normal person, but when seen clairvoyantly, it is seen as an exceptional glow in their aura. There is specific shade to this glow, which we call the *Brahma Tej.*

Lord *Brahma* is responsible for creation. Every thought, every action, every word, every material, every element, every aspect of creation has been created by him. The Creator has the ability to manifest his thoughts to create. Similarly, as a human being, you too have the ability to manifest your thoughts in creation, the difference being that you will not create thoughts but catch them from the environment and recreate something or transform something into something else. It is very easy, but you need to have that force in you.

In *yog*, this energy is called *sukra*. It is from *sukra* that *ojas* comes into the body and from *ojas* comes *tej*, the *Brahma Tej* —dazzling glow in a person, which sets him apart from an ordinary being. Certain people are born with this *tej* owing to strong *karmas* of previous births and because of this *tej* are able to attract physical comforts, name and fame towards them with relative ease. Others have to collect this force through austere practices of *yog* and *Sanatan Kriya*. For an ordinary person it is difficult because it takes a long period of time to collect it but for a person who is born with this glow, it's very easy. If such a person maintains celibacy for just 30 days, he will develop and radiate phenomenal glow, because he has already come with those kinds of *karmas* and so his ability is manifold. A person is ordinary not because of any other reason, but only because he does not have that *karmic* balance with him, and one of the main forces of that *karmic* balance is celibacy.

Glow and radiance is one aspect of manifestation of this force. Another aspect is sound, for example, chanting *mantras*. You will observe that when certain people chant a *mantra*, you feel something inside your body and are able to experience that energy. It could be anywhere — in a *mandir*, *masjid* or a *gurudwara*, you will find that when certain people chant, there is something different, something very strong about it. It is not the voice... the chants of the one who can sing well might sound melodious, but they may not generate that effect in you. Why is it that the chant of a singer, who knows the *surs*, articulates his voice beautifully, has no effect on you whereas someone, who has no background in music, is able to create a stir in the environment with his chants? What is the energy that makes an ordinary voice so powerful? It is again the force of celibacy. A bullet is just a piece of metal until the gun-powder is put into it. The gun-powder disintegrates into the atmosphere and the metal remains. Your body is like that metal bullet. You have to generate that gun-powder within it and then you can use it to reach any heights in the physical, as well as the spiritual planes. As this force develops inside you, the manifestation power of your thought becomes manifold. That is the manifestation of the *Brahma Tej*, of *tejas,* which originates from *sukra*.

A person who is successful, who possesses the *Brahma Tej*, can manifest anything very easily. If you have got something important coming up in a month's time or two, just celibate for that time duration and connect with your *Guru*. There are specific *mantras* for specific *chakras* and by chanting those *mantras*, you can pull the energy so generated to the *chakra* that you desire, and from there you can manifest anything. At *Dhyan Ashram, sadhaks* have done many experiments on this — from conception of a child to the physical manifestations in a *havan kund.*

Patanjali gave *Ashtang yog* and as the first limb of *Ashtang yog,* he gave the five *yams.* If just these five *yams* are practiced in totality while connecting with your *Guru*, anything can be achieved by the body. This is the power and the ability of a *yogi* and of *Ashtang yog*. One can just begin by fixing a period, let's say, one week or ten days. In that period, speak only the truth, do not collect, do not steal, do not harm anyone and celibate in thought and deed. If just for one week you are able to maintain the five *yams,* immediately, something will happen, because then Divine shows you the light and there occurs a dimensional change in you.

I have personally experimented with all this and experienced the force of the *yams*, and if someone is desirous of pursuing higher *yog* with me, he/she needs to follow these, because it is these *yams* that will fuel the force of your *karmas,* otherwise the body will perish. For how long can you hold it? You cannot hold on to the body, no matter how much wealth, power or influence you wield in society. And then what? Then there is just pain, because when you fall from a height, it is extremely difficult to take that hurt. But when you ascend to greater heights from where you are, there is immense pleasure. So whatever your stage or state, you should strive for an upward progression. If you are leading a normal life, then every day is a regression, a step lower, because a normal life consists of collecting and enjoying pleasures of the five senses, which would have to be paid back for. But if you lead a yogic life, then every day is a progression, a higher pleasure, unexplained in words, only to be experienced.

The body works on the force of the Kundalini and the Kundalini is a semi-dormant force that rests at your mool chakra and sends out pulses of energy. The strength of these pulses determines whether they get consumed at the lower chakras or are able to penetrate and reach the higher chakras. To activate your higher senses and thought manifestation power, it is imperative to pull this energy till the Agya/Sahastrar.

SERMON 11

TATTVA GYAN AND ATMA GYAN

" *We are all connected to each other with the five elements or tattvas. The elements that are constant in creation keep remodelling themselves to form different bodies. The elements that compose your body today could have once formed the body of Lord Ram.* "

11

All religions, all faiths, all cultures emphasise upon the importance of *karma*. The whole of *Gita* rests upon *karma*. In this creation, *karma* is foremost. It is *karma* that governs the running of creation. Ever wondered what is it about *karma* that makes it so important? After all, salvation is the ultimate goal of the soul and for salvation all that is required is *dhyan* on the *param tattva*. At that time there is no thought and hence no time (since time is created by us when we think; it is the distance between two thoughts) and when there is no time, there is no question of *karma*. That is a state of rising over *karma*, a state of *vairagya*, and yet *karma* has been called as *pradhan*. Even after reaching great heights, most people do not understand the concept of *karma*. It is only the *sadhaks,* who do *dhyan* and have had revelations, can understand and appreciate the importance of *karma*. You will not get to read about this in books.

Once when I was asking about the importance of *karma* in a session, a learned gentleman explained quoting the *Gita* that *dhyan* is greater than *gyan*, *karma* is greater than *dhyan* and that by foregoing the fruits of *karma* one can get liberation. It sounds very good but then how many can give up on the fruits of their *karma*? (Including the gentleman who lectured me on this, for he also was looking to heal his body.) *Yog* is a subject of self-experience and therefore at *Dhyan Ashram*, we only talk about that which is practical and can be followed. You are in the physical and everything is done through the physical only, the state of *shunya* is also reached through the physical because that is what you understand and relate to.

Coming back to *karma*, when you slap someone, the person feels the pain because he has a body and the five elements. But would you agree with me when I say that you too will feel the pain of that slap in return?

Is there something that connects a human being to the other?

We are all a combination of *purush* and *prakriti*. *Purush* is the soul (*atma*), which is individualistic and *prakriti* is the five elements (*tattvas*) that are common to all of us. When *atma* combines with the *tattvas,* it becomes a *jeevatma*. We are all connected to each other with the five elements or *tattvas*. The elements that are constant in creation keep remodelling themselves to form different bodies. The elements that compose your body today could have once formed the body of Lord *Ram*. This is the basis of the philosophy of *karma*.

If you have inflicted pain upon someone that pain will travel back to you since the elements remain the same. There will come a time when you will connect to the elements on which you had inflicted pain or those elements will come inside you, and when that happens, you will experience that pain. The pain might change its form and return to you in the form of an accident or a loss, but you will definitely experience it, in this lifetime or in some other birth. Because, your body is changing constantly, every seven years all the cells of your body die and are replaced by new ones, i.e., all the *tattvas* change and this is what causes the body to age. The pain you feel, is the pain you have given to someone sometime. That is why *karma* is *pradhan*.

It is foolish to think that nobody saw you when you did what you did, because nobody is required to see it. You think like that because your consciousness level is presently in the physical, not in the *sukshma*. You do not have the experience of the subtle, you have no *gyan* beyond physical. The *Patanjali Yogsutras* state that *abhnivesh* or fear of death resides even in the biggest of *gyanis,* because even he does not have the experience of what lies beyond, no matter how big he talks. It is important to understand our current state because only when we understand it can we go beyond it. Otherwise we will keep going in circles, thinking we have got a lot of *gyan*. Unless you experience the basics, you will not understand how you are supposed to go ahead.

The fear of death exists because you do not have the experience of *tattvas*. A clear indication of this is that you cannot think beyond yourself. Everything you do from morning to night is for your satisfaction or the satisfaction of your own five senses. This is the reason why in *tantra*, the practice of *Tattva Shuddhi* (it is detailed in the book, 'Sanatan Kriya, The Ageless Dimension') is prescribed to first purify the elements so that the person can experience something beyond.

Karma is considered *pradhan* because every person is connected to the other through *tattvas.* When you cause harm to or benefit someone, that 'someone' too is you only. Is there any difference between the two?

Long back when I was a student, we were having a discussion on *yog* in the class. I had returned from the field and was feeling uneasy. When my teacher asked me the reason, I told him that I had just seen carrots being uprooted and did not feel good seeing that. The whole class started laughing on hearing this; they jibed at me saying, "You do not feel bad while eating chicken but you feel bad when carrots are being cut?" Even I was confused. My teacher was listening to all this very carefully and he told me, "Now your sensitivity level has increased." I still did not understand. So then he explained further, "You can now experience within your body the *tattva* that has yet not become a part of your body."

The question is not what one should or should not eat, the question is where your sensitivity has reached. Do you get affected by someone else's pain? Think about it — how will you react to the killing of a human being? Would you react with the same intensity if it were an animal? What would be your reaction if you see carrots and radishes being cut?

When you are in a state of detachment you rise above both pain and pleasure. Mind you, it is rising above both pain and pleasure and not pain alone... do not think a vairagi escapes pain and enjoys pleasure, a vairagi is above the tattvas.

If something bad is happening to someone and it does not have an effect on you then no matter how many times you have read the *Gita*, no matter how many *shlokas* you have memorised, you have reached nowhere because *tattva gyan* is the first stage of *yog*. The *tattvas* are the same in all bodies; when any *tattva* is harmed, even if it is a cloth being torn, it has an effect on you. That is why *yogis* in the Himalayas leave everything including clothes and live in the caves, and ordinary men travel far and wide to meet them...

Once I happened to be staying with a *babaji* when an affluent family after taking much pain came to meet him in his cave from a remote end of the world. *Babaji* asked them the purpose of their visit. They narrated a whole list of problems — health, money, family etc. *Babaji* simply said, "I neither have food nor clothes nor a house nor people around me, then what is it that I have, which you have come to ask me for? Either you are a fool or a *gyani*. *Gyani*, you do not look like, and fool, I cannot call you. So you yourself understand what you are..." This is something to understand. What is it that you will get from someone who does not even have clothes to cover him? What does that *baba* have? The *baba* has the *gyan* of *tattvas*. You need him because you are still not familiar with *tattvas*. The one, who has *tattva gyan*, never asks for anything from anyone because a *tattva gyani* can create anything he wants for himself, it's not difficult for him. But an ignorant, remains stuck in *tattvas*, and even when he goes to a *gyani,* he still asks for *tattva* only, for the solution of a pain due to *tattvas,* because he knows no better. It is ironic he goes looking for *tattvas* to someone who apparently does not have the *tattvas* that he wants. Such an interaction is of no use because you do not have the slightest idea of what such a person has to give you, you are just not ready to make a *Guru*... you could have got the entire energy of the creation, but you asked for a small candle.

People ask me what is the need to go to a person, if your thought is pure you will find divinity even in a stone. Yes, if one has the *bhaav*, then there is no need. But in order to bring that *bhaav*, to bring that kind of confidence in a stone is a little difficult because a stone cannot communicate with you. That communication is required to tell you the path. You will bring the *bhaav* only when you find a path, if there is nobody to tell you the path then what *bhavna* will you bring? So first a path is told and by walking on that path one gets the experiences. After that a state comes when one can even have faith in a stone but a stone certainly cannot tell you a path.

Aseeker once asked me that in today's time when there exist so many TV *babas* who rise and fall with the same speed and when everyone has a 'shelf-life', how one finds a real *Guru*. This depends upon your intent. If you are going, to get a cure for a disease or solution to some relationship or business problem then you will get someone with a shelf life only, but if you are getting into *yog* for *yog* only, without any other temptation, only *for atmic unnati*, then you will find the one who does not have a shelf-life. If you are looking for *'upays'* for the problems you are facing because of your bad *karmas*, then you will only reach someone who will fool you. Here it is important to understand that whenever something unpleasant happens with you, it is simply the *tattvas* that you had once harmed that are coming back to you, there is no other *upay* but to improve your *karmas.* That is why *karma* is considered *pradhan*. The state of rising above *karmas* is called *vairagya*, as then one does not harm or benefit anyone. It is not possible to reach this state till you have the *gyan* of *tattvas*. And once you reach that state, *tattvas* will no longer affect you. What you will see or feel then, you cannot understand that now, because right now you are only limited to the *sthool*, the five *tattvas*. You may believe in this intellectually, but you do not have the *gyan* as that sense is not awakened in you as yet.

The basic difference between a normal and an evolved being is that the latter has experience of *tattvas*. When your *tattvas* expand, then you feel the pain when anything happens anywhere. At a basic level, you feel the pain of a human's death, if you are a little higher then you can feel the pain of an animal's death, if your sensitivity has increased further then you can even feel the pain of a vegetable being plucked from the field and there comes a time, when you feel the pain even while breathing... because breathing too is eating into someone else's share of air. In fact, in later stages of *yog sadhna*, as you sit in *dhyan* in detachment, the state of *kumbhak* comes naturally, where breath gets suspended automatically. That is the state of *yog* and *vairagya.*

One might argue that everything is the will of Divine and so why should one feel the pain of someone else, after all it is His wish... true. But that is a later stage of *yog*, the stage of a *gyani*. At a basic stage when your awareness is very much in your *tattvas*, such an attitude is indicative of shamelessness and insensitivity. In between the two is a third stage, which is as you are progressing in *yog* and your *tattvas* are expanding, at that time you connect with all the elements of creation and feel the pain of each one. This is a subject of *tattva gyan*. After *tattva* gyan, *atma gyan*. Only that being can be an *atma gyani* who is a *tattva gyani*. *Atma gyan* can also happen if your *Guru* is a *gyani* and he gives you *shaktipath*. After *atma gyan* the state comes where you feel that what has to happen happens, he has to go and so let him go. That is why *Gita* is the most misunderstood book, because everyone knows it yet nobody has its *gyan!*

These days you will come across people who have given up wearing clothes and yet want a huge crowd around them, which simply reflects their state and the levels of deception in *Kaliyug*. Recently I was looking up the ratings of various engineering colleges for someone's admission, as I went through the list, I was surprised to see that the ratings were based on the actors and actresses that studied at those colleges. Common sense told me that if someone wants to become an actor, they should enrol themselves into an engineering college and by reverse logic, maybe to become an engineer one has to attend a film school. This is the state where we have reached today, actors and acting is at the top these days, those who take a thousand retakes to give you two hours of unreality are the ones who help you make your career decisions. That is why *yog* is not a subject which can be understood by all and sundry because there is no acting or drama in this. If you want to gather crowds around you, then just take off your clothes, wear *maalas* and make a weird hairstyle, there would be a huge crowd around you, but that does not make you a *yogi.*

One of my teachers came to meet me from the Himalayas and was staying with me. He does not wear clothes. Once we were strolling in a quiet place and he told me, "Just see what is about to happen." As I wondered what he was referring to, there was a crowd of 500 around us. Just by seeing a fat person wearing *maalas* people thought 'what a *mahatma* he is' and hoping to get something from him, flocked us. Even I have gone through a similar experience with a *gyani* who stays *in Gyanganj*. *Gyanganj* is a small village enroute Kailash Mansarovar where there are still some *rishis* and *munis* doing *tapasya*.

One of them had come to Delhi long back and while in a conversation, I had enquired about the *Mataji* who stays alone amongst crocodiles in Madhya Pradesh. So then he told me, "What will you get from meeting her? What she has is her *sadhna* and you will not understand one bit of it. It is not a circus that you go and see it." It does not work this way. You have to have the right *karma* to meet such people and then you ask them for what they can give you, rather than think what you need and if they can give that to you. What they can give you is best left to your *karmas* and their assessment of you.

Tattva and *karma* are inter-related and so is reality and unreality. Anything that you do has an effect on *tattvas* because you do not have the *gyan* of *tattvas* as yet and when what you do is effecting the *tattvas*, then its counter effect is bound to come back to you. If you do charity thinking how much benefit you will get out of it then that charity will be of no benefit to you because you have put its effect on *tattvas* and its effect will come on *tattvas* only. I do not consider this as a benefit because what you already have you are unable to take care of, what good will it do to get even more in the same sphere? You will only get more stuck and go further down. That is why charity should be done in *vairagya* and as per *Guru vakya*, and not by using your own brain. Your brain will only do the math of profit and loss. I find so many people who tell me, "I have fed 500 people but have not got benefited till now." There is no bigger foolishness than this.

Try and rise above the *tattvas* and the *kriya* to rise above *tattvas* is called *yog*. It is these *tattvas* that keep you here or take you beyond. The major cause for you taking birth again and again is because you are tied to *tattvas*. Every pleasure that you take is destroying your *tattvas.* Every *bhog* has a *rog* attached to it and *rog* is there to balance your *bhogs*. When you are asking for pleasure, if you have some state, then ask for pain along with it. The one who is asking for pain is a *gyani*; only he is above *tattvas*. The one who is asking only for pleasures has not reached anywhere, no matter how many books he has read. *Ramakrishna Paramhansa* underwent a surgery without anaesthesia. Getting cancer was his destiny but he did not feel the pain because of his *gyan* of *yog*. When you are in a state of detachment you rise above both pain and pleasure. Mind you, it is rising above both pain and pleasure and not pain alone... do not think a *vairagi* escapes pain and enjoys pleasure, a *vairagi* is above the *tattvas*.

Your *tattvas*/elements are attached with your power, money, health, family, friends and social status, which are six very dangerous things because when any of these reduces even slightly, it pinches a lot and — reduce they will. They cannot keep on increasing forever, they may increase for the time being but after that they would lessen gradually. Till the time you are expanding your *tattvas*, remember, it is at the cost of someone else. There is a simple law in Economics, that resources are limited but wants are unlimited. When you take someone else's share, then you are certainly harming that someone, and when you harm someone, the effect of that will surely come back to you because *tattvas* are common to all of us.

It is not possible for you to grow endlessly in the physical because every time you get something, it is at the cost of someone else. Even when you are breathing, you are competing with someone else's share of air. You bypass so many people while getting promotion or business contract, are they not experiencing pain then? When you bribe a bank or submit a false report to take an extra loan, do you realise the damage you cause to the nation? You do all this because you are stuck in *tattvas* and the one who is stuck in *tattvas* can never understand *yog*. That's why *karma* is *pradhan*. When you harm someone you bring harm to yourself as those *tattvas* will surely come back to you. And when you do well for someone you get stuck even more because then you will get back more and how will you take care of that? So either way, whether you do good or bad, you are stuck. There is only one-way out — the *gyan* of *tattvas*. Not weekly, daily or hourly, but with every second that you pass for yourself, you prepare more trouble for yourself which will lead to another painful birth. That is why *munis* donate everything belonging to them and turn their face and go away. They have the *gyan* of *tattvas* and can see that whether they do good or bad, they are still getting stuck. That is why *karma* is *pradhan*.

Charity should be done in vairagya and as per Guru vakya, and not by using your own brain. Your brain will only do the math of profit and loss. I find so many people who tell me, "I have fed 500 people but have not got benefited till now." There is no bigger foolishness than this.

SERMON 12

LEADING A SPIRITUAL LIFE?

" *If you identify yourself with anything that you possess, including your body, then remember, it is soon going to end. Just try holding onto sand with both your hands and see what happens. Seconds later you will be wondering where did all the sand go...* "

12

You hear people saying that they want to lead a spiritual life, but what is a spiritual life? A human being is combination of *purush* and *prakriti*. *Purush* is the *atma* and *prakriti* is the five *tattvas* — *prithvi, jal, agni, vayu* and *akash*. When *purush* enters a body, it becomes *jeevatma* and that is called a spirit.

Tattvas in themselves are *nishkriya* (inactive), whereas *atma* is *nirantar kriyasheel* (active). When *tattvas* come in contact with the *atma*, for some time, they become active due to the *tej* (glow) of the *atma*, however, it is not possible to understand the *atma* through these *tattvas*.

An ordinary human being takes the body (or the five elements) to be the reality and continues to chase the *tattvas,* which are constantly changing form. The same *tattvas* constitute this wall, that chair, you and me, and are constantly undergoing a change from one form to the other. And when that change of form happens, the person is unable to understand what happened and gets scared.

A senior bureaucrat of this country had been practicing *Sanatan Kriya* with us. She is nearing 80, and recently, we got the news that she is admitted into a hospital. The news was disturbing since if anyone doing the *kriya* in the right manner lands up in the hospital, it is a matter of shame for us. When we enquired about her health, we were told that she had a severe stomach ache, but her energy body as seen through *yog* told a different story. On probing further, we found out that she had gone there to get plastic surgery done... at the age of 80. In two decades of teaching *yog,* my experience has been that as the age of a person increases, especially as he crosses 60, his wants become funnier by the day. By funny, I mean, physical, that which is directly connected with the *tattvas* — money, business, looks, staying in shape, curing disease etc.

After 60, one should be looking to take the journey backwards, what is called (and what most do not understand) as the 'spiritual' journey. Majority of you think the *tattvas*, that make up your physical body, as the truth and want a spiritual journey with them but *tattvas* will not take you on a spiritual journey. It is like asking to be at two places at the same time, that 'everything should happen while staying here'.

The *tattvas* will remain here only, and those of you who relate to them as yourself, will also remain right here, you will not go anywhere. You will take another similar body and go through similar experiences and this will go on till you are attached to the unreal. It is the *tattvas* that come under the effect of *maya*, the *atma*/spirit is not affected by *maya*. The one who is tied to the *tattvas*, is under the effect of *maya* and veiled by *maya*, he walks in the opposite direction and so he stumbles upon something, falls and gets hurt. This is the reality of the physical world, the reason why every person is troubled, because he wants the spiritual through the physical.

A *Guru* can make you have the *darshan* of *atma* in a moment, provided you also have the desire for the *atma*. You consider the *tattvas* as reality and say that you are spiritual, you want something else and the reality is something else — the *darshan* of spirit does not happen this way. Everything in the physical world, the world of *tattvas* is temporary, it is bound by time. Today, it is with this soul, tomorrow it will be with that one. The soul thinks it is changing the body, while in reality it is the body that is changing souls, as it is constantly changing forms. Because every single thing in this physical world is *nashwar*, everything is bound by a specific and limited time. So if you identify yourself with anything that you possess, including your body, then remember, it is soon going to end. Just try holding onto sand with both your hands and see what happens. Seconds later you will be wondering: where did all the sand go?

Majority of the people even after crossing 60, 70 or even 80, talk to me only about the physical, "Tell us the cure for this". What will happen even if you get a cure? What will happen if that cure makes you live for a few more years? What feats will you achieve in those few more years that you could not achieve in the last half century? These few more years will also pass, much faster than the last half century and you would still want more 'few more years'. It is imperative to understand here that this is *maya* and the only reason for creation to go on, taking you down by the birth by ensuring your attachments don't leave you and you remain stuck to the unreal even much later in age. At that time and age, all you can think of is to save the body, somehow. You have no idea if there really is something called a spirit or if there is anything besides the body at all and you do not even want to find out or know. You have no confidence in yourself or your *Guru* figure. You do not know what you are doing, where you are going, what are you wanting, so what should I show you? How can I make you have the *darshan* of the *shakti,* which you do not believe in? You neither believe in the medium, nor the channel or the *shakti,* you understand *tattvas* as real.

What you call a spiritual life, is only possible when you have the belief that these *tattvas*, your body, is *nashwar*. Everything that you have will slip away from you, just like sand — when you believe in this, only then can you go beyond it, otherwise you cannot.

So, be sure what side you want to be on — the side of the spirit or the physical? Once you have made up your mind, let me know, and I will tell you what to do to achieve it.

What you call a spiritual life, is only possible when you have the belief that these tattvas, your body, is nashwar. Everything that you have will slip away from you, just like sand – when you believe in this, only then can you go beyond it, otherwise you cannot.

SERMON 13

DHYAN

"*When you sit for dhyan, you get plenty of thoughts — about business, friends, physical health, maybe even a scene from the last movie you saw... Does anybody get a thought that there are five hungry men waiting to be fed or that he/she has forgotten to put grains for the birds today?*"

13

There is a lady who has been doing *dhyan* for quite some time. Everyday without fail she would write to me seeking my blessings, so that she can move ahead in *dhyan*. She has been doing this everyday for three years now. A couple of days back, I got a mail from her asking if I could help her find a camera that got lost recently…

Such emails, especially from those who have been long practicing, set me thinking. Why do you do *dhyan*?

As I am asking this question, all of you are blank because some of you want to pass an exam, some others want a better job or relationship and the rest have a heart trouble or a factory that is about to shut. There are two or three who have a slight understanding of meaning of *dhyan* and know what I am talking about and so are silent, but the majority is not answering because they have one of these problems.

I know this because I keep getting your emails and as I read them, I wonder if I really am a *Yog Guru* or am I a consultant to whom people come for solutions to their various problems… Most people take me to be a consultant and so nothing happens. They keep going round and round and later put the blame on me. They know they are only facing the effect of their own *karmas*, but they keep looking for someone to blame for their present state, even if that is me.

For example, recently someone who used to come to the Foundation passed away. His entire family and extended family came to the *ashram* and created a hue and cry. They demanded that how could he die when he used to do *dhyan*. I told them, "Everyone has to go, and the ones who do *dhyan* are the ones who get to go earlier, I mean do not die, but understand what lies beyond the limitations of the physical body. And then they have a choice of continuing in this rut or go beyond, many choose to go beyond..." But they kept on hauling and accusing. Their behaviour came as a shock to me. That's when it struck me, that do you people even know what you are trying to do? I later got to know that the person was a chain smoker and had high blood pressure and a weak heart. I had received a call from his family the day he was admitted to the hospital but when I communicated with the soul, by then, it had already left the body and it refused to come back despite me telling it that he has a family and children to look after. I communicated the soul's wish to the family but could not understand why it refused to come back. But when I saw the faces of his family members, it was clear... Each of them had placed a long list of demands on him and troubled him and lied to him. He would spend maximum time outside the house, got addicted to the cigarette and was relieved to get out. The family on the other hand had a sinking feeling, on losing someone who was doing so much for them.

It is foolish to think that *dhyan* would make you immortal or help you recover a business loss or make your ailing heart hale and hearty. The creation is based on certain laws, and neither you nor I, not even the trinity, can violate those laws. Anybody who attempts to violate those laws will have to bear the brunt of it. It is not possible to go on leading a seamless life without any ups and downs just because you come here and do *dhyan*. If you want to make your life better in any way, then focus on social activities, not *dhyan*. If you direct a fair percentage of your income and time to charitable activities, your physical life will improve automatically. There is a gentleman from Punjab who owns a big factory and has been bothered about the poor returns for quite a few months. He told me he does a lot of charity and yet his business is going down. When I asked him what he does, he told me that he feeds cows and birds everyday... that would amount to 10-20 rupees a day and a 500 per month. If you earn 50,000 every month, and take out a 500 from it for charity, the factory is bound to shut after sometime. You cannot escape that because that is your *karma*, the basic law of creation. I cannot change your *karma* but yes, I can transfer some of my *karmas* into you. But if I have to put energy into someone, there has to be a strong reason for it — if someone will aid and work with creation, it makes sense to transfer that energy into him/her but if someone has to only live for himself/herself then that energy exchange is of no use because with one pleasure that you take, that energy will balance out and go to waste. So if that person, who just passed away, was even brought back into the body, it would have been purposeless for he would have continued with his old ways.

Everything in creation is a combination of the five elements, including your body. You are tied to this creation with those five elements through specific centres in the body called *chakras* — *Mooladhar, Swadhisthan, Manipoorak*, *Anahad*, *Vishuddhi* and, to a certain extent, *Agya*. Along with the five elements, you are also tied by your senses, which too are controlled by the *chakras*. For example, the sense of touch is linked to the *Anahad chakra* governs organs in the chest region, if someone has a heart or a lung problem his/her sense of touch reduces considerably. When there is depletion at the *Manipoorak chakra*, the vision deteriorates or if there is expansion at the *Vishuddhi*, auditory faculties improve such that you are able to hear sounds from distant dimensions. Similarly, *Swadhisthan* chakra enhances your sense of taste and *Mooladhar chakra* is related to sense of smell. In this way, you are tied to the creation through the elements as well as the five senses. Think of a situation when all your senses are shut. What will remain then? You might think 'nothing' but actually, everything will begin after that only. Till that happens, you will keep asking funny questions and like most of you have experienced, my answers will be restricted to two-three words or maybe a line.

Once, I wrote a detailed mail to someone in reply to his query about a property matter. Looking at my reply, the person could not help asking that how come when he writes to me about *yog*, he gets a one-line answer but for a property matter, I wrote in such detail. I replied, "To comprehend a detailed answer on *yog*, you have to have that degree of awakening in you, and when you have that, you will not be asking questions via the physical route and I would also be replying to you in detail as per your understanding. Your interest and understanding for *yog*, vis-à-vis property is minimal, hence my reply".

You are tied to this creation through five senses and the five elements and cannot think beyond. When you sit for *dhyan*, you get plenty of thoughts — about business, friends, physical health, maybe even a scene from the last movie you saw... Does anybody get a thought that there are five hungry men waiting to be fed or that he/she has forgotten to put grains for the birds today?

People often tell me that I judge them. In fact, once I got a wonderful compliment that I am a 'spiritual dictator'; that I dictate the way it will happen and refuse to budge. Well, if this is the way it works, what can I do about that? When someone comes to me, the responsibility is on me, if she/he does not do what I am telling him or her to do, there would be no results. Then that would be my failure and I have never failed in anything that I have touched in my life so far. So, the one who wants to walk the path of *yog*, should be ready to accept my dictatorship. (In matters of property, if you listen to me even 10 per cent, it would do. But in *yog*, you have to listen to me 100 per cent, else you will make a mistake and cause harm to yourself.)

The thoughts that come to you during *dhyan* indicate the *chakra* or sense with which you are tied to the creation. That thought will keep coming back to you and when that thought comes, only the lower regions of brain (that control the five senses) will be active. That is, the brain will function at a normal level only and you get into a *samvad* (dialogue). When you get into a dialogue, can your brain think of anything else besides that? So you are in a dialogue and yet you keep thinking, 'I have reached some high state'... then that is nothing but daydreaming or pure entertainment. But it is not your fault, you are bound by your desires and those desires tie you to the thoughts that you get, not allowing you to see that with every passing day the time is slipping out and your body is becoming less and less capable.

You can have only five kinds of thoughts, relating to the five senses. In *dhyan* you block those thoughts, because those are your *vrittis* and the basis of *vritti* is desire and you fulfill those desires through your thoughts. So if in *dhyan* you block your thoughts, your *vrittis* get blocked, that *samvad* (dialogue), which is going on with yourself stops. Then the lower thoughts get converted into higher thoughts. Then those higher thoughts are blocked and they get converted into super higher thoughts. What are super higher thoughts? For instance, during the day you saw someone breaking the leg of a dog and while sitting for *dhyan*, the incident generates anger in you and you think that you should have intervened and prevented that from happening. That is a super high thought, but that too is a disturbance in your *dhyan*. Even that should not come, as everything that is happening is *poorva nirdharit*. So after a stage, even the super higher thoughts are blocked to reach a state of thoughtlessness. But remember, it is a journey from lower to higher to super-higher to no thoughts. People usually use this as an excuse not to do charity and service thinking that it is a *bandhan* and so should not be done. Yes, it is a *bandhan*, but what about the *bandhans* of all the wrong things that you do? You are not ready to forego them but would rather forego charity and service. This journey has to be treaded step by step and to ascend the steps you have to improve your *karmas*, only then will the thought of *dhyan* and *yog* come to you, only then can you reach a thoughtless stage. Thereafter the state of *dhyan* comes, before that you can keep sitting with your eyes closed for as long as you like, nothing will happen.

Till the time you have a physical thought, you will not be able to access the higher centres and as a result you will not understand anything beyond the five senses. It is okay to first indulge in the five senses and to experience them for a while, but disastrous to make them a basis for your journey into *yog*. They are only a transition and not the basis. So you must change. In order to awaken higher senses, you first need to close the lower senses and only then the energy will rise upwards giving you higher experiences. Before that, you will continue to get foolish thoughts like, "when I get up from *dhyan* today, there will be a windfall in my business" and when such things will not happen, you will blame me that "I am doing *dhyan* for over two years now and no such thing has happened." Or, "My relationship with X person was this, why is it not so today? Has the person changed?" Yes, the person has changed. In comparison, he has evolved and you have devolved. If you had continued to evolve with him, then the relationship would have got deeper and better.

I reduced my own business involvement to minimum long time back despite it giving me phenomenal returns. It might seem illogical to most but when I sat down to do the math of the number of days I spent roaming around, the tension that I took, the debates and arguments it got me into and the meals that I missed to work out business plans, then the money earned seemed of little value in comparison to the damage I caused to myself. I was convinced that it is just not worth it and reduced my working days from 30 to three in a month as that much would be enough to meet my requirements. Same goes for my relationships also.

Think about it, even if you earn that extra money you will only spend it on wasteful indulgence as you do not really need it, you will not only damage your health but also spoil your *karma* and *janam* by hoarding on to resources and eating into someone else's share. It is a misconception that good *karmas* bring you large fortunes. An honest person, who follows the *yams*, even if he is earning bare minimum he would be satisfied with it. To make super profits and hoard, you have to make strategies and lie to people, and the one who does that can never spend the money so earned as he knows of the 'effort' that has gone into making it. Such a person would also not do charity and I can assure you, he would not be enjoying his wealth, he would be dissatisfied and troubled, trying to guard it all the time. That money is spent by his children who are only concerned about their life and they would do it in front of his eyes and he will not be able to say anything to them because after all he earned that money for them only! I am yet to meet someone who is happy with the way his/her children are. So when you do not think your children are good, then for whom are you earning and collecting? You very well know what will become of your hard-earned money and yet you are sacrificing your *janam* and *karma* in earning a little more and not sharing it with creation. This is *maya,* which will not let you enter *yog* or go beyond. It is okay to earn, it is okay to enjoy, it is okay to spend but it is not okay to not share.

If you observe the thoughts that disturb you most during *dhyan*, they would be centred on the people who are closest to you – spouse/children/parents, the next would be financial problems and third would be office problems. None of you will be disturbed or get up early from *dhyan* because you have to feed someone or help your neighbour. If that is happening, it is a progression; otherwise you are simply disturbed by the play of *maya* and are ruining your life and birth under its influence. Understand that whatever is disturbing you is temporary; it will disappear sooner than you will think it would. Everything in the physical is bound by time and whether you are 20 or 40 or 60, that time will pass very soon and since time will pass, so will that object of desire that is disturbing you. What will not pass is *dhyan* because when you go into the state of *dhyan*, time ceases to exist. And when there is no time, nothing passes. Time is the *swaroop* of *maya*, for you it is the five senses and the five elements constituting your body. Once you still your thought process, i.e., when the mind stills, then your five senses become *shant* and so do the five *tattvas* and once that happens there is no time, your body does not age and you have no problems. The period for which you sit in *dhyan* that much time doesn't exist for you and the result of that is that the effect of *maya* starts declining on you. Till there is effect/influence of *maya*, you cannot do *yog* or *dhyan*. And the effect/ influence of *maya* is what I mentioned before – you earn and someone else spends it, you take tension and someone else enjoys it. Have you ever seen tension on the face of the one who is spending your money?

King *Yudhishtir* was deeply troubled by his children's behaviour and sought advice of *Bhisma Pitamah*. *Bhishma* then explained to him that the more he gives his children, the more they would expect out of him and more their expectations rise, the lesser they will care for him. For example, if someone has been serving your house for many years, you take that person for granted and assume he will do everything that you ask him to. On the other hand, if a new servant comes and warns you that he will leave if you raise your voice while speaking to him, you will be polite with him out of fear that if he runs away who will do the dishes. *So Bhishma* advised *Yudhishtir* to give them less because when you start giving them freely, they take it all and expect more and never have any tension. You become like that servant who will do everything for them no matter what. You can continue giving them more and more and see for yourself what happens. This is the *bandhan* of *maya* that keeps you tied.

When you sit for *dhyan* and thoughts of the physical trouble you, there is a very simple way of getting out of them. Let's say you get a thought of money or an asset, then simply take your awareness to the *Manipoorak* chakra and cut your connections from that *chakra*, the thoughts will disappear immediately. Similarly if you get a sexual thought, cut connection from the *Swadhisthan chakra*, for a thought of food or drink, cut connection from *Mooladhar* chakra and for a thought of relationship, friend, spouse, children or parents, cut connection from *Anahad chakra.* The cutting process is explained in detail in *Sanatan Kriya.* But before trying this, you need to be absolutely sure that you want to get out of these thoughts because when you start cutting connections with these thoughts, the things which are not in your thought, will automatically start moving away from you. And if you cut the connection keeping your *Guru*'s *smaran*, then there is no way that that person/thing will return to you otherwise there is a chance that in the morning you cut, and in the evening the thought is back again but when you connect with your *Guru*, his/her thought supersedes your thought and then even if your thought is there, that thing will not be there. So whenever you get the thought, just remember your *Guru* and visualise that the person/thing has gone to the other end of the earth and you are on this side. And see what happens, but after that don't blame your *Guru* because this is a path of *vairagya* where one is allowed to do everything, provided they do not get attached to it. The state of *poorna vairagya* is when you are not concerned with anything around you, including your own body. All those who stay at the *ashram* have crossed the state of *vairagya*, you cannot attract them with anything, no matter what. They have merged with me completely. They have seen the reality of every person, why she/he is with you, what is his/her purpose. When you see the reality, it causes great pain. For instance, if you are in a relationship with someone but if you find out he is in a relationship with three others as well, think how much pain it will cause. So if you are in a state/condition to see the reality then only cut the connections.

You need to be sure that you want that but also be informed that there is no other way! If you cut connections that thing/person will go away and if you don't, it will keep troubling you, time will keep passing and the body will keep ageing. This is the*swaroop* of *maya*, which keeps the creation running. There is no other reason for creation to run, there is only one reason — *maya* and by these thoughts, *maya* keeps you tied to the creation. If you shut your five senses, what will you remember then — money, person or relationship? And these five will surely shut, in a matter of years, your body will be put to fire and your senses will shut. What is bound to happen, you think that it will not happen and so you keep going on, stuck in *maya* without any *gyan* or *darshan*, because you are tied with your thought, which does not let you progress in *dhyan*. *Maya* always takes you away from your path, away from your *Guru*. There is a very simple way to understand *roop* of *maya*, whatever your *Guru* has told you not to do, the reason (person/thing) because of which you are still doing that, that person/thing is the biggest *roop* of *maya* for you, that is your biggest enemy. That person will never let you evolve or go beyond, he would get you stuck in the physical, would exploit you and would say a bye to you, when he gets something better.

Dhyan is the control of the senses, blocking the modifications of mind and awakening of higher senses. It is done to limit and eventually stop your thoughts and *vrittis, 'yogah chitta vritti nirodh'*, but most people come to me for those *vrittis* only. Even if I can, I will not increase those *vrittis* for you because that will only get you stuck more and more and take you further down and a time will come when you will not be visible to me at all. Always remember onething, you can never make anyone happy, no matter what you do. This is *ghor Kaliyug*, a time when if you perform a *havan* at your house, neighbours will be suspicious of your intentions and your family will get irritated by you for spoiling the paint of the house; if you do charity, the neighbours will complain that you have bred beggars in the colony; if you feed an animal, people will throw stones at it to make it run away lest it dirties the surroundings; if you invite people home for a dinner they will go back criticizing what all you did not do or if there is nothing that you left, they would be jealous of you. So while you are ready to waste your life and birth to make people happy, in the process you are only increasing your enemies.

When a young woman dresses up, wears the finest makeup and jewellery, walks out of the house thinking that she is looking pretty, she does not know that she is only creating jealousy in her peer group and those who will get attracted to her will be attracted only physically, to fulfill a physical desire because external beauty will only attract people with physical desire. What is the point of doing all this when at both sides you are at loss? When you purchase a big car, people around you wonder with jealousy where did you get all the money from. What's the use? After all, it is just a medium of transport. When there is a marriage at home, and you do five to seven functions and invite everyone you know, to show-off your wealth and status, you are only creating enmity and jealousy for yourself. So what are you trying to do?

If you are coming to me, come for the reason of removing that influence/effect of *maya* by doing *yog*, do not come for any other reason because you will only waste your time and nothing else would happen. Removal of that influence of *maya* might include me asking you to leave a very dear friend or to do charity for a specific cause. I know what I am doing, you don't. If you have come to me, either trust or don't come. I cannot take responsibility of someone who is unsure of me.

Time is the swaroop of maya,
for you it is the five senses and the five elements constituting your body.
Once you still your thought process,
i.e., when the mind stills, then your five senses become shant and so do the five tattvas and once that happens there is no time, your body does not age and you have no problems.

Original/unedited pictures of manifestations in *havan* performed by *sadhaks* at *Dhyan Ashram*.

OM

Since the *puranic* times, *asurs* have been known to disrupt *havans* and create obstruction in invocation of *devic* forces. That is the nature of an *asur*. The nature of a human being is to aid the positive forces, the *devs* and *devis*, by protecting the *havans* for the peace and prosperity of one's home, surroundings and creation at large. The *devs* and *devis* do listen to a call made with pure intent and reveal themselves in manifest form. If someone is preventing you from doing a *havan* then that person's *asuric* side is predominant, a good way to check someone's and your own nature.

SERMON 14

THE PURPOSE OF DHYAN AND MANTRAS

"*A shishya is a reflection of the Guru. If the shishya is connected with the Guru, and walks the path shown by the Guru in totality, in accordance with 'mantra moolam Guru vakyam', then whatever his/her activity is, is the state of the Guru.*"

14

Why do you do *dhyan*? What is the purpose of *mantras*? All of you saw certain colours and forms when you were made to close your eyes for five minutes. How could you see these colours when your eyes were shut? Some might say it is the subconscious mind at play, but even for that to happen it takes at least twenty minutes, you just sat for five minutes...

Understand this; it is not just the eyes that are seeing, or the ears that are hearing... there is more to you. The *mantras* that you just chanted, every *mantra* is a *dhwani* (sound) and *dhwani* is what you are, what your body is. When you chant or listen to a *dhwani,* it brings a *jagriti* (awakening) inside you. Then every cell of the body experiences this energy in the form of *prana*. When you hear an unpleasant noise, you feel disturbed. You can try shutting your ears at that time but the sound will continue disturbing you, because the sound is not just affecting your ears. Similarly, if you are watching a beautiful sunrise, even if you shut your eyes, you will feel the pleasantness inside you, because the visual is not just affecting your eyes.

The five senses are controlled by the brain and are only involved in the physical act, and you have tied yourself to this physical act. For example, when you eat food, you tie yourself to the taste of *masalas*. Try eating the food without spices for some time; you will get to experience the actual taste of food. Once, I had gone to a Chinese restaurant and while ordering food, I asked the waiter not to put ajinomoto, chilly sauce and other spices. He expressed his concern that without these, the food would have no taste. I told him, that had I wanted the taste of *masalas*, I would have ordered just the *masalas*, why bother ordering food? Baffled, he got the food as ordered, but as soon as he placed it on the table; he poured the sauces over it. I asked him, what did he just do? He replied, that if he had not added these, the food would not have tasted good. So that was the level of his consciousness/awareness.He could not comprehend that food has its own flavour.

If food did not have a flavour, it would have been colourless. Though colourless too has a flavour, which can be experienced at a higher state of consciousness. The people who do *tapa* on the mountains observe fasts for long durations and take in the *prana* from the atmosphere — that has its own flavour. Everything has a flavour — the deeper and darker the colour, the grosser is the flavour. The same holds true of experiences of life — the more colour you add to them, the more you try to enjoy, the grosser they will become and the more disappointed you will be, as desires and expectations can never be satiated. Take the example of *golgappas.* You enjoy the spicy flavor, but at the same time, ruin your intestines by consuming the hydrochloric acid that is added to its water. Every fun takes you one step lower than your present state, leaving you disappointed. The things with which you have maximum expectations, disappoint you the most. Those who excel in academics are the ones who are most disappointed with it. "I only got 99 per cent; I could have scored 1 per cent more!"

There is a student of mine who was a topper throughout her school and college. She even cleared the CA finals with good marks. Today, she is doing a business in organic food... Her biggest regret is having studied for the CA exams. So what was the use of all those marks? Ask the ones who pass with great difficulty, they are never disappointed with their marks. Once, I remember, in college we were checking our results on the notice board. I was the happiest among all those around me. One of my co-students, who seemed most dissatisfied, thought that I had topped and enquired about the same. I had scored a 50 per cent, while he had scored an 85 per cent. He had an expectation of 100, while I had none. I was just happy to pass. When you have no expectations, there is no question of disappointment.

The people who enjoy good food and make efforts to render it tastier are the ones who crib the most after eating it because it never meets their expectations. At times, the sadhaks at the *ashram* even forget to put salt in my food, but I am never disappointed. I have no expectations from the food, because its taste can only please the taste buds and that too for a couple of minutes. That's it. What is the point? Not just food or academics, you may also look at your relationships. When you establish a relationship with a lot of excitement, there is a lot of expectation from it, but then the same expectations become the biggest source of your disappointment.

The bottom line is, the more attached you are to something or someone, the more disappointed you will be. This holds true even for your *Guru* figure. The more attached you are to the *Guru* physically, the more you relate to the physical body, the more disappointed you will be. That is why it is said that one must relate to the *Guru* as energy and access that energy in totality. Those who expect physical things out of me are the most disappointed; those who access me in the realm of the ether stay content. Why? Because spiritual is *satvic,* there is no taste in it. So, if even the body of *Guru* can do nothing for you, you can be rest assured that everything else in life is surely a disappointment.The more you expect, the more you go down. Develop a taste for the tasteless...

With every passing year, your disappointments will grow and your life will fade away. Each day deducts the time that you have at hand; every birthday means one year less. In earlier times, birthdays were celebrated not because you were born that day, or you have lived one more year, or your life has decreased by one year (as you grow in *yog*, you will realise that your being in the body is immaterial), they were celebrated to mark your growing wiser by a year. When people did a *havan* for their birthday, it was a means to express gratitude for one more year of *gyan*. The process of acquiring *gyan* starts the day you make a *Guru*. Before you make a *Guru*, everyday revolves around 'what more fun should I have', 'what is the plan for the day' or 'how to make a fool of myself today'. When you are with your *Guru*, every passing moment is a new learning experience, a new *gyan*. In earlier times, education revolved around natural sciences, these days however, the children learn about newer technologies and sciences to destruct the planet. It is a pity to see the bespectacled, lack-lustre and aimless youth of today, who are deprived of *gyan* and made to learn foolish things.

If you want to grow in yog, if you want to increase your attraction, then keep your dhyan on sukshma and on vairagya. Only then can you attain the state of attracting devs. And let me assure you, when your attraction increases, all the physical pleasures will be at your beck and call.

Coming back to the colours, sounds and their effect on you... the colours that you just saw with your eyes closed, are indicative of your frequency, your state of being. You will be attracted to the people, things and energies that fall in your spectrum of frequency, and repel those that lie outside it. And your level or frequency is determined by the energy that you follow and the connection with your *Guru*.

Your *vritti* (activity) is a clear indicator of what your *Guru* is. Let us understand this with the help of an example. There is a particular sect, which has a huge following. Once, a member of *Dhyan Ashram* encountered a group of followers of that sect, driving down the road. They were singing and clapping. Suddenly, they sped their car to overtake and in turn hit the car of the person in question. Next, they got out of the car and instead of apologisng, they took out *lathis* (wooden sticks) and tried to intimidate him. The person called the police, who in turn informed the office of the sect. The office first denied having any bearing with the group and later, conceded that they will have a word with them... but nothing came of it. So you must understand, whatever is your activity directly reflects upon the energy that you follow. Sadly, many spiritual organisations now are actually political organisations — power, that too physical, being their basis.

A *shishya* is a reflection of the *Guru*. If the *shishya* is connected with the *Guru*, and walks the path shown by the *Guru* in totality, in accordance with '*mantra moolam Guru vakyam*', then whatever his/her activity is, is the state of the *Guru*. Whatever is the frequency of the *Guru* figure, people who have a *vritti* that falls in that spectrum will be attracted to his energy, and be able to come close to it and become a *shishya*. Others will only come to get their problems solved and as soon as they get what they want, they would leave. They can never become *shishyas*. Every cell in your body vibrates at a particular frequency and according to that frequency (or *prana*) attracts and repels other frequencies. The purpose of *yog* and *mantras* is to increase the attraction of that cell and tune it to subtler frequencies so that you can attract *devs*. *Yog* is done to achieve that state, not to solve your physical problems.

In *yog,* it is said that if you have a strong desire for something and if you get it, it is a warning bell for you; as then your chances of leaving the path are maximum. And if someone is walking the path and is still not getting what he/she is wishing for (there is a fraction of people like this), then that means they have a lot of *shakti* in them and God himself is telling them, that it is high time that they turn towards higher attractions and leave the grosser attractions, lest they should waste this birth as well. So if you are walking the path of *yog*, and your physical desires are not getting fulfilled, it is a good sign. However, if you have had no experiences of *yog*, if your *vritti* is not changing towards *satvicta* and *vairagya*, if you are not able to rise above the *sthool*, then that is a cause of concern. The purpose of *yog* is to attain a state of *vairagya* and not to attain physical pleasures. If that is not what you are looking for, you must not waste your time in trying to do *yog*. You can only move with me if your thought is of the *sukshma*. If your thought is that of the physical, you will move away from the subject and me, with every passing moment.

A gentleman from Bengal once brought his grandson to me to teach him *yog*, so that he could 'progress' in life. I told him, that the progress he is looking for, does not come with *yog*. If he wants his grandson to run his vast empire and make it prosper, he must not put him in *yog*. The grandson understood, but the grandfather continued to argue that both things go hand-in-hand. He had come across a lot of *'yoga' Gurus* who had promised him that... Well, it does not happen that way.

A *Guru* never pushes the *shishya* towards physical recognition and growth. A *Guru* knows that every increase in your bank-balance and business is a deduction from your *karmic* balance. You must understand that that you are collecting none of it is going to go along with you. It will leave you sooner or later. In the process of collecting all this, you will collect negative karma that will eventually lead you to hell. I actually feel happy when any of my *shishyas* suffer a loss. I try so hard to reduce their negative *karmas*, and when God does it himself, I could not be happier — for I know, that after this loss, there would be a manifold gain.

You relate to everything in the physical. When you see yourself growing physically, you think your frequency is increasing. I, however, can see your shades becoming grosser and darker, from pink to red to brown to... You see from your five senses, from the physical. What I see is — you want to see more and more of what you are seeing, but your vision is reducing. You want to taste stranger things with every passing day, but your taste-buds are becoming weak; you want to listen to a new music every day, but your hearing power is diminishing. Is there anyone, who is not in *yog,* who is wanting physical pleasures, and yet his/her senses are becoming sharper with age?

The path of *yog* is that of *vairagya*. If you want to grow in *yog*, if you want to increase your attraction, then keep your *dhyan* on *sukshma* and on *vairagya*. Only then can you attain the state of attracting *devs*. And let me assure you, when your attraction increases, all the physical pleasures will be at your beck and call, but by then you will have the *gyan*, and you will not want them anymore. *Yog* is not about leaving, it is about satisfaction in what you have and materialisation of desire. As you grow in *yog* and understand the science of colours, you will be able to alter your body and life events, your pains and pleasures, by using these colours. Whether you alter it or not will be at your discretion. At that time, you may choose not to alter and go through the pain instead because that cancels out your negative *karmas*. In fact, there is a therapy in *yog* where pain is given to the body by sitting on nails, lying on ice, intense fasting and so on, in order to move over the effect of negative *karmas*. When you give yourself pain, it is instantly visible to a clairvoyant, in the form of change in your colour frequency from grosser to subtler.

Ramakrishna Paramhansa chose to undergo the pain of cancer because he was on the path of *moksha*. He knew that he needed to rid himself of his *karmic* baggage in order to attain *moksha*. All those who walk the *satvic* or *satya* path, those who have a *Guru*, they get the *gyan* at a very young age and take to the path of *vairagya*. The rest make plans to live for at least 100 years, so that they can enjoy a little more, collect a little more. Whether 100 or 80 or 50, all this will come to an end, but by then it will be too late for *yog*. No effort would be enough to alter your state of consciousness then.

Identify your purpose in life. What is it that you want to achieve and decide a time period to achieve it. But if you are with me and want to move in *yog*, then after that time you will have to leave it. And let me tell you, at that time you will not be able to let go of it and will devolve further. It is best to reverse your thinking right now and start walking in the opposite direction. It is the rule of creation; whatever you turn your face away from, starts following you and whatever you try to chase, makes you chase it more and more.

So keep your focus on *yog* and alter your consciousness level; let's see what happens then...

The things with which you have maximum expectations, disappoint you the most. Those who excel in academics are the ones who are most disappointed with it. "I only got 99 per cent; I could have scored 1 per cent more!"

Original/unedited pictures of manifestations in *havan* performed by *sadhaks* at *Dhyan Ashram*.

GANESH JI

Sadhaks who have been seriously practicing the various *mantra siddhis*, have had physical manifestations of the various gods. When they did the *Ganpati mantra siddhi* and did its *havan,* the complete form of *Ganeshji* was created in the *kund*. This is how manifestation happens when you do *mantra sadhna*. Lord *Ganesh*, the master of *ridhi* and *sidhi*, resides at the *Mooladhar chakra* and is the guardian of the doorway to higher *loks*. During a *havan* while doing *mantra uccharan* for *Ganeshji*, the energy in the *Sushumna nadi* rises upwards.

SERMON 15

PERFORMING A HAVAN

“ *Yog is your relationship with your Guru. The number of intermediaries and instructions that intercept this connection indicates your state of evolution.* ”

15

Yog is your relationship with your *Guru.* The number of intermediaries and instructions that intercept this connection indicates your state of evolution. At a *Ganpati havan*, those who were performing the *havan* were asked to complete 11 *maalas.* Once the 11 *maalas* were completed these people asked the ones who were standing to assist them, as to what they should do now. Those who were standing in turn called up someone else to ask what they should do. Finally after much passing-the-parcel they decided to continue counting the *jaap maalas* till they got the next 'instruction'. It is almost like a surgeon asking the compounder on how to perform an operation and the compounder in turn, asking the receptionist if she has any idea. The patient will surely die.

These people had performed *havans* many times in the past and knew I always come at the time of *poorna ahuti* at every *havan*. So if I was not there at the end of eleven *maalas* there must have been a reason. An important reason was to make them understand that nothing happens from counting. If while doing a *jaap* your thought is focussed on the numbers, then you are simply wasting time. Through all these practices, we are trying to awaken a force inside us. Will that happen by counting numbers? Instead of depending upon your internal connection with the one who has given you the *jaap*, if you rely on external instructions from those who are standing to assist you, surely you have not reached anywhere.

At another instance, someone who has been into the practices for the last five to six years enquired about further 'instructions' regarding her *dhyan* from someone else in the Foundation. In *yog* and *dhyan*, there is nothing called as an 'instruction', there is only a relationship. If you are connected internally with your *Guru* figure then what is the need for any 'instruction'? This person asked for an instruction not from me, but from someone else in the Foundation. That someone else then asked me what to reply. I told her to ask for '*Guru dakshina*'. On hearing this, that person shot a mail to me saying that I had asked for *Guru dakshina,* which is such a big thing. I sent her a question mark in reply. In the next mail, she informed that she had been asked to give *Guru dakshina*. I answered back that it's between her and the one she received the instruction from. Now this person told the one she received the instruction from, "What can I give? I have nothing to give. I am ready to give the *dhyan* that I have done for so many years..." I told the person to tell her to give it. After that I did not feel the need to ask because I got my answer. She got so scared that in an instant she was ready to part with her *yog* and *dhyan* without even bothering to ask what I wanted. She was nervous about how much money I might ask for.

If that is your state after six-seven years, you surely have got nothing to give. You have only wasted your time. In all those years the person must have heard at least 500 times from me to not keep anyone in between. Whenever someone else comes between you and me to give instructions, then your *Guru* figure is that person and not me. This is the reason, the experiences, the level you should have attained by now, you have not been able to. It takes many years for you to complete the *jaap*, which otherwise gets completed in two months. You keep counting the *maalas* and asking me if your *jaap* is complete. But, whenever you count, be rest assured you are only wasting time. When the *jaap* goes on for this long, then the person should not be aware of anything else, just a continuous process that keeps going on and that is your connection. If that time is wasted in counting, then what experience can you have? Does an experience of *yog* happen from your mind? What is it that makes you experience? Whatever that is, you are not able to reach it, because you have tied yourself to a number game.

So understand, if you are walking with me, then walk with me only. One person in the *havan* is for synchronisation only; if you make him the leader, then that's your connection. Always remember, energy follows thought. Whatever is your thought, your *prana shakti* or *chitta shakti* will follow that thought. Especially, when you try to walk with me, whatever thought comes to you, your life starts progressing in that direction only. Whatever you are walking with me for, that thing will manifest immediately and that indicates your connection with me. Whatever aspect you are able to connect with, that is your truth and that is your connection, nothing besides that. I never judge anybody, I don't have that right. Your actions, the most minor of them, speak of your level, your reality.

Let me narrate a small story. There is a person in the Foundation who has an expansive business but is not getting the kind of returns that are expected. He has also been trying to do *dhyan* with me. He also follows some other

Guru, who is not in the body anymore. I have tried explaining to him many times that it is important to follow one path, if you put your feet in two different boats, nothing will come of it. (There is no ambiguity in this philosophy, if you do not like my face then make someone else your *Guru*, but that *Guru* should be in the body, otherwise you will keep going round and round.) He, however, refuses to change his thinking. Recently, he was discussing with me the reasons as to why his business was not growing. He came to the conclusion that it was because he does not bribe anyone. I told him to follow whatever were the norms of business. Instantly, the idea clicked with him and he asked me when he could come to discuss this further. For years I have told him to follow just one *Guru*, but he could not absorb that but the minute I told him about his business, he could connect with me.

Why was there a difference in the receptivity of the two things, when both were being said by me only? How you relate with me is what your level of evolution is. It is a clear concept. Just like business runs on certain principles, so does *yog*. If you do not follow those principles, you cannot do *yog*. If you are doing *yog,* then first make a *Guru* who is in the body.When *Ram* and *Krishna* took birth as human beings, they made a *Guru; even* though they were incarnations of Lord *Vishnu* because this is a *niyam*, a law. And I, or *Ram* or *Krishna* did not make these laws. They were given by the Creator and so one cannot overlook them because of ego.

Once I was lecturing in England when a person from the media asked me to define *yog*. I said, '*Yog* is *Guru*.' They said if you talk like this, we will not be able to publish anything because 'in this part of the world we don't think like this.' Later when I made them experience the power of the science and the energy of *Guru*, they all carried full-page articles on the subject. Initially they had inhibitions for they feared that a *Guru* will charge a huge sum, teach them some funny thing and later they would be exploited. These days there are many in the markets who sell weird practices in the name of *yog.* If you are getting fooled by them, you yourself are responsible because you are going to them for finding 'solution' to your problems. You have to understand that it's your own *karma* that comes back to you in the form of a problem. What solution can anybody give? Just improve your *karmas;* make use of your birth.

I know the power of the science of *yog* and I do not want its name to be spoilt. If you are engrossed in the physical, you will not be able to comprehend the subject and would take to old age, disease and problems while chasing the physical. This will cause you to doubt the subject; you might leave my hand and lose *yog*.

A person did *yog* with complete focus for three years with the sole intention of moving to the *ashram*; we even got a room made for him. But in spite of coming so close to me, he could not come here to stay, as one day his father threatened that he would commit suicide if he does not get married. The person asked me what to do. I knew nothing would happen but I let people choose for themselves, it is your individual journey. Now the person is married to an ideal spouse with high status, lots of money and every luxury in physical, the room at the *ashram* is still empty... When you do *yog* and *dhyan*, you are earning positive *karmas*, it is like increasing your bank balance. When the time comes, if you spend it in the wrong direction, then it is all over. A person, who could not even stay a minute without *yog*, was involved in every service and charity, and who was just 50 yards away from my place, suddenly vanished from *yog.* Whatever his desire was in the physical world got fulfilled and now he is unable to leave it. He completely forgot about the room. It is good that you have formed a relationship with me on the level of the physical, but simultaneously don't forget that it is a very low level, whereas the level of *yog* is very high. With a connection of that level, you can manifest anything in the physical but if you do not have that, then remember, physical is destructible. You are associating yourself with something, which is constantly moving towards destruction; it will perish sooner or later. *Ramakrishna Paramhansa* and *Ramana Maharishi* never thought of accumulating physical pleasures though they could have done it easily. Each of them had a *karya* and a *karya kshetra*. Once their *karya* was completed, they left their body. What would they have done with the body after that? The body is for *bhog* and *bhog* always brings *rog* with it. But it can also be used for *yog*. While it takes you towards destruction (*tamas*), you can also go towards light, *tamaso maa jyotir gamaya*. The darkness is this physical — your body, your assets — and the light is *gyan*. My job is to show you light in darkness, to put you on the path of gyan, not just show the way, but put you on it. Some don't see a torch in my hand and disagree with me. Some don't need a torch, they agree...

There is another acquaintance of mine, who has been trying to walk with me since the time I started *yog*. Once, when I went to his house, I could hear the sound of Sanskrit *shlokas*. Upon entering the house, I saw a *Guruji* sitting who was introduced as his Sanskrit teacher. When I asked him about the need for having a teacher, he replied that he wanted to understand the *Gita*. I just said, "Good. At least, you are understanding from someone. How does it matter who that is..." Today he has memorised the *Gita* by heart and lectures a crowd of 4000-5000 people whereas not even 400 come to listen to me. One day, I called him to one of my sessions to give a lecture. Some people came to me after the lecture and told me, "Yogiji why do you take the pain to give a lecture, you should call him only, at least it is interesting." After that feedback, I invited him to give lectures since people understood what he says, whereas hardly anybody understands what I have to say. He thought I am joking and never came after that. (I never joke with anyone. Everything I say is very serious because *yog* is no laughing matter; it is a very serious subject. With every passing second of your life, you have no idea what you are losing. Had you had the slightest hint, you would have become a *sanyasi* by now.) Recently, someone very close to him was seriously ill and so suddenly, I started getting calls from him. I had not received a single call from him for months together, but in those two hours he called me many times. Whenever I get a mail or call from you, I understand that you are facing a problem and the number of mails/ calls tells me the seriousness of the problem. I returned his call around 2 am, he was wide awake. He told me that the doctors had given up and only I could help his situation. The person in question was a 70 year old... I told him "You read and teach *Gita*, you know so much. If he is 70 and critical then just pray for him and let him go." My reply shocked him. Then I asked him if he thought that person would stay forever. He said, "No... just let him live for ten more years." I asked, "What will he do in those ten years that he hasn't already done in the past so many?"

There is power in *yog*, he had seen many cases like this before where the *sadhaks* of the Foundation had revived people through *yog*. But all the people who were revived have only gone deeper into the physical aspect of life, into more *bhog;* what was the purpose of that extended life? I told him not to do such things and let him go. His reply was, "Don't be so practical and logical. Just do it because I know you can do it." I told him I can only try, whether or not it happens is upon the Almighty. This person, who was asking me to shun logic, is a super specialist and there were some very critical cases pending in his department that required his immediate attention. I asked him to leave his problem to me and attend to those cases first. He told me, he will first have this person cured and only then attend to those cases.

The crux of *Gita* is *karma*. He did not do the *punya karma* by which he could have changed the course of events. He had more faith on the doctor's treatment than *karma* as described in the *Gita*. He could not see the pain and trauma of the 50 whose life depended on his being at work. He could only see his own pain and that too a pain for which he could do nothing. The doctor would not have permitted him inside the operation theatre, he could at best be biting his nails sitting outside. So what *Gita* did he learn and what *Gita* did he teach? God gave him an opportunity, an opportunity to do *punya karma*... *Punya karma* can evade all the pains that you are going through. That is the only way... Have I ever told you to take ten black seeds or five wheat grains and throw them in so-and-so direction to solve your problem? How will such *'upays'* help? If you have come to me and I am telling you the way, then at least walk it.

The subject of *yog* is a very serious one; it is the subject of entire creation, never mess around with it. If you mess with it, then nature will mess with you.

There is an English proverb; 'Birds of a feather flock together'. In terms of energy this means that people with similar energy patterns stay together. There are organisations where people who want to have fun come together, at others people with political aspirations collect under the same roof, but here... majority of you have no idea about what you are doing here with me. With every passing day the distance between you and me is increasing because you are not ready to walk the path of *yog* and *seva*. A day will come when you will suddenly move out of my spectrum, leading to a dimensional difference between you and me and then you will not be able to meet me because we will be in two different dimensions.

Remember, there is only one *mantra*, one *maala*, one *Guru*, one *asan* and one *isht dev*. These can never be two, otherwise it is considered an adultery in *yog*. In *yog*, adultery is not a person getting married to two women, but this is considered adultery and will take you away from the path because when it becomes two, then you have two ways. Which one will you take? It has to be one.

Once we went to *Gangotri* towards *Gaumukh*, along with a couple from the Foundation who was very influential in that area. In the mountains we met a *babaji* seeing whom the two got really enamoured. I knew it right there that their mind has gotten diluted. While talking to him, they introduced me as *Yogiji*. The gentleman looked at me (I was in my tracks and t-shirt) and laughed. I did not say anything but his action was indicative of his *shreni*. Later when we came back to the hotel, I said that let us call him down. The in-charge started laughing and said he never comes down; he always stays in the mountains. I just told him that he will come down tomorrow and we will have a conversation with him. I could make out from their faces that they thought I had lost my mind. Next morning, I went for my *sandhya* practices (normally I do not wear anything at that time, just a loin cloth). The *babaji* was also there and he started observing me carefully. He could not recognise me as the person he had met a day before and people had to reintroduce me to him. A person who judges you by your appearance and clothes and is unable to sense the energy body, has definitely not risen above the physical and the five elements. He came down and spoke to me for ten minutes. Even he did not know why he came down and was very embarrassed.

That couple, because of dilution and adultery, is no longer in *yog*. The moment they believed that *babaji,* who was mocking me; that very instant it was over for them. Once you look down upon the path which is giving you experiences, what else can happen after that? If I wear T-shirt and track-pant, that is my wish. I can be without them too. It does not matter to me either ways. The one who judges me by my appearance, what can that person do? I gave him full respect but got to know his *shreni*...

The subject of *yog* is very simple and at the same time the most difficult subject because in this you have to practice what you preach. Has anybody seen me preaching what I don't practice? The fact is that this body is perishable and so is everything related to it and this is slipping from your hands with every passing day. With each day, this physical aspect is increasing the distance between you and me. The choice is entirely yours — whether you want to stay in that spectrum or you don't want to.

The crux is that you have to practice what you preach. You have to move from what is perishable/mortal towards what is immortal and you cannot do that till the time you keep holding on to the perishable. No doubt physical achievement is important but *gyan* is far more important, both of these should be there together. A lack of any of the two will make your life incomplete and your soul will keep wandering. Now that you have tasted *gyan*, when the time comes for you to leave this body, you will search for a body, which is similar to this. And since you will not find such a body, you will keep wandering in different *yonis*, troubled and in pain. Because once you have tasted good food, would you eat stale or less tasty food offered by someone? No. You will keep looking for that tasty food only and you will always be unhappy, searching for the same quality but you will just not find it, as it will not be available then. Understand this and wake up now.

Sadhaks who have been seriously practicing the various *mantra siddhis*, have had physical manifestations of the various gods. When they did the *Ganpati mantra siddhi* and did its *havan,* the complete form of *Ganeshji* was created in the *kund*. This is how manifestation happens when you do *mantra sadhna*. But if there is no focus or intensity, then nothing will happen. Lord *Ganesh*, the master of *ridhi* and *sidhi*, resides at the *Mooladhar chakra* and is the guardian of the doorway to higher *loks*. During a *havan* while doing *mantra uccharan* for *Ganeshji*, the energy in the *Sushumna nadi* rises upwards. The *agni* moves in *Mooladhar* and the *abha* or *shakti* of *agni* activates all the *chakras* and opens your *Sahastrar*. When you have formed a connection with *agni* and the *havan kund* and while you are invoking that energy, how can you count? At least I cannot do it.

Connect with the *agni* and you might as well ask somebody else to count, you just move your *maala*, that is important. When the *maala* moves, the *shakti* of *mantra* gets accumulated in the *maala* and its *meru*. All these are *tantric mantras* and have their *prayog* later in *sadhna*, you use them for a specific purpose and the use happens through the *meru*. That is why the *meru* is never crossed over while doing *jaap* with a *maala* and since *shakti* gets accumulated in it, it is important to keep rotating it. If your *jaap* has been completed, wear the *maala* upside down, which means, the *meru* should be behind the neck. This region is seat of the soul, also called as *pindli*, where spine curves and goes into the head, into the medulla oblongata. Often in *dhyan* you see a blue pearl or the *neel bindu*, that is a reflection of this only.

Along with the *havan*, it is important to do service and charity, to open your blocks and to lead you to a state of *vairagya*. Only when you start parting with something, give something to someone or devote your time for someone else without expecting anything in return, you realise the futility of it all. What you are yourself giving away is useless for you and gradually you find everything physical as useless.

Let me share a personal experience. I hardly move out of the *ashram*, but once there was some work which required me to go out. As I reached and decided to park my car, I realised that I had absolutely no money with me since I never carry a wallet, card or a cheque book. When I saw the parking guy, I did not know what to do. I just opened the ashtray and by chance found some change, which summed up to exactly rupees ten!

Once you start giving, your mind starts to get off it; what to give, what to take, becomes a matter of lesser concern. Not that you do not want it, but the attachment finishes. It hardly matters whether it is there or not. You know it is important, but it is of no value to you — if it is there, good. But if it is not, you will not regret it not being there or feel bad or get tense. Again this is an indication for you. If you are attached with a person or your money or property or car, then you have not attained the state of *vairagya,* no matter how highly you may think of yourself. If you are losing your hair over a drop in your salary and contemplating becoming a *bhikshu* so that you can manage in the meager income, then you do not have the state to become a *bhikshu*. The state of *bhikshu*, the state of *vairagya,* is a very high state. It is the most difficult thing. I am talking of *bhikshu* and not a beggar, so do not mock it.

Whatever you are walking with me for, that thing will manifest immediately and that indicates your connection with me. Whatever aspect you are able to connect with, that is your truth and that is your connection, nothing besides that. I never judge anybody, I don't have that right.

TO ACHIEVE *SRI* YOU WILL HAVE TO PLEASE ALL THESE GODS AND GODDESSES. THERE EXISTS NO SHORTCUT, FIND A *GURU* TO KNOW THE PATH FOR THIS.

SERMON 16

THE PROCESS TO ACHIEVE SRI

*" There are rishis whose life spanned many centuries.
They did not merely sit for 500 or 1000 years, they transgressed into the subtler dimensions where time moves faster and so while for them only 100 years would have passed, in Earth years it would be many thousand years. "*

16

A month before my lecture (for most it's only a lecture) at the Indian Medical Association, I received a mail from a person in Mumbai saying that, "I am very troubled; I am not able to prove myself." So I asked how I can help him. To which he replied, "Tell me some technique of meditation by which everything becomes fine." When I asked him about his problem, he told me that he had done *Sri Vidya*. I told him that is very good and asked him who his *Guru* was. He mentioned some complicated name, (similar to the trend these days where one puts many titles before and after the name) — *Avdhoot* something... I have forgotten. He asked if I knew him.I told him that I was not familiar with the name. I knew of a *Shivanand Avdhoot* but he is no more in the body although his place is still there enroute Haridwar to Rishikesh. He replied back saying, "No, he is still in the body." I told him that I knew mostly all the *avdhoots* and he told me that this gentleman has *shivirs* in India and abroad. I knew something was wrong because no *avdhoot* moves from his/her place. He also told me about some other *vidyas* that he had learnt, about which I had never heard. I told him that when he knew so much, he should be the one giving me *gyan*, why was he still troubled. He responded, "That is exactly what the problem is. I do not know what I am supposed to do now." So I finally told him to forget all this *tamasha* (drama) and start doing *yog*. He asked me what *yog* was. He had done so many *vidyas* and yet no one had told him about what *yog* is, and that to enter *yog* one needs to first leave aside all this *tamasha*. He told me that there were many like him there, who had done many such *vidyas,* which left me thinking that I was headed for a tough time in Mumbai.

Asurs have been there since the beginning of creation. In every *yug*, *asurs* have come in different forms and in every form that they assume; they have cheated, duped and harassed people. That is the basic nature of an *asur*. *Asurs* pertain to the lower dimensions, the dimensions below the Bhulok. As the various dimensions co-exist, it is important to understand what dimensions are, who is it that we are going to learn from and how to distinguish between *yog* and *tamasha.*

The *vedic* masters revealed to us that when you go near a heavy or grosser object i.e. the one that has more weight, then the speed of time slows down. One might argue that the speed of the second hand of a watch remains the same irrespective of your location on earth and so time moves at a constant speed. However, recently an American scientist, Stephen Hawking, did a study on this and said that time travel (which involves moving from one dimension of time to another) is possible and that is only because time is not the same everywhere. Somewhere time moves faster and somewhere it moves slower. And this gap between slow and fast is determined by the speed of light. If you move with the speed of light, then in every half an hour, you will move one hour, which means that if you are travelling at that speed, then if half hour has passed in your watch, one hour would have passed in the life of normal people. So if 12 hours have passed for you, then 24 hours would have passed for them and because of those 12 hours of time, a dimensional change will occur within you.

Did you know that the satellites that orbit the earth have a specialized program which adjusts time after every day for one-third of a billionth of a second? They do that because time moves faster in space, if they do not, all our global positioning and time systems will become erroneous. If you go higher than where the satellites orbit the earth, then you gain time, and if you go near a black hole and orbit around it with the speed of light at a distance where you will not get sucked into it, then in every 16 minutes you will gain eight minutes, that means, while you would pass eight minutes, 16 minutes would have passed for others. So, if you circle the black hole for five years and come back to earth, 10 years would have passed by on earth, there would be a dimensional change in you and it would not be the same time as you had left. So time travel, according to Hawking, is possible like this. It is a dimensional change, the whole dimension changes.

All these things which Physics tells us today were clearly laid down in our texts 18,000 to 20,000 years ago. You must have heard that a day in *Brahmalok* is equivalent to four *Mahayugs* on earth (a *Mahayug* comprises of *Satyug, Tretayug, Dwaparyug and Kaliyug)*. And for Lord *Vishnu*, it is said, that when he blinks once, then four *Mahayugs* pass by, so this is what dimensional change is. Physics now acknowledges the fact that the more we go upwards towards the subtler layers, the faster the time will move. Our *rishis* thousands of years ago said that in the heavier and grosser dimensions, the speed of time will be slower and in the subtler dimensions, time will move faster. This is the reason why there are *rishis* whose life spanned many centuries. They did not merely sit for 500 or 1000 years, they transgressed into the subtler dimensions where time moves faster and so while for them only 100 years would have passed, in Earth years it would be many thousand years.

Every being is tied to time according to the dimension it is in. An insect's entire life passes in a few days, it takes birth, procreates and dies. The same life for a dog passes in 13 to 15 years. The basis of *yog* is these dimensions. An *asur is* a heavy dimension. Going back to the incident we discussed earlier, there are people who set up *shivirs* and teach all kinds of *vidyas* and there are those who wander troubled and frustrated after learning them. Both, those who teach and those who learn are in a state where their *karmas* do not allow them to rise above a certain limit and hence they are tied to their dimension, because *karma* is the basis of the entire creation. All the *shaktis* of creation perform their *karma* and that is why the creation is functioning. The *jeevatma* is a reflection of the creation; it is energy, it has to do its *karma* to progress. Talking about *jeevatma*, let us look at another Law of Physics. Einstein told us that energy can neither be created nor destroyed, it only changes form. The same was stated by our *rishis* and in the *Gita* about the soul, that it cannot be destroyed by a weapon, it cannot be burnt by fire, withered by wind or wetted by water, and that the *swaroop* of the soul is *anant-akhand, ajar-amar*. So when energy can neither be created nor destroyed, that means every person here is tied by *karma* and he/she is only changing his/her form.

To rise above one's karma, Guru kripa is required and that does not happen just like that. To get a Guru, you have to have the intent for a Guru, a Guru is there to make you rise above the sthool and not to solve your physical problems or tie you more to the physical..

Let me share an experience with you. There was a lady who came to me sometime back in a very bad state, she had never done *yog* or *dhyan* in her life, all she did was fly between Italy and India and think of herself as nothing less than an Italian princess. She told me that she had never had an experience of anything beyond, so she was made to experience her past lives through *yog*. After the 20 minute session when she got up, I asked her what she saw. She just stared at me blankly contemplating whether to tell me or not. With much hesitation, she finally revealed that she saw herself standing on the roof of an old house, in the heart of a village. She was of ordinary appearance, her clothes tattered, her hair oiled and braided. The house where she was had two-three broken *charpais* and on one of them sat an old man. And as she was trying to figure out where she was, someone called out her name... *Shakuntala*. So I asked her what happened to her views on being an Italian princess in her last birth, she just kept quiet and I explained to her that the reason for extreme desire for money and a mate stems from here.

Every person thinks that he/she is above *karma bandhan,* that except for him/her, everyone else is tied by *karma*. And this is where one makes a mistake. Every person, the whole creation, all the dimensions, except the *sanchalak (*controller*)*, are bound by *karma* and because of that, they have to move in accordance with *karma* only. At that moment, I thought to myself, that had she really been a princess then her *karmas* would have been so bad (she would have sent so many down the gallows, exploited so many) that she would have never been able to reach me in this birth. It must have been good *karmas* like service to the elderly in her past birth that got her to me in this life. No person thinks that he/she is less than the other in any way. Infact, each one is of the view that there is no one bigger or better than him/her. You take yourself to be the ultimate, that you will always remain here, which is true, because you will not go anywhere, only the body will change. And the body you will surely change.

It is necessary to have the *gyan* that you are not this body, but something beyond it, and that from wherever you have come here, it is because of your *karmas*, and you cannot rise above the ties of your *karma*, you can only go as high as your *karmas* allow. It is also important to understand that the plethora of *vidyas* and *kriyas* that are being sold across the globe are not given at the drop of a hat (or for a few thousand rupees). A *sadhak* has to work hard to generate the capacity to receive a *vidya* and become worthy of it. These *vidyas* are steps or stages in the journey of *yog*. What we call the *Sri Vidya* is the ultimate science, next only to *Gayatri Sadhna*. These sciences are not taught or told just like that, to anybody, because all these sciences are for evolution, and not for any physical gains like business expansion or curing a disease or a better body or a happy relationship etc. If somebody is claiming that you will get physical gains out of a particular *vidya*, or is charging a fee to give it, be rest assured it is only a *tamasha.*The gentleman that person mentioned in the mail, was a property dealer sometime back. His business was drowning and so he was advised to become a *baba* (these days the *baba* business is flourishing). Today he is a *baba* and setting up *shivirs* where all kinds of *vidyas* are sold, leaving one confused and frustrated. The mail-writer from Mumbai is not an isolated example; such things are very common these days because we forget that we cannot go above our *karma*. If our *karmas* are like this only, if this is what we are asking for, then we will get that only. If you have been cheating and fooling people throughout and are hoping that the resultant problems will end with certain *kriyas* and *vidyas*, then you will only find such *tamashas* and drain the little money and resources that are left with you on them. It is foolish to expect a *kriya or vidya* to make things alright for you when your *karmas* are so polluted. It does not happen this way. To rise above one's *karma, Guru kripa* is required and that does not happen just like that. To get a *Guru*, you have to have the intent for a *Guru*, a *Guru* is there to make you rise above the *sthool* and not to solve your physical problems or tie you more to the physical. Even though modern science confirms that energy cannot be created or destroyed, that is, you neither die nor take birth, yet you run after such *tamashas* and not the *sukshma* or *adhyatmic.* This is *maya* and *karma bandhan.*

The more you tie yourself into physical knots, the lower becomes your level and dimension and you do not even realise it, just like a clerk, who takes bribes to make money and enjoys thinking he is progressing, without having a clue that every *bandhan* of *maya* is taking him further down. There are so many scams and incidences of embezzlement and bribery that one comes across in the papers these days. This is the dimensional difference that we referred to earlier, a person makes money by cheating and finds nothing wrong with it because there is no *Guru* to make him realise it. And why is there no *Guru*? Because the *karmas* do not allow. This becomes a vicious circle. It may also happen that a *Guru* is there, but you cannot see him, and sometimes when the *Guru* is not there, you think he is there, because your *karmas* do not allow you to rise above.

There are many who come to me and say they have a family *Guru*, but he is no more in the body. To them I say, "Good that you have a *Guru*, but then why are you here?" These people just do not know the meaning of the word *Guru*. A *Guru* is like food. When a person feels hungry, then that food is *Guru* and once you have eaten your food and your stomach is full, then you do not need to eat for some time. So once you find your *Guru*, then you get satisfied, the experience that you desire gets fulfilled and you do not need to eat again. And a *Guru* gets to know a long time before, when it is time for him/her to leave the body, so they tell their prime disciples beforehand what and how they need to do. And there is only one *Guru*, not multiple *Gurus*. It is a misconception that our grandfather's and father's *Guru* will be our *Guru* and also of our child. If this was the case, then the *Gurus* of earlier times *Rishi Vishwamitra, Sandeepan Rishi, Parshuram,* only their *aradhna* should still be done. Why consider the ones who were there only two-three generations ago as *Gurus*? So it is absolutely necessary for the *Guru* to be in the body and *Gurus* do not go down from generation to generation.The problem in present times is that there is an *abhaav* of *Guru* because of which one is unable to get out of the *bandhan* of *maya.* A body has to go and in its place a new form will be taken, but you do not have the *gyan* of either the form after it, or of the one before it. You just go and listen to lectures, read books, some even give lectures, but if you do not have the *gyan* of this form itself, then all of it is useless. The term *shareer* itself means that which is heading towards destruction constantly. No matter how high your position is, no matter how much money you have, how good-looking you are, eventually, 'you' or the body (which you think is you) will fade away and will be put to fire or buried. All the things will be left behind. Understand that body is not forever, it is destructible, and so instead of wasting your time on that which is temporary, focus on *yog* as only *yog* will take you somewhere. No matter how *gyani* you are, unless you have the experience, you cannot reach anywhere. If your *karmas* do not allow then even if you are blessed with the *sakshat darshan* of Lord Shiv you will not recognize him. And if *karmas* are there then there can be *sakshatkar* in any form.

So, I would suggest, that for the time being, let these *vidyas* be, do not get impressed or enamoured by them. These are just ways for evolution that take you towards higher states or dimensions. They are meant for dimensional change and not for making more money or curing diseases. The people who initiated these *vidyas*, for instance, *Shankaracharya* who left his body around the age of 40 and *Vivekanand* who also left his body early, none of them led a leisurely life. In fact, all the *Yog Gurus* — *Shankaracharya*, *Ramakrishna Paramhansa*, *Satyanand Paramhansa*, *Sai Baba* — the ones who had *vidyas* and *shaktis* — they never lived in *vaibhav*, rather they chose the life of *ekant*. You would never hear a *Yog Guru* telling people that he will teach them this *vidya* or that. *Vidyas* are neither taught nor learnt en masse, it is a private relationship between *Guru* and *shishya*, never to be discussed with someone outside, no matter what the circumstance, for it is considered a breach of faith, for which punishments are severe. That is why a *Guru* gives *shakti* to a limited few and not en masse. Anyone giving en masse is only doing a *tamasha*, avoid it.

Nothing in this creation is constant, everything is in continuous movement and that movement is either up or down, so you have a choice whether you want to go up or go down. If you want to go up, you search for a *Yog Guru* and if you want to go down then you search for a business *Guru*. If you are searching for a *Guru* to solve your business problems then you are looking for a business *Guru* and not a *Yog Guru*. The *karya* (work) of a *Yog Guru* is to open your bondages and not to tie you further. When you start *yog,* you immediately start having experiences, and your experiences show you the way. There is no *yog* without experiences. So do not go by words, only go by your own personal experience. It is a misconception that we can read and understand *yog*, because that is knowledge, not *gyan.*

What is the difference between *gyan* and knowledge? Let me explain with an example. Some senior members of the Foundation are not present as they 'had to' attend a party. Mind you, none of them is below the age of 60 and they have had all kinds of experiences and have all the knowledge, but today, I feel they have had no *gyan*. Because even after crossing 60, they are at a party today and enjoying it. If you ask them, they will call it a social obligation. But remember, there is no such thing as a 'social obligation'. When a child is born, the social obligation ends right there. It is up to him/her to decide whether he/she wants to keep any social obligations or not. These are just ways to fool yourself because if you have done everything in life, then where is the question of social obligation now? It is these social obligations that tie you to another birth, another life because you still want to enjoy a little more.

There is no energy/*shakti* bigger than a human being in the whole creation, so no matter what happens, if you have your *Guru* then no *anisht* can happen to you, this is the first thing. The second thing is that if we have and are taking birth in this *yug,* that means our *karmas* are not very good and that is why, we are being born again in this *yug.*And just look over the generations, what state we have brought the creation to and the beings taking birth now, what state will they take it to. In the name of music they love to make noise, the outdoor sports have been replaced by artificial play stations and by burning black oil, we are polluting our environment. We have not left anything. So for any intelligent person, there is no scope for taking birth here now. In another 10 years, just see the state of affairs. There is no scope for being born here again, so do not waste your time — by planning on taking another birth. You can do that also as there is nothing good or bad in this creation. It is said, that in Lord *Shiv*'s abode everyone is allowed — *sur-asur, dev-danav, yaksh, kinnar, naag, manav.* No matter what you are doing, you are still eligible for *moksha*. But still, if you are not ready to leave, then that *karma* of yours takes you towards hell, that is a wrong *karma*. This is the difference between a *gyani* and an *agyani.* Till the time you are an *agyani*, you can do anything, nothing is forbidden. But once you have the *darshan* of *gyan* and even after that you do not stop doing it, then that is a wrong *karma*. Otherwise everything is allowed at all stages, you are stopped from doing nothing. *dharma, artha, kama, moksha* — simple and straight forward.

You can only go up till where your *karmas* allow, or till where your *Guru* chooses to lift you. So if you want to reach somewhere, the only thing you can do is improve your *karma*. When you do that, then for whichever *vidya* your state is ready, I will individually call you and teach that to you, but then, even you should want it. You just do not want it; you only want solutions to your business and relationship problems and for these you do not need these *vidyas* and so they are not discussed with you. But yes, if you are into service and charity, if you are a part of this creation, if you are with the *paramatma* in a positive way, then all these sciences are accessible to you, otherwise not. You can read about these *vidyas* in books —*Saundarya Lahiri* of *Shankaracharya* gives a clear description of all these *vidyas,* but you will not achieve them by reading it. Nor by sitting with your eyes closed, or chanting *mantras*. The only way to evolve is by improving your *karma* and finding a *Guru*.

Even a thought is a *karma*. If you think about something, then even that is considered a *karma*. That is why in the state of detachment, *vairagya* or *kevalya*, one's thoughts go into *shunya and* he/she does not think anything. Acting or doing anything is surely a *karma,* but even thinking is a *karma*. Thoughts also tie you in bondages, which is why the *rishi-munis* would live in isolation, and stayed here only if they were given a specific purpose by their *Guru*. If no purpose was given, they took themselves into the state of *shunya* and returned back to where they had come from.

This is the play of *karmas* and dimensions, and it is the dimension of time that you need to cross. Length, breadth, height and time are the four dimensions and everything happens within these four dimensions only, and all of them including time, are physical. You can measure all of them except time. When you cannot even measure time, how will you go beyond it? How will you reach the levels beyond it, by only talking of the *vidyas*? *Sri* is the mother of all and all the *loks* are *sthit* in her womb. If your basics are not in place, if you do not have the *karmas*, then what is the purpose of talking about *vidyas*? It is nothing more than a *tamasha*.

Sri Vidya is the ultimate science, next only to Gayatri Sadhna. These sciences are not taught or told just like that, to anybody, because all these sciences are for evolution, and not for any physical gains like business expansion or curing a disease or a better body or a happy relationship etc.

Original/unedited pictures of manifestations in *havan* performed by *sadhaks* at *Dhyan Ashram*.

HANUMAN JI WITH HIS MACE

Agni is the first word of *Rigveda*. It is the only element that cannot be polluted and also the only element that rises up (against the pull of gravity). It is the element that holds within it the power to purify and transform. No wonder it is the chosen medium for *devs* and *devis* to interact with us, during a *vedic havan*.

SERMON 17

PRADAKSHINA KRIYA

“ *Thus, the moon does the pradakshina (circumambulation) of earth and earth does the pradakshina of sun so that they become the sun but they are unable to do so as they are tied by their bondages of maya.* ”

17

Creation is run on *shakti*. The entire science of *Tantra* is based on *shakti*. All the *tantric vidyas*, *Dasmahavidyas* etc are all centres of *shakti*. A centre is that which runs other things on its energy. This means that the *shakti itself* and the *shakti* on which it is *ashrit* (dependent) together form a single *oorja*. In other words, if you are doing the *upasana* of something, then your *shakti* and the *shakti* of whose *upasana* you are doing are one. This may be understood with the example of planets revolving around the sun; together they form a single *oorja*.

All the planets run on sun's energy. They are the materialisation of sun's energy and have the potential to become the sun. However, they are not able to become the sun due to their limitations or attractions.

There are no mountains, plants or rivers on the sun, but there are certain *shaktis* that reside on it. These are known by different names. The name of one such *shakti is Pooshan,* which runs the *Chandra dev.* You must have observed that on a full moon night, at times the moon glows like the sun. This is because of that one ray from the sun, called the *Pooshan kiran* that falls on it. The moon has the capacity to become the sun but it remains the moon because it is tied to its bondages of *maya*. The moon has an attraction towards the Earth due to which it cannot become the sun even though it runs on the sun's energy.

Earth too is run on the *shakti* of sun but is unable to become the sun because of its own attractions — that of *jeev-jantus* that inhabit the Earth. It fears that if it becomes as *tejomaya* (radiant) as the sun, then its children (flora and fauna) will get destroyed as they will not have the capacity to tolerate the sun.

Thus, the moon does the *pradakshina* (circumambulation) of earth and earth does the *pradakshina* of sun so that they become the sun but they are unable to do so as they are tied by their bondages of *maya*.

Just like the Earth and the moon, a human being too has the potential to become the sun or any other *shakti* that he is desirous of. For this, there is a specific kriya in *Tantra* called the *Pradakshina Kriya* in which the *Guru* prescribes certain *mantras* to the practitioner. By chanting those *mantras* while doing the *pradakshina* of a *shakti — Surya, Chandra, Das Mahavidyas*, etc — *the oorja* of that *shakti* comes inside the practitioner and he/she starts becoming like that *shakti*. However, to become *shakti,* the bondages of *maya* need to be opened and so it is important to practice the *kriya* under the *sanidhya* of a *Guru* who knows your attractions and guides you as per your individual capacity.

The most important and powerful *pradakshina kriya* is the *pradakshina* of your *Guru*. *Guru* has been given the foremost position in the *yog-sutras*. A *Guru* is considered beyond God...not because he is beyond God, but because for you he is beyond God, as he will take you to God. A *Guru* is neither a businessman nor an entrepreneur. He is the giver of gyan, love and bliss. Normally love and bliss in most of the schools today is considered as sexual gratification and physical pleasure, but it is not so. The bliss and the state of *anand* cannot be described in words, as it is beyond words...it is to be experienced and the experience will happen only if while doing *pradakshina* and otherwise the thought is undiluted, of your *Guru* only.

Energy follows thought. The thought draws the energy towards you and there is *anand*, an indescribable experience. Having thoughts and doubts on the *Guru* will make this *kriya* wasteful. Do it only when you are ready and have the permission of your *Guru*.

Nothing in this creation is constant, everything is in continuous movement and that movement is either up or down, so you have a choice whether you want to go up or go down. If you want to go up, you search for a Yog Guru and if you want to go down then you search for a business Guru.

SERMON 18

SIDDHASAN AND A STRAIGHT SPINE, PRE-REQUISITES FOR YOG

" *Dhyan needs to be taken, and done, seriously. If your back is bent even slightly, and if your thought wanders even remotely, then dhyan will immediately come to an end, and you will go into a state of sleep. And when you go into sleep, you get to see beautiful dreams.* "

18

Y*og* is a subject of *shakti*; it is a powerful science and must not be taken lightly. *It* is the final frontier, in which lies the essence of the entire creation. It is, therefore, imperativethat no aspect of it is distorted.

In present times, we have learnt to simplify and distort everything to suit our comfort. If you are not able to do a certain thing, instantly an alternative method is provided for. For instance, if you cannot sit cross-legged on the floor, you can sit on a chair. If you cannot keep your spine straight, you can sit with a hunch, and if you cannot even do that, lie down. Do whatever you are comfortable doing, but 'the show must go on'. Today, the subject of *yog* has become the very embodiment of such quick-fixes and easy alternatives. You will be disappointed to know though, that there are no shortcuts or cheat codes in *yog*. If you want *yog*, you have to do it as it is. There are certain pre-requisites that must be met with, for the experience to happen.

Several years back, a couple who had done *yog sadhna* and *tapasya* for many years came to see me. They were dressed in plain white clothes. Looking at them, I asked, that they must have gone real deep into *dhyan.* The reply came, "We do *dhyan* for five hours every day." I told them, "Even I don't do *dhyan* for five hours, so then what will I teach you? Instead, you should teach me. Five hours of *dhyan* is a lot of time..." We then sat for *dhyan*, during which I noticed that both were sitting with their backs bent throughout the session. When I inquired about this after the session, they asked me the reason for asking. I told them, that there are certain pre-conditions for *yog* and *dhyan.* Hearing this, they revealed that they sat like this all the time, at times, they even lie down. I told them, "If you lie down, then why do you say you do *dhyan* for four or five hours?

You should say we do *dhyan* for ten to twelve hours; because a person easily sleeps for ten to twelve hours, and that should be considered as *dhyan* as well."

There is a story of *Satyanand Paramhansa*, the founder of Bihar School of Yoga. *Satyanand* used to sit for *dhyan* in the evening, and once, in the initial years of his *yog sadhna*, he kept sitting till morning. In the morning when he opened his eyes, he ran straight to his *Guru*, *Shivanand*, and told him, "You know what? I have achieved *samadhi* today." He was then asked, "How is that?" He replied, "I sat in the evening for *dhyan* and got up only in the morning. I did not realise the time at all." So *Shivanand* told him that it is not *samadhi* he had achieved, but that he had fallen asleep. Also, that he must have heard of a small *sutra* in *Rudrashtakam* — *'Nidra samadhi sthiti.'* The *sthiti* of sleep is the *sthiti* of *samadhi* only, but the *avastha* (state) is not. The *avastha* is different.

At one of the *dhyan* sessions, I saw a young boy, aged 20-21 years, sitting for *dhyan* with his eyes tightly shut. Upon asking him what was it that he was trying to do, he told me he was trying to see. When I asked him what was it that he was trying to see, he said he did not know. When I probed further, he shared, "I just wanted to see all these *shaktis*." I asked, "Who told you this?" He mentioned that his parents followed somebody who also features on the television, and always asked them if they had seen something. So I asked him if he had seen something, and his response to me was that he hadn't seen anything till now. Then I told him, "Don't worry, even I have not seen anything till now."

All this 'seeing' is a mental state and it operates from the sub-conscious mind. Initially when you grow in *yog*, you do get some visions, but only initially. Once you reach the state of *dharana* in *yog,* then all these cease to come. After that it's a different state that cannot be described here, but in that you see nothing. If something is visible, and you are getting nice *darshans*, then it means you have slept and the subconscious is at play. This is a very clear indication, as the mind can play and show you anything, anytime.

Point here is that *dhyan* needs to be taken, and done, seriously. If your back is bent even slightly, and if your thought wanders even remotely, then *dhyan* will immediately come to an end, and you will go into a state of sleep. And when you go into sleep, you get to see beautiful dreams. If you can't sit straight, then you cannot do *dhyan*, the *sthirta* (stillness) that comes with *dhyan* will not come, nor will the *shakti.*

I have noticed that there are very few people who sit in *Siddhasan*. When we talk of *yog*, it's a subject of *shakti* and *shakti* has to get awakened inside you. I can give you a *mantra* and a method to awaken it, I can also awaken that *shakti* in you, but your fragile bodies will not be able to hold it. Sitting in *Siddhasan* is the very first and the most basic step to awaken that *shakti* inside you. When you sit in *Sidhhasan*, your one heel is on the *moolsthan*, closing the *Mooladhar chakra* and the other on *Swadhisthan*, closing the *Swadhisthan chakra*. And both the heels are kept, one atop the other.

During *dhyan*, slight heat gets generated in the body that is emitted from the *Kundalini*. This heat can be understood as hunger pangs that are emitted in the form of a series of pulses from the bottom — the *Mool chakra* (which governs the basics of life — food, drink and good living). If your focus is always on the basics, then it means you are at the level of *moolsthan* only, and haven't risen upwards. So when the heat is emitted, it gets consumed at the *Mool chakra* itself. It makes you *bhramit,* creating a desire for an even bigger house, even better food, etc and in the process, the *shakti*, which you awaken by doing *dhyan*, gets exhausted at the *Mooladhar* only. Sometimes, you are able to control the urges of the *moolsthan*, but then the *Swadhisthan*, the seat of sexual desires gets fired up and so the remaining heat gets finished there. It cannot go beyond that. It is only when we keep the *Swadhisthan* and *moolsthan* under control for a long period of time, that the *shakti* or the heat can rise up, but it still has to cross *Manipoorak, Anahad, Vishuddhi* and *Agya*. And a pre-requisite for this heat to rise through the *chakras*, is a straight back. Your back is a reflection of the *Sushumna nadi*, through which the pulses of *Kundalini* rise from *Mooladhar* to the *Agya*. It is only when the pulses rise till the *Agya* that the experience happens; otherwise it is simply day-dreaming or the subconscious at play.

If somebody is at the level of *Manipoorak* and you are at *moolsthan*, then you will be attracted by the things he says, or the *tej* (glow) he emanates. But you will also be troubled thinking, why he has it and you do not. You will not be able to understand his actions because you are at a level lower than his.It is because in your case the heat is being consumed at the lower levels of *moolsthan* or *Swadhisthan*, due to your desires. You can only experience *yog* when the heat crosses all the levels and reaches the *Agya*. And that can only happen when your body is straight and still like a stone, affected by nothing — a state of complete balance, where you're capable of everything. But that balance cannot be attained till you develop a control over your *chakras*. If you keep tripping here and there, or if there is a lot of hyperactivity in you, you keep shouting or crying, it means you still do not have that control. And when you don't have control over your basic *chakras*, then you cannot channelize that *shakti* till the *Agya*. Till that time, you will only see the physical aspect of things. Even when you talk to me, all you will think of is getting just one more work done.

To rise above the level of *Mooladhar* and *Swadhisthan*, *Siddhasan* is important. *Yog* is not a subject of comfort. It cannot be done by sitting comfortably or while sleeping; that is a waste of time. When your back is straight and you can maintain *Siddhasan*; that is when experiences of subtler dimensions or *loks* begin…

Let me explain what *loks* are. Right now, you are in the *Bhulok*, which comprises of five basic *chakras* and desires corresponding to those *chakras*. To rise above *Bhulok*, you need to rise above the desires of these five basic *chakras*. Next comes *Bhuvahlok*. In *Bhuvahlok* there is only one *moolsthan/chakra* or desire, gaining control of which, you reach *Swarglok*. After that are *Maha, Jana, Tapa* and finally, *Satyalok*. However, for measuring the journey through the *chakras*, which we call *atmic unnati* or spiritual evolution, we take *Bhu* as *Mooladhar*, *Bhuva* as *Swadhisthan* and *Swah* (or *Swarglok*) as *Manipoorak*.

It is difficult to understand what these *loks* are, because these are dimensions of existence. For instance, right now you are at *Bhulok* but when you begin to evolve spiritually, it is only then that you can experience the *Bhuvahlok;* in this body itself. Same is with *Swahlok*, although this *lok* can be experienced without the body too. Each lower *lok* is controlled and run by the upper *lok.* There also exist still lower *loks* called *taals,* below the *Bhulok*. Just like the insects living below the ground are completely dependent on you, similarly these *taals* (*Bhutaal, Rasataal, Pataal*, etc) are dependent on the *Bhulok*. A human being starts from these lower *loks* and then reaches *Bhulok*. His *moolsthan* in *Bhulok* is his connection between lower *loks*, and the higher *loks*.

Till *Bhuvahlok* there are pleasures, the five pleasures, which are your five *indriyas* (senses), five desires. After *Bhuva*, comes the *Swahlok* or *Swarglok*. I have heard many a times, people say that when you reach *Swarglok*, you will get all kinds of delicious food to eat and beautiful *apsaras* to entertain you (especially the men)... The idea is quite foolish. *Swarglok* is above *Bhu* and *Bhuvahlok*, which means that it is above the basic desires of food and sex that are governed by the *Mooladhar* and *Swadhisthan*. This means that in *Swarglok*, there is neither food, nor drink nor any sexual activity. And yet, *Swarglok* is called the *Bhoglok*. *Bhog* here refers to some other higher pleasures, above the desires for food, drink and sexual activity, and only those people can go to *Swarglok*, whose basic desires in the *Bhu* and *Bhuvahloks* have been satisfied completely.

When somebody dies, people say that he has gone to *Swarg* — *'Swargwasi ho gaye'*. It means that people believe that *Swarglok* is only meant for those who are *phal kaami*. *Phal kami* means people who look for physical pleasures in everything. Take for example, the television. Every channel today is telling you of newer ways to earn more money and enjoy even more. Such people are called *phal kaami,* who target innocent people with no understanding of *loks*, spiritual evolution, *yog* and *dhyan* and the *shakti* that comes with them. They cannot understand because they are still stuck at *Bhu* or *Bhuvahloks* and cannot think or go beyond these, to the *Manipoorak chakra*, the pleasure of which cannot be explained. *Swarglok* is a gateway to the pleasures that your limited *buddhi* cannot comprehend, because of the *loks* you are at. These three are the most basic *loks*, the ones who do *yog* think of *loks* above these. And you cannot think of the *loks* above these until you sit straight and in *siddhasan*.

If you notice in a *dhyan* session, the most meaningless questions come to me from those who sit on the chair with a bent back. Those who sit on the floor, speak less. This is because the former groups' minds cannot go beyond that; the heat of *Kundalini* gets consumed at the lower centres in their case. Once all the centres are in one's control, his/her body exudes that control through the glow, stillness and *shakti*. No disease can touch such a person, and that is the state to start *yog.*

No amount of *yantras* you buy and keep in your house, or *puja paath*, *havan* or *yagya* you do, will make things happen. If you sit with a bent back or in an *asan* in which you can do '*dhyan*' for 10 to 12 hours, then you can't do *yog*. Yes, sitting in Sidhhasan can cause pain, but at that time, if you still don't move and instead, just remember your *Guru*, that pain will stop after reaching a level, and you will experience nothing after that. Once you have given that pain to yourself, then the pleasures that follow, the *anubhutis* that happen, do not have a limit. Every pleasure is a new high.

But right now, all you know are the pleasures of the *Mooladhar* and *Swadhisthan* and cannot understand the pleasures that lie beyond. So sit straight in *Siddhasan*, as only then can you tread on the path of *yog*.

Once you have given that pain to yourself, then the pleasures that follow, the anubhutis that happen, do not have a limit. Every pleasure is a new high.

SERMON 19

BHAKTI YOG

"Bhakti yog is so powerful that if you are in Bhakti yog, it is impossible that something that you wish for, say or try to do does not happen, gets stuck or goes the opposite way. It is just not possible and I can say this not with 99 per cent, but 100 per cent conviction."

19

Yog is a rigorous *sadhna* — it is a constant practice, *nirantar abhyas* and if your *sankalp* breaks, that is, there is a break in your practice, you have to start all over again. There are many things that one needs to be careful of — the ego needs to be kept in check, detachment has to be maintained from the physical attractions, one-pointed focus on *ek tattva,* stillness of thoughts, etc. The various kinds of *yogs* cater to different kinds of people with different kinds of desires. A beginner comes with lots of desires, and for him there is *Gyan yog.* Other forms of *yog* like *Hath yog* are for those who can make a *Guru* and also have desires. But within the various forms of *yog,* the most difficult is *Bhakti yog*. There is no *yog* above *Bhakti yog* because it is *nishkam* and *poorna*, and this is the *yog* for adept. There was only one *Meera*, who was completely immersed in the b*hakti* of her *Guru*, her *isht*, *Krishna*.

In *Bhakti yog,* there is complete surrender to the *Guru*, there is 100 per cent confidence in the *Guru* and there is no scope of 'ifs' and 'buts' that 'let us do it this way and see what happens'. A *Guru* could be a book or a stone or human being or anything else in which you have 100 per cent faith in and through which that energy is channelized into you. If you consider your *Guru* as a book, then it becomes book, if you consider *Guru* as a human, then it is a human and when you believe it to be a stone, then it becomes a stone. If the *Guru* is a human being, then since he/she is in the body, there has to be something lacking in him/her; because if nothing is lacking he/she cannot stay in the body. The problem in *Bhakti yog* is that when a human is teaching you *yog* and you are following him/her, you see that weakness/demerit first. And when you see that, the *bhaav* of complete surrender cannot come because a thought stays in the mind. Chances are that you will discount your experiences and undermine them and give pre-dominance to the physical aspects of the *Guru*, which is a gateway to hell. So, whenever you think your *Guru* as a physical form whether it is a human being, *granth or* stone, you will start looking for weaknesses and start interpreting it your own way. Whenever you go into interpretations of the *granth*, stone or human, that interpretation is only yours, not of the *Guru.* And since it is your own interpretation and you yourself are full of so many lacunae, your own weaknesses will be visible to you in your *Guru*. A *Guru* is like a mirror in which you see your own face. And once you see that weakness, then *Bhakti yog* is so dangerous that if even once there is the slightest of doubt in your mind, that is enough to be considered as disrespect of the *Guru (Guru niradar*). Once that happens, you cannot do anything about it, it all goes to waste.

Guru niradar also happens when you have a *Guru* but you go somewhere else looking for solutions to your various problems — physical, mental, emotional, financial. It is considered disrespect because a *Guru* is not as per your convenience — today this is convenient so you are here and tomorrow some other place is more convenient so you go there. This does not happen in any *yog*, leave aside *Bhakti yog.* If you consider someone as *Guru* and He asks you do something, but you start looking elsewhere that 'let us try that instead' then it is deemed as *Guru Niradar.* When you have a *Guru* and if you have asked for or said anything, then that will happen, it is an impossibility that it does not happen. If that is not happening then either something is lacking in your *Guru* or something is lacking in your *Guru bhaav* and if it is the latter, then go inside you and trace what is lacking.

Bhakti yog is so powerful that if you are in *Bhakti yog,* it is impossible that something that you wish for, say or try to do does not happen, gets stuck or goes the opposite way. It is just not possible and I can say this not with 99 per cent, but 100 per cent conviction.

Just go back in history and see who all were in *Bhakti yog* — *Meera*, *Hanuman*, *Prahlad*, *Draupadi*, *Meghnath*, *Shravan Kumar*, *Panj Pyaare* of *Guru Gobind Singh*... Now compare yourself to these, can you? Even one wrong step can bring the *yog* of many-many years together to a point zero. It is a very big thing, you do not understand it but I know what that means. So *Bhakti yog* is a very distant thing, it is not so easy. In *Hath yog,* there is forgiveness and you can come back. But in *Bhakti yog* there is none.

There are misconceptions about *yog,* that being in *yog* means doing nothing, that 'we have *bhakti*, so automatically everything will happen.' It does not happen like that. When you have *bhakti,* then you do not see anything except the *sadhya*, your whole mind is focussed on it only, not here and there. *Bhakti yog* does not mean you are given instructions, in *Bhakti yog* you are merged in that *ek tattva* completely and your *bhaav* is selfless.

SERMON 20

A THOUSAND NAMES OF LORD SHIV

"*With the progression of times and change of yugs, men started losing touch with the creation and became self-centered. As a result, the eight forms of Shiv were not enough for them and so newer names began to emerge...*"

20

Mount *Kailash* is the source of *shakti* for the entire creation. At the time when *vedic* sciences were given, Mount *Kailash* corresponded to the north-east direction. With the change of *yugs* and the shift in the tilt of earth's axis, it has assumed the north direction in present times. In the *vedic* times, directions were given by looking at and measuring the congruence of energies. Directions played a pivotal role in the process of creation. Even though now Earth's axis has tilted, directions still play a determining role, of course according to the present position of various entities.

You must have observed that all auspicious tasks are performed in the north-east direction. This direction has been called *Ishan* in our ancient texts. Even when Muslims do *namaz,* they do it in a particular direction and time called *Isha* (indicating that all religions have similarity and religious beliefs should not be a reason for intolerance towards each other). Interestingly, *Ishan* is another name for Lord *Shiv*. In *vedic* times there were only eight names of Lord *Shiv — Sharva, Bhava, Rudra, Ugra, Bheem, Pashupati, Ishan* and *Mahadev* — representing various aspects and forces that play a pivotal role in running the creation. Take for example, *Rudra. Rudra* is the form of *Shiv* that is required for destruction. There is a specific *mantra 'Rudra-Rudra-Maharudra,'* which when practiced in the *sanidhya* of *Guru*, stops the effect of all adversities that are to happen. As one completes the *sadhna* of *Rudra jaap*, the body develops the capacity to change anything. Then he/she can change the direction of anything coming towards him/her or anyone else. However, such things should not be done; as the purpose of a *tantric sadhna* is evolution of the being, and nothing else. Similarly, *Bheem* represents the strength aspect of *Shiv;* strength not of the muscles but the strength needed to go from one dimension to the next. *Pashupati* epitomises the abundance of nature, the flora and fauna. *Pashupatinath t*emple was made for this purpose only but later corruption seeped in and they started the incorrect practice of performing ritualistic sacrifices. This and other adulterations in the authentic *vedic* sciences have led us to completely forget our culture.

With the progression of times and change of *yugs*, men started losing touch with the creation and became self-centered. As a result, the eight forms of *Shiv* were not enough for them andso newer names began to emerge — *Mrityunjay* being one of them. Earlier there was no *mrityu* but *'iccha mrityu',* i.e. a person would leave the body at will. Therefore, there was no need for the name *Mrityunjay*. But when people started performing wrong acts, they started fearing death. As a result, the name *Mrityunjay* originated. Similarly, there were no *jyotirlingas or shaktipeeths* in *Satyug* because they were not required. Their need was felt when the civilisation started its descent. Today, the condition of human beings has deteriorated to such an extent that he has moved on from the *swaroop of Shiv* to worship of lower beings like *rakshas, pishach, bhoot* and *pret.* And with every passing day, the situation is becoming worse. Men can no longer see anything beyond themselves and or their limited circle. That is why today we have a thousand names of Lord *Shiv*. All these are readily available on a CD in every marketplace. People who play them think they are worshipping Lord *Shiv* unaware of the fact that *Shiv* has only eight names. Few years from now, the names of *Shiv* would multiply to such an extent that it would be difficult to contain them in a single CD...

People keep asking me strange questions and at times I am just not able to understand, which direction to steer them in. I try to take them north but they want to head south. If I talk of something, whereas your direction is some other, you will get confused and not be able to reach anywhere, which is a failure for me. The thousand different names of *Shiv* pertain to different *isht devs. Yog* says that there is only one *mantra,* one *asan*, one *maala*, one *isht dev* and only one *Guru*. If you make any of these two, then it is adultery in *yog* i.e. you are being unfaithful to the creation. And if you are unfaithful to creation then the creation will be unfaithful to you. So before embarking on the journey of the spirit, you need to be sure of what it is that you are seeking, only then can the path to achieve it be carved out by your *Guru*. If you don't know what you want then we have a thousand names of Lord *Shiv*, you can start doing thousand *sadhnas*... where do you think you will reach?

Original/unedited pictures of manifestations in *havan* performed by *sadhaks* at *Dhyan Ashram*.

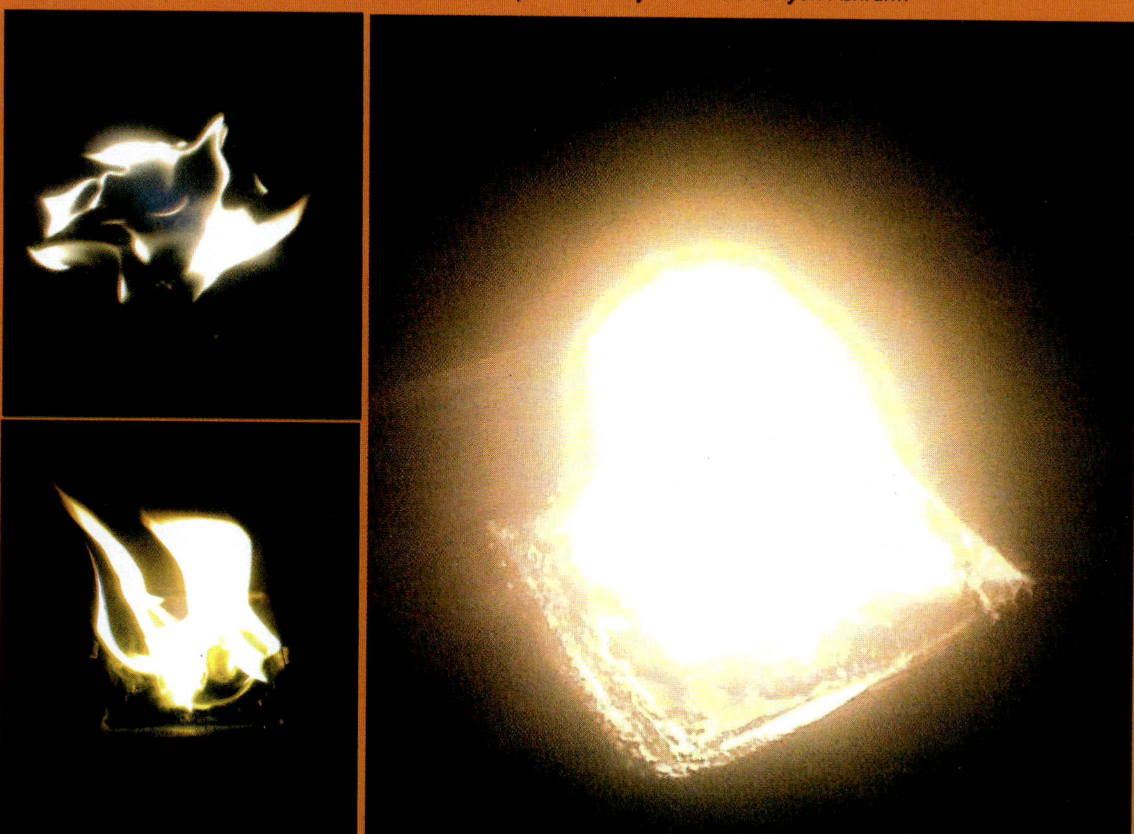

TRIDENT; LORD SHIV; SHIVLING (clockwise from bottom-left)

If you want to know whether the *havan* was performed properly or not, just watch the *havan-agni* at the time of *purna-ahuti*. You will be able to see the form of *dev/devi* if the invocations were successful. But don't get attached to manifestations, focus should be on the *havan*.

SERMON 21

SAKSHATKAR OF SHIV

“ The concept of maya is the concept of entire creation.
Maya is the glue that binds us to the world around us - our body, family, friends, job, relationship, etc.
All these things exist for us because we are attracted to them. ”

21

The concept of *maya* is the concept of entire creation. *Maya* is the glue that binds us to the world around us — our body, family, friends, job, relationship, etc. All these things exist for us because we are attracted to them. The moment that attraction (*maya*) for a particular object ceases, that thing leaves us. This is true even of the body. The body exists because of maya. What is the body?

The body is essentially the five elements — earth, water, fire, air and ether combined with the ego and certain other gross senses. These elements form the basis of the major *chakras* that govern the body — earth for *Mooladhar*, water for *Swadhisthan*, fire for *Manipoorak*, air for *Anahad* and ether for *Vishuddhi*. The controls for the various elements in our body lie at the fingertips — the little, ring, middle and index fingers representing earth, water, ether and air respectively while the thumb represents fire.

We know that things expand on heating and contract on cooling. The thumb represents fire. If you touch any element to the tip of the thumb, it expands and when you touch it to the base of the thumb it reduces. In this way, we can very easily increase or decrease the various elements in our body, depending on the need of the situation, using our fingers through the science of *mudras*. For example, in situations of extreme tension and anxiety, like in the case of appearing for an interview, or an exam, or an important meeting, the *vayu tattva* increases in the body leading a feeling of uneasiness in the chest. If at that time, you place your index finger at the base of the thumb (where you will feel a pulsation), the air element will normalise and you will feel better. The *Gyan mudra,* which involves touching the index finger to the tip of the thumb, has a diametrically opposite effect. If the one increases the *vayu tattva,* but the body is not prepared for the increase, tension in the body increases and one develops problems of the nerves. That is why it is not advisable to sit in *Gyan mudra* in the initial stages of *dhyan*. The *mudra* is introduced by one's *Guru* at a later stage, after the body has attained a specific balance. All problems related to the nervous system have their origin in increase of *vayu tattva;* even hypertension is a problem of the nerves. If a person, who is at the verge of a heart attack, sits in the *Amrit mudra* — that is the tip of index finger touching the base of thumb and the tips of little and ring fingers touching the tip of thumb — within minutes he/she will normalise. *Amrit mudra* increases the earth and water elements, which are the basis of the body and reduces the air element, thereby normalising the body. The science of *mudras* is a perfect and precise science, however, it is not taught en mass. It is given by the *Guru* to the *shishya*, individually, as per his/her individual needs and capacity. The science if used incorrectly can do more harm than good. The purpose of *mudras* is to bring the body in a state of balance but if you perform an incorrect *mudra*, the element, which is not supposed to increase, might increase, resulting in an imbalance, instead.

Our body is a reflection of the entire creation with its five elements. Earth forms the core of the creation, similarly the muscles and bones comprise the earth element and form the core structure of our body. Above the earth surface, one finds water — rivers, oceans and other water bodies. Similarly, in our body, *Mooladhar* gives way to *Swadhisthan,* which represents the water element. There is absolute darkness at the bottom of the ocean. As one rises through water to the surface of the water body, there is light. As one rises up the *Swadhisthan* chakra in the body, there is *Manipoorak, chakra* of agni *tattva*. *Agni* is not just fire, it is also light (responsible for vision), the digestive fire (responsible for digestion) and sexual energy (responsible for procreation). *Manipoorak* is the *adhaar* of all the *kriyas* of *drishti*, especially the s*haktipath* through *drishti*. In fact, the ability of *door-drishiti*, which we call clairvoyance, also originates from the *agni tattva* because we can take the energy of light to any distance even with our eyes closed. We can see wherever and whatever we want to because there is light, there is an awakening. If *jaap* of *Manipoorak chakra* is done properly, then the eyesight can never deteriorate.

On the surface of water there is light, and above that winds blow, that is the air element. According to *Ayurveda*, two-third of the diseases of the body, are caused by an imbalance in the *vata dosha or the vayu*. If you observe air element in nature, you will notice that it moves swiftly traversing large distances in a matter of seconds. Of the three *doshas* of *vata*, *pitta* and *kapha*, *vata* is the most mobile. Diseases caused by it become severe in no time. That is why air element needs to be handled with care and should not be increased arbitrarily by sitting in *Gyan mudra.* If it goes out of control, then a disease will manifest in the body. After the atmosphere, there is sky or ether.

As one moves up the elements, lower elements merge with the higher elements. That is, element above holds the capacity to include the elements below. Ether contains within it air, fire, water and earth, air contains fire, water and earth elements, fire contains water and earth elements, and water contains the earth element. Mahapralay involves merging of the earth element with water, leading to end of physical creation. To effect a change in any of the elements one need not go to the level of the individual element. The elements can be easily controlled and modified by accessing the element that lies above the five elements, the *partattva* or *Shiv*, under the *sanidhya* of *Guru*. All the elements can be controlled from top. That is why it is said '***Omkar bindu samyuktam...***' which means, everything is there in *omkar*, it is a *bindu*, the *partattva*, nothing else. **'....*Nityam dhayanti yoginam*'**, which means, a *yogi's dhyan* is always on that *partattva* and not on the elements below. A *yogi* has an association with the lower elements also but he controls them from the *Agya*. He has control over his senses and the associated urges, and he is able to do that from the *Agya*. This is the point of the *bindu* in which everything is present. That is, the entire creation is in *Shiv* or *partattva*. One can experience the five basic elements in the body through the science of *mudras*. If you increase the air element, you start feeling nervous and will start burping, if you increase the fire element your temper will shoot up suddenly, if you increase the ether element you will have a feeling of expansion. But how does one get the experience of the *Shiv tattva*, which is the *adhaar* of all these elements?

The *Shiv tattva* is not experienced by an ordinary person because he does not need it. A basic person spends his life in the pursuit of the five senses, which pertain to the five basic elements and the five basic chakras. Sense of smell is controlled by *Mooladhar*, sense of taste by *Swadhisthan*, sense of sight by *Manipoorak*, sense of touch by *Anahad* and sense of sound by *Vishuddhi*. These five are sufficient for the daily pleasures, which one indulges in from morning till night. There is no need for anything beyond for experience of basic pleasures. When there is no need, then there is little incentive to look further, and so, an ordinary person remains unaware of the *Shiv tattva*. *Shiv* is beyond the five *tattvas*, the *partattva*, in which all the *tattvas* reside. Experience of *Shiv* requires the awakening of *Agya* through *yog*. You may be given the experience a couple of times forcefully, but till you have control over your basic senses, till you elevate to the level of *Agya*, it will not happen to you naturally. Till you keep evaluating everything in life with these five senses, you will not be able to go above them. Even the thought to find *Shiv* will not come to you. Even though *Shiv* is right here, *sakshat*, but you will not be able to see *Shiv* because that vision is not there; the third eye has not opened because you are bound by the other five senses.

Shiv is in the whole of *brahmand* and the whole of *brahmand* is in *Shiv*. A *yogi* has the *sakshatkar* of *Shiv;* a *yogi* is above the domain of five senses and their related pleasures. An ordinary being is tied to one or more of the basic senses, because of which this experience eludes him. Let us understand this with an example from daily life. If you see a man and a woman walking, holding hands, some will think they are having an affair, others will take them to be brother and sister, still others may think them to be a mother and child. Different people seeing the same thing will have different perceptions about it depending upon the *chakra* by which they are bound. A person at *Anahad* will see them as brother and sister, the one at *Swadhisthan* will think of them as lovers. A *yogi*, the one who is at *Agya,* will call it a relationship of *Shiv-Shakti.* He just will not see anything except *Shiv and Shakti.*

The merger of *Shiv and Shakti* is creation and separation is dissolution.

An ordinary person cannot see that because he is stuck at some other *chakra* and bound by the thoughts of that *chakra* he is unable to think beyond a physical relationship. What you see, tells you your level and capacity. The day you see *Shiv and Shakti,* understand, that you have come in *yog*, whatever anyone may say. But before that you may meet the most powerful people of the country every day, you might know everyone in the whole world, but you are still here, you are nowhere beyond this because you cannot think beyond this. You do not understand *Shiv*, you do not know *Shakti* because there is no awakening in you.

Yog is done for that awakening and not for the basic senses. When the awakening happens, all the pleasures of the five senses come within it. You can get anything you want just by accessing the *Agya* but for this *yog* needs to be done. You cannot do *yog* by merely thinking with your brain, it doesn't happen that way. If you want to travel somewhere, you do not have to pack your bags for it. The one who is in *yog* will sit here and travel around the world and beyond, just by closing his eyes because he is beyond the five elements and not bound by them. The one who is still stuck here will be happy packing bags and thinking about the trip he is going to take.

It is important for you to understand what *yog* is, and take it seriously, otherwise you will waste your birth. The entire creation is right in front of you, the body is just this and this body is inside *Shiv,* which is making the body function. *Shiv* is at *Agya* but where are you? Till the time you do not give first priority to *yog*, you will not see *Shiv and Shakti*. You will only see these senses and you will keep moving in circles in these senses only, even after doing *yog* for 100 years!

Question: Where is *Shiv*?

Answer: You will not get this answer like this; till you have that awakening, you cannot see *Shiv*. *Shiv* cannot be explained in words, because what I say or you see will be these five elements only. For *Shiv darshan* you have to reach the sixth element otherwise it will not happen. *Shiv and Shakti* are not a subject of words, they are an experience and the experience will not happen, till the time you rise above the basic senses.

The West has got all the *vedas and tantric* sciences in a CD. They know much more than us and have got much more knowledge than us but it is only literature for them, nothing more than that. It is not being translated into an experience and if there is no experience, there is no evolution. That is why they are just stuck there. Even today if you go to the West with the concept of the *Guru* they will not accept it. And a majority of people who have gone there to teach the *vedic* sciences have also said the same thing, that you don't need a *Guru;* because if they tell them about *Guru* then nobody will follow them.

The *darshan of partattva* cannot happen until you have the *Guru kripa*. You have to be one with the *Guru*, you have to finish everything and become one with the *Guru*. You become your *Guru*'s reflection and when that happens then that *partattva* starts to become visible on its own. Without *Guru kripa* you cannot see the *partattva*, it's impossible. You will remain stuck here.

SERMON 22

EVERYDAY HAS ITS SHAKTI

"There is always a specific purpose to every birth, not even one person is born to just eat, drink, make merry, have fun and go back. We are all born with a specific purpose; we are all born with a specific shakti. We need to understand what that shakti is and then we need to work with that shakti to achieve what we have been sent here for."

22

What does the word '*shakti*' refer to? At times we use the terms *shakti* and energy synonymously, but actually, they are not the same. What is it that the two terms indicate?

Think about it. Is today same as yesterday? Is every day the same or is there a difference in two days? Or not even two days, just observe different parts of the same day... Are they the same or is there any difference between different parts of a day?

Each day is different, every part of the same day is different, and the difference lies in its *shakti.* The energy patterns are constantly undergoing a change; what they were in the morning is not the same as what they will be in the evening, is not the same as what they are going to be tomorrow, is not the same as what they were on the same day some hundred years back... The *vedic* philosophy is a highly sophisticated and complex science encompassing within its purview the minutest detail of the creation as also the cosmos as a whole. Often, the *vedic* culture is joked about saying that 'these people keep doing something or the other all the time, all the time they are busy pleasing some god or the other.' Here one must delve a little deeper and understand what is the science and energy behind all that the *vedic* seers have handed down to us. Why they gave us so many gods and goddesses and why did they emphasise upon different times of the day, month and year. There is a definite science and energy behind it and this science is unsurpassed till date.

You must have observed that the Earth rotates and revolves, but it does so at an angle. Why is it not straight? The answer lies in the *vedic* concept of dimension or *yug,* which is determined by the tilt of the axis of earth. When creation began, the Earth was straight and that was a dimension. Then *yug* changed, energy changed and hence dimension changed and with the change in dimension, Earth tilted and took its beings to the next dimension. Then again, it was tilted and once again there was a change in dimension. The dimension we are going through right now is the *Kaliyug,* before this there were *Dwaparyug, Tretayug* and *Satyug* respectively. If there was to be even a slight shift in the axis of Earth right now, we will immediately enter a different dimension, that is how powerful this *shakti* is, and when it happens, something new will come…

As students of *vedic* sciences, you need to understand that the creation is governed by *shakti* and *shakti* is in its every aspect. It is *shakti* that makes this creation function and *shakti* that makes it transform into something else. As students, you do not have to understand *shakti*, you have to experience that *shakti* and what it is all about. Once you understand that, your day-to-day practices will become very simple. You will forge ahead with that *shakti,* rather than going against it. But for that you need to appreciate the fact that the energy of every day is different and that of different times of the day too is different. Let us take for example the day of *Janmashtmi.* The *vedic* seers told us that on this day Lord *Krishna* was born and hence it is a very powerful day. Hearing this, we rush to the temple and start worshipping. Why? The Divine never incarnates, there is no such thing as incarnation of Divine; it is just energy. Each one of us, individually, is also divinity, is also energy, which is going through a human experience. However, the ultimate energy, the subtlest of the subtle, it does not incarnate. There is no need for it to incarnate because it functions on the concept of consciousness, it does whatever it has to through that consciousness. And every person is a flash of that energy but not that energy. The flash of that energy is incarnated into the body for a specific purpose. There is always a specific purpose to every birth, not even one person is born to just eat, drink, make merry, have fun and go back. We are all born with a specific purpose; we are all born with a specific *shakti.* We need to understand what that *shakti* is and then we need to work with that *shakti* to achieve what we have been sent here for. It is very easy to get misled and waste your life in normal mundane pleasures. It is very difficult to identify yourself, to be able to see who you actually are. And for this very reason you need *yog* — to make you realise, to make you see right in front of you, to make you experience that 'this is what I am, this is what my purpose is'. And you will actually see it, if you go with the *vedic* philosophy; it is a very powerful science. If you go with the philosophy, if you just practice as you are told, you will find that one by one the veils will be removed and you will start experiencing each and every aspect of Divinity. It will be right in front of you, there will be no question of your mind playing tricks with you. That is my job, not yours; leave that to me. But you need to do the practice right, when you are talking about *shakti,* you also need to be with *shakti.*

Let us start with a day of 24 hours. What is so special about the early morning time of four o' clock? What is special about noon? What is special about the evening, the time when sun sets? What is special about midnight? In *vedic* philosophy, we call these four times of the day as *sandhya*. The word *sandhya* means a conjunction. It is a transformation; the energy is transforming and merging into the next one.

There are two kinds of forces in the creation — one is the positive and the other is the negative and both the forces are vital to keep each other in balance. The *asurs* and *devs* are both part of this creation, both are divine. If there is no negative, the positive will have no meaning. In the human body also, there is nobody who can say that I am only positive or only negative, you have an aspect of both — the positive and the negative — inside you. It is up to you to realise what you want to be and then to use that aspect for general good, for the betterment of human kind.

The four *sandhyas* mark the transformation of the various forces in creation. At the time of sunset the negative energies are at their peak, while at the time of sunrise it is the positive energies that reach their peak. As the day progresses and the sun starts rising in the sky, positive forces are on a decline. By around noon time, there is a complete merger where both the forces — positive and negative — are equal, in a state of balance. After this there is transformation yet again, negative starts to go up reaching its peak at evening *sandhya* and declining thereafter. At midnight, once again the positive and negative reach a state of equilibrium and then positive starts to rise till it reaches its peak at the morning *sandhya.*

All these times are for a specific purpose. For instance, the practitioners of dark arts use the time of evening *sandhya* for their *prayogs*. You will observe that most accidents happen at this time and also the lower urges, like that to get drunk or plot a conspiracy, are usually on a rise around the evening time. You might be wondering that why then do we meet for *dhyan* during this time — it is to seek protection from the negativity, which is there in the environment. The practitioners of lower sciences use the time of evening *sandhya* for their various *anushthans*, when negativity is at its peak. If you are in a state of *dhyan* at that point of time, you will get protection from these negative forces. That is why this *dhyan* is done at the *sandhya* time.

Diametrically opposite to the evening *sandhya* is the time of early morning, which we call the *Brahm muhurat.* It is the time when positive forces are at the peak and it is time for higher practices, for those who have reached a level in *yog sadhna*, not for ordinary people. If you want to do something, which is charitable, for social good, then that is the time you sit down to conceive it. It will never go wrong, it will happen smoothly and this is the meaning of moving with the *shakti.* Similarly, if you want to do something negative, evening *sandhya* is the time to put the *shakti* behind you to do something negative and it will happen.

The *vedic* seers were highly scientific beings and there was a reason for all that they said or did. They knew of the existence of oil, of all the natural resources, but they did not exploit these bounties of nature. We call ourselves advanced with all the industries we have set up, but we are being told that at this rate in the next 40 to 50 years, there will be no oil left on earth. In the last merely 400 to 500 years we have used up all the oil that was available, something which was conserved and preserved for so many million years. The *vedic* people were masters of creation who gave us advanced concepts of *shanti* and of the various *shaktis* that run this creation, they were not fools. They knew about the existence of oil but they also knew that it is a resource, which cannot be replenished. They realised the need for something different and that is the energy they worked upon.

The *vedic* seers have given specific time, depending on which energy you want to use for what purpose and what do you want to do in a day. You must have experienced that you cannot look at the sun directly in the afternoon where as in the evening and in early morning you can. What happens in a few hours that you are able to see a heavenly body so clearly, which you just could not look at few hours back? It is the energy, which has transformed completely. It is that energy which you can use for your betterment, that is why, at evening *sandhya* and morning *sandhya*, certain *mantras,* certain chants are prescribed for a specific purpose. Some of these practices are detailed in the book, 'Sanatan Kriya, The Ageless Dimension'.

Moving from the energies of single day to those that span the whole year through, you will find that every day is different from the other. The day of *Janmashtmi* was marked by the *vedic* seers not because Divine incarnated on this day, but because the energies associated with Lord *Vishnu* are at their peak on this day. It is a very good day to ask for riches or pleasures and similar *anushthans.* I normally say that there are four days in a year when you must see me and if you do not see me on these days, you will miss out on something very strong in your *sadhna* and those four days are — *Shivratri, Holi, Guru Purnima and Diwali.* It is because the kind of practices that we are doing, the energies for these practices are at their peak on these four days. As these days pass the energy starts receding, and as they approach, the energy starts increasing. Similarly, there is a day called *Ganesh Chaturthi,* which is thought to be the day of Lord *Ganesh's* birth. But Lord *Ganesh* is not a human being, nor is he half-man-half-elephant whose head was cut and stitched back again. Lord *Ganesh* is an energy; it is a force and you see that force when you do the *Sanatan Kriya*. When you practice all the eight limbs of *Sanatan Kriya* consciously as told, all these energies start manifesting in front of your eyes, one by one.

The science of *yog* is a 100 per cent accurate science; there is not an iota of doubt in that. If the manifestation has to happen, it will happen. If it is not happening then either you are going wrong somewhere or I am going wrong somewhere and we need to correct where we are going wrong, The *vedic* philosophy cannot be wrong. It is not a physical science; it is a science of creation, a science on which this whole creation is resting. This science has to be utilized for our own good and for general good and that is why every day becomes very significant, and what you need to do on that specific day is clearly laid out by the *vedic rishis*. If you can just use the energy of various days to your advantage then there is nothing in the world of the spirit which is away from you. The world of the spirit is the real world and to access it you have to take the right path, you have to take the right route, and that can be taken only if you are with the energy. If you take the physical to be supreme and base all your actions on the physical, you cannot reach anywhere in the spiritual world.

Be with the *shakti* and see what happens. You will be given a time and a day and at that time and on that day, if you will do something, it is just going to happen like that. I know there is no dearth of astrologers who will tell you all this, but there is slight problem in that. The *vedic* philosophers were not commercial people, they were not businessmen. When they gave these sciences they put a rider to them — if you commercialise these sciences, they will lose their efficacy. When you put an angle of *maya*, you get stuck in that *maya* only. *Maya* is the physical attraction, something, which is unreal but you think it to be real and remain stuck. Just look at the people around you, everyone from 20 to 80 is searching for something. But if you are 80, and if you are still searching, there is a very slim chance of you finding it unless you change the philosophy on which you have passed the last 80 years. You have to understand that there is something drastically wrong with your approach to life and you have to change and you have to go with that *shakti*, you cannot go against it. You cannot go ahead with your own thoughts, 'that I say so and so it is going to happen because I have been successful in the world'. No. What you say is not going to happen. What is going to happen is what the laws of creation say. .

When you are out to do something auspicious or something negative, you can be your own astrologer. You can calculate the time, which is best suited for that purpose on your own, on the basis of which energy is prevalent on which day at what time. You do not need to go to an astrologer who is caught in the web of *maya*, because an astrologer who is caught in the web of *maya* can take you nowhere. That is why the *vedic* seers were non-commercial people and it is them who gave us the power of each day and every *shakti*.

SERMON 23

DEVS AND DEVIS IN YOUR SPINE

" *Till the time one does not improve his/her karmas, gyan is a far cry. For the sake of understanding, think yourself to be a glass, but on that glass keep a lid and ask me to fill your glass. How will I fill it? Even if I try, the water will spill and it will create a mess.* "

23

When you sit for *dhyan* or even otherwise, the spine should always be kept straight. The spine comprises of small bones called vertebrae that are connected to each other. Each vertebra is a reflection of a *dev* or a *devi*.

What is a *dev* or a *devi*? So many of you keep idols and pictures in your house and pray to them from morning to night. There are people who organise huge functions and *puja-paaths* with loud-speakers placed in the entire neighbourhood. I asked one of these people about *devs* and *devi*, he replied, "*devs* and *devis* reside within us". I then asked him, "If they are within you, then what is it that you do outside?" It is very important for us to understand all this because we are approaching the end of *Kaliyug*. There is chaos everywhere and it is only going to get worse with time because the *vedic* culture is being forgotten and only *tamashas* are happening in its place. His reply was, "My consciousness level is not high, it is to increase consciousness that I organise pujas." This is the corruption of present yug, where everyone wants to increase something or the other, even if it is consciousness. The basic thinking is flawed because that is what is being taught across the globe — to increase everything. There is hardly anyone who talks of balance, or reaching the optimum level, which is the basis of *vedic* thought. One should strive for a state of balance from imbalance, from *vikriti* to *prakriti,* for that is *yog*. Once the various imbalances in you are harmonised, you climb the first step to *yog*, before that there is no *yog*. No matter how many *puja-paaths* you do, till the time you are in a state of balance, you can never understand what is inside and outside or how to move inside. Balance is the key. And every *shakti,* which we call *dev* or *devi*, is a balance and this balance is at different levels and corresponds to different *shrenis*.

We cannot say that there is only one state of balance in entire creation; there exist different kinds of balances. One moves from a state of balance to a state of imbalance and then a new balance is established. The balance that you are at, first you have to bring that into a slight imbalance, only then the next balance can be established. For example, if a person is enjoying different kinds of foods and his/her body is able to digest all those foods, then that person is in a state of balance and will not be able to think beyond food. Every day he/she will think, "What new dish should I try today?" Or till the time a person does not have a problem in breathing, he/she will not think of getting into a state of *kumbhak*. Or if the body is in comfort and completely healthy, one will not think of doing anything more with it or taking to *yog asans*. Similarly, if hypothetically (because it does not happen in reality anymore) a person is satisfied with or happy on all fronts, then such a person will never think of *yog* or *dhyan* or search for any *shakti* as he/she is in a state of a balance. Till the time a person is in balance at a particular level, till that time he/she does not require anything else. Once an imbalance sets in, only then he/she sets out in the search for something else. So, to rise above anything, first you need to introduce a slight imbalance.

Yogis or those who do *yog*, create an imbalance within themselves voluntarily, out of their own wish, in every *kshetra* (area) and *shreni* (*level*). Only when they do this are they able to reach the next level of balance and this is what the entire journey of *yog* is all about — to get something you wanted and then to leave it. That is why at *Dhyan Ashram* we neither hold onto something nor leave anything. If something is there, it is good. But if it is not there, then it is even better. This is balance. However a slight imbalance has to be created so that you may think ahead and search for anything beyond. Otherwise, if everything is going fine, you will neither think ahead nor go inside yourself to search. Till the time, you are in your balance, you are least bothered about anything else. Only when you see that you are ageing, or that disease is setting in, do you get nervous and start thinking of searching for more, this nervousness is termed as *abhnivesh* in *Patanjali Yogsutras* — the fear of death.

In the two decades of teaching yog, it has been my experience that anyone who comes to me with a wish, comes with a small wish and when that wish gets fulfilled and he attains that level of balance, he forgets about everything else till he gets a wake-up call from above. So every *kasht* (pain or trouble) you get is an indication that someone is watching you from above and he cares for you. You are being given that pain to remind you that there is something beyond, so you can move towards that; move towards Him. *Patanjali Yogsutras* list certain pitfalls for a *sadhak* and luxury and comfort are regarded as one of the major pitfalls. It is very difficult for someone who is sitting in the lap of luxuries to do *yog*, as he does not feel the need to see or do anything else. Such a person is content in that comfort only and wastes his lifetime in enjoying them, living under the misconception that the body will not perish among those comforts. The very meaning of the word *'shareer'* is one, which is constantly moving towards destruction, it is getting destroyed every second. To think that 'nothing will happen to me while I am in the comforts and because I have everything' is foolishness and is referred to as *asmita.*

Do not forget that even the most renowned and able doctor, the one who knows everything about the body, even he does not know if he will survive the next moment. I have travelled far and wide and lectured the leading medical practitioners of various states on the science of *yog.* Every time I have discouraged them from using or recommending *yog* as a cure to diseases. And yet after every such session, at least two-three doctors have walked up to me to ask for a cure for their sinus, spondylitis, diabetes, or some other sickness. And this is not the case at one place, but at each of the 10 hospitals that I have lectured at in the past six months.

Recently, we were in Kolkata and a highly qualified gastroenterologist was among the group who attended a past-life visitation session with us. Every member of the group, except for the doctor, reported what they saw or where they went. Later, I asked the doctor individually, if she had experienced anything. She responded with a yes but said that she could not have disclosed in the group as the rest of them were her patients and would have thought her to be mad. And, even before I landed in Delhi, I got an e-mail from her asking for a solution to her 66-year-old mother's illness. Reading her mail, I wrote back to her saying that the problems she described were all gastrointestinal and that she was an expert in it. Her reply was that she had tried everything but it wasn't coming under control and so she needed help. On asking about the treatment that the lady was going through, she mentioned some "Silva method" and pills (I am basically trying to tell you how all the *vedic* sciences have become a joke today). I asked her what Silva method was. She was surprised to know that I did not know about it and told me that it finds mention in the *vedas*. She explained that this treatment taps into the brain wave and creates alpha waves to treat the patient. I told her that alpha waves are waves in the brain when it is in a fully conscious state, everyone has them. She then told me that I do not know anything and that we function on theta waves. So then I told her to ask a neuro-surgeon about alpha waves and also let me know the *veda* in which 'Silva method' is described. I am yet to receive a reply from her.

This is the reality of *Kaliyug*, everything has been made into a *tamasha*. Someone talks of *devi-devtas*, another of consciousness, and some about 'Silva method' — everyone talks big, but nobody knows what they are doing, where they are headed and keep going in circles. They do not know because they are tied to their *karmas.* They are not ready to improve their *karma* and till the time one does not improve his/her *karmas, gyan* is a far cry. For the sake of understanding, think yourself to be a glass, but on that glass keep a lid and ask me to fill your glass. How will I fill it? Even if I try, the water will spill and it will create a mess. And this is exactly the state today, every person is in a state of mess because the *karmas* do not allow them to access *gyan*, and they keep going round and round, still confused what *devis* and *devtas* are and whether to find them inside or outside.

Devis and *devtas* are only the *sanchalaks* of the various *shaktis* of the creation. They do not have anything for their own self, each *dev or devi* is just a *sanchalak* of a particular *shakti.* A group of *devis* and *devtas form a dev-samooh to* collectively channelise a particular group of *shaktis* and one *dev* watches over the functioning of the *samooh*. Above the various *dev-samoohs* is the trinity – *Brahma*, *Vishnu* and *Mahesh*, who do the *sanchalan* of all the *samoohs* below. It is a pyramidal structure and we are at the base of the pyramid and while being here we want to be at the top. Can that happen? You are at the *nimn sthiti*, you do not have the time to do anything besides earning for yourself or enjoying your food and drink but you have hung a big photo of *Shiv* in your house. Nothing will happen by that. Stop fooling yourself. To reach there you have to gradually move up, from one *shreni* to the next. And those *shrenis* are there in your spinal column.

The spinal column is a reflection of the *Sushumna nadi*. Each vertebra is the sign of a *dev* or a *devi.* By doing *yog* under the *sanidhya* of *Guru*, you gradually move up each vertebra and reach the top. You cannot jump from the lowest to the highest. There are many in the markets who claim to awaken your *Kundalini* and take you to the top, by just paying a fee and doing their 'course'. Be rest assured that such courses will take you nowhere. The *kriya* to reach the top is fixed and for that you have to open your *bandhans*. The three main *granthis* or *bandhans* are the *Brahma granthi, Vishnu granthi* and the *Rudra granthi.* No matter which *dev* or *devi's aahvaan* you may do, wherever you may go, nothing will happen because you are tied by that *bandhan*. Until your *bandhans* or knots are opened, you cannot go above them.

Through *Mool, Udyan* and *Jalandhar bandh* heat is generated at those points to open the *Brahma*, *Vishnu* and *Rudra granthi* respectively. But only your *Guru* channelises that energy; that *granthi* will not open till the *Guru* puts that much force inside you. If your *Mool or Brahma granthi* is closed, then you will just not be able to think of anything beyond food, sleep and sexual activity. Your mind will be stuck in these and even if you go to a *Guru*, you will only think of asking a new way of doing business or about a job problem. If this is your thought pattern then that simply means even your basic *granthi,* the *Brahma granthi* is is not open. So first it has to be opened and only then you proceed further.

If you think that by lighting incense sticks or

diyas in front of idols or by ringing bells every morning and evening, you have done your duty and you need not do anything else, now you are free to go to your shops and fool people, then you are mistaken. Nothing will happen from all this (except that your lungs might suffer because of the chemicals they put in incense sticks these days). By doing all this you will just keep going round and round and get troubled and irritated by looking at others — "*Guruji* does not tell me anything at all, I have been after him for so many years." But how can I tell you? There is a *maryada* among *Gurus* that they don't interfere with the *shishya* of other *Gurus*. There are never two *Gurus* and a *Guru* is always in a body. This is the fundamental point in the entire philosophy of *yog* because if it was ok to not have a *Guru* in body, then there was no need for *Ram* and *Krishna* to make a *Guru* when they took birth on earth. *Krishna* was born with all 16 powers, and he could have created many *Vashishts*, but still he made a *Guru* because without a *Guru* you can't get *gyan* — only a *Guru* can get that *jagriti* (awakening) in you and he being in his body is most important. If you think that being in the body is not important for the *Guru*, then you should consider someone like *Parshuram* as your *Guru*. It is of paramount importance for a *Guru* to be in a body, as without him being in the body you cannot get *shaktipath*.

The word '*Guru*' means the one who has already merged in the *Brahm*, *brahmleen*. He is merged when he is in the body and when he is not also. Till he is in the body, he can channelise *shakti* in you, once he leaves the body he cannot channelise *shakti* in you because then there will be a huge distance between him and you. Even if *Brahm* wants to channelise energy into you he cannot, a medium is certainly required and that medium is *Guru*. *Guru* is not God, he is only a medium through which that *shakti* flows in your body. When the *karma* or path of the *Guru* is complete only then he leaves the body and then he leaves his *shishya* with some other *Guru murti*. And even that *Guru murti* is his own *ansh*.

The *shishya* has to follow the path of his *Guru*, if you don't go by that path then you will just keep sitting troubled and irritated. Either you change your *Guru*, which your ego will not allow — "I have been with him for so many years, how to change the *Guru* now?" If you don't have that strength then keep walking on the path that you are walking on, it is your *karma* and your own *Guru sanidhya*. There is a *maryada* of every *Guru,* which cannot be broken. No *Guru* ever tells a person to leave his/ her *Guru* and come to him as that would amount to breaking the *maryada*. It is your own decision. There is no competition between *Gurus*. If there is competition somewhere, then there is no *Guru*, there it is only a *tamasha*.

Dev and *devis* are *sanchalak* of *shaktis* and you cannot progress in *yog* till you experience these *shaktis*. When you have the capacity for *sanchalan* of these *shaktis*, then gradually you start rising. When the *shaktis* awaken, they move one by one up through spinal column. However, this cannot happen by attending courses on '*Kundalini* awakening'. It will only happen when you open your *karma bandhans* and *granthis* by doing *yog* under a *Guru*. No matter how powerful or rich you are, the path of *yog* will not change as per your wish, the *maryada* of *Gurus* will not be broken. So leave that path and come to *sadmarg*. It took me 10 years to understand what *yog* is, before that I too was going round and round, although I used to do my practices very seriously and search for it very seriously. I have been to numerous places — mountain peaks, isolated desert regions, shores of oceans, to understand it; but the result was ultimately the same — nothing. Why? Because nothing can happen without the *Guru sanidhya*, you may keep on doing whatever but without the *sanidhya* of the *Guru*, nothing will happen. And the sign of *sanidhya* of a *Guru* is very simple, it is exactly what happens once you have food. After eating the food, you don't feel hungry. Similarly, after meeting your *Guru*, your search ends. But if the food is lying in front of you and you just think that you have had all of it without really making any efforts towards consuming it, then you will certainly remain hungry. What can I do about that? It is not because of me that you are still hungry, I have not done anything in that, it is because of your own foolishness that you still remain hungry despite food lying in front of you. You cannot have two *Gurus* because once you have food and your stomach is full, then you do not eat again. So take one path only.

In *yog*, it is said "*ek tattva nirantar abhyas*". Focus yourself at *ek tattva*, whatever has to happen will happen from there only. If you have *anubhav* at one place, then stay there only, then no need of going here and there. But, if there is no *anubhav* then do not waste your time. A *Guru* is not good or bad, nor does he teach you anything, he just makes you experience. You are yet to understand what *Guru* is.

You do not find the *Guru*, the *Guru* finds you because he/she needs you more than you need a *Guru*. A *Guru* always has an *aadesh* (order) to follow; he is bound to a *karma*, which is the *aadesh* of his *Guru*. To fulfil that order, a *Guru* needs extensions. So you and I are extensions of a *Guru* because can you work without your hands or *karmenderiya*, even though you have the energy? Similarly a *Guru* cannot work without his extensions and so he finds you and not the other way.

A *Guru* is not chosen, he/she is experienced. When you see your *Guru's chhavi* for the first time, you experience or feel something inside you. Never go by words or what others are saying, or what is written in the book, go only by your experience. What you experience within by looking at *Guru-chhavi* that is your *lakshan* (sign). If you have no experiences then you are wasting your time in *yog*, nothing will happen as experience is the basis of *yog*. From experience only you come into *yog* and from experience only you go beyond it. Only a *Guru* will make you experience, you on your own cannot.

If you don't experience anything within you, then probably the *Guru* you have gone to is not your *Guru*. Then start improving your *karma;* it is possible that your *shreni* is very high or very low. Every *Guru* has a *shreni*. So as per your *karmas* you go to that *shreni*. if you have very good *karma* then you will have an *uttam Guru* and if your *karmas* are not good enough you will get *nimn Guru* or *madhyam Guru*. So *Gurus* have different *shrenis* and you get the *shreni* as per your *karmas*. And *Guru* finds you on his own, you need not set out to search for him. A *shishya* never comments or tries to assess the *shreni* of a *Guru*. For a *shishya*, a *Guru* is complete, the ultimate. The *shreni* is for his *Guru* to judge and not for the *shishya* to judge.

The *yog* of *Kaliyug* is *seva*. Every *yug* had its own *yog* — *gyan, karma,* etc. If you are doing service, if you are helping those who are weaker than you or if you are helping people who depend on your *seva*, then correspondingly *Guru* will call you on his own. But if the *seva* is not there, then it is plain waste of time, nothing will happen.

You must understand what *yog* is and what is the importance of your spine. The *dev* and *devis* will gradually move up your spine. The first bone corresponds to *Ganeshji* and his *siddhi* is the first step in *yog* and *tantra*. You rise as per your *sadhna*, your path. The *Sushumna nadi* is divided into three parts — the inner most is the *Brahm nadi.* It is the path which takes you to *moksha.* There are two outer layers which are known as *Chitrani and Chitrangda*. You may tread either, as prescribed by your *Guru* upon assessing you and then accordingly your *Guru* gives you the *siddhi* of that *dev* and takes you up. The entire *yog sadhna* is a subject of pure experience and your own experience, not of anybody else. It is your own experience, which will tell how much your *yog sadhna* is or if it is nothing at all.

The judgement of *Guru* is prohibited for the *shishya*, it is your own experience which tells you the *shreni* of your *Guru.* Attempting to judge the *Guru* while discounting the experiences one has had is a gateway to hell.

The word 'Guru' means the one who has already merged in the Brahm, brahmleen. He is merged when he is in the body and when he is not also. Till he is in the body, he can channelise shakti in you, once he leaves the body he cannot channelise shakti in you because then there will be a huge distance between him and you. Even if Brahm wants to channelise energy into you he cannot, a medium is certainly required and that medium is Guru.

SERMON 24

THE BEGINNING OF CREATION

“ *Your swaroop is not this body. Understand your swaroop and understand who or what your near and dear ones are, those sitting around you are not your near and dear ones. To understand that, you will have to go beyond the effect of the five senses; till that happens you will just find yourself in a loop, going round and round.* ”

24

Time is the distance between two thoughts. When you think of one thing and then the next, the distance between the two thoughts is measured as time. What can be measured cannot be ultimate. There is something beyond time. Time was created, it did not exist forever. There was a stage in history when there was no such thing as time.

Time was created when the first desire was created. When there is a desire, desire for anything, that first desire is the beginning of time for a being. When a baby is in the womb there exists no time for him/her. I once received an e-mail from someone stating that he gets fearful thoughts that after he dies; he will be born again and will have to spend nine months in the clustered space of the womb. It sure is scary to be tied and stuffed into a small compartment for nine months; I doubt if you can even survive nine minutes, nine months is a far cry. I wrote back to that person saying, "Don't worry, because for a child in the womb there is no such thing as time as the child has not been manifested into the physical world as yet." Time begins with the physical world; time begins with the first desire. Even when the baby is born, when it comes out of the womb, even then there is no time. Time begins when the child makes his/her first decision, that "I want this."

So time was created with the creation of desire. But then, what was there when there was no time? What and where were we?

Just think of: one, strong energy and a lot of energies revolving around it because of its attraction. When you see light, even at distance, you look towards it because there is an attraction in that light. So, there is a strong light and a lot of smaller lights moving around it in its attraction. This attraction keeps them moving but none of the small lights has the capacity to merge with the big light as then there will remain no small light, only big light. There is no desire at this stage, no thought, only an attraction that keeps the smaller lights moving around the source. They do not know why they are there or what they want and that attraction is so strong that no desire is able to enter them and so they carry on.

At that point there is no time, since there is no desire or thought because there is nothing to want or to have. Because there is nothing, there is only a very strong attraction and a feeling of euphoria, happiness, bliss, joy and this is the natural state of the lights. It is a state, which has no desire attached to it and this cannot be described in words. From this state, suddenly, among the cluster of lights, one small light gets a thought — 'I want'. It is immaterial what it wants because that light itself does not know what it wants because nothing has been created till now. There is absolute silence, there is no time, there is no dimension... there is only one stillness, one light and all small lights around it, which are part of that light. They all emerged from that light and they are moving around it, in the attraction of that light. That one desire makes that small light think 'let me go and see what is happening'. Since there is nothing, it does not know what it wants, and so it goes searching for it.

The situation of that light is like most of us — we do not know what we want — that's basic human nature. Is there anybody who can say, "I want this, and I will be satisfied after I get it"? I am yet to meet someone who knows exactly what he/she wants because whatever you want or whatever you think you want at this point of time is based only on your senses and the present state of your desires. Because what is the maximum that you want? Social status — "My status in the society should be enhanced. Nobody should do anything which hurts my social status." It is a desire that is inside you, and that is again limited to one of the five senses and the ego, of course. Even that one desire is linked to the physical — the five senses or the ego because you know that these things exist at that point of time and you know only that. You might have been doing penance for the last 100 years but that is immaterial because you do not know anything else that exists over and above that physical. From morning to night and night to morning you are only going after your basic desires — just your five senses. When you go to sleep at night you are worried about what is going to happen tomorrow and that is directed towards the five senses. When you wake up in the morning, you are worried about the day and that too is directed towards your five senses. So every desire is fixed and targeted towards the five senses.

But here, at this stage, for these lights, there is no sense; there is nothing, only attraction, only *anand*, only bliss — the ultimate state. So when that one light leaves, it starts travelling and searching aimlessly. And then it comes back because there is nothing — there is no time; there is nothing to go to. When it leaves, it just creates its own space, its own time in that one desire. It goes here and there, it does not know what it wants but it wants something, so it creates space and time for itself. But there is nothing in that space and time because that light itself cannot manifest. It then comes back and tells this ultimate force that, "I desire an experience." The force asks, "What experience?" The light says, "I don't know what that is. But I desire an experience." The force says, "Ok! Go there and you will find something, which will give you your desire." The light then starts to travel, creating space and time for itself and as it starts to move, few more lights decide to join this light — "We will also come with you. Let us do something different." The same way as we all have this desire to do something different — if somebody has black hair, he wants to colour them red, if someone is dark, he wants to be fair, if someone is fair, he wants to get a tan... It is actually a desire where you do not know what you want to do or where you are headed.

These lights then move across to a place, which abounds natural beauty, and see something different about the place. So they go and see it. But when they go there they are not able to experience anything, they see everything but are not able to experience it, so they come back and tell everything to the main force, "We went to this beautiful place... we want to be there, but we are not able to experience it." To experience a thing you need a sense, whether it is the five senses, which you want to experience or something more than that. If you want to experience something more than the five senses then you need to have the sense to experience that. Something, which you think is there but because you do not have the sense you are not able to experience it. You do not know what that experience is because you don't have the capacity to experience it as you lack that sense.

The main force (or light) then tells this group of lights, "Ok, you go again and this time I am going to give you a special suit and that suit will enable you to experience all that." So, all these lights go back once again, this time with special suits. When they reach that place, they are able to experience it and start enjoying that experience. They taste fruits, inhale the fragrances of fresh air on the mountains, hear the sound of flowing river and they find everything very beautiful. So many sights, sense of touch, taste... They get absolutely enamoured by the place and set up a base there to experience it all with the help of the five senses. But to experience all that they have bound themselves with those five senses as they have put that cover, that suit, on themselves and now they experience only those five senses. After some time, they get so engrossed in experiences of those that they forget about the main light and that experience, which they were having in the state of small light because now they are tied to the enjoyment of the five senses. Now they are a body, no more a point of light.

As time passes, some more lights come to join them. The ones who are already there enjoying it become worried upon seeing more lights, as they will now have to share all this with the new visitors and have less for themselves. Initially they had divided space among each other and compartmentalised the space and everyone experienced their own share but as more and more lights join, no space is left. Then one group of lights gets an idea to break the suits of another group; as without suits they won't be able to experience anything and return to the main light. And so they break the suits of another group and get more space for themselves. Seeing them, everyone starts breaking each other's suits. So a few remain, but those who go want to come back again and so they get another suit and return. Again clashes happen; again some go back and come again. Ultimately in due course, clash becomes so severe that the place for which they are fighting starts getting destroyed. When this place is destroyed and the suits are destroyed, the lights come to their actual form and they realise what they have done — "Is this what and why we had actually come for, having travelled so much distance and having left our ultimate source? Did we come for this? NO! We had come for something bigger." Only once they are out of it do they realise this, when they were still in it, they were not able to realise this. So they go back to the main light and say, "We are very happy here, we don't need to go anywhere to get any other experience." And again the same life begins — they are in bliss and revolve around the main source of light... Again one of the lights gets an idea — "I want an experience!"

So, what does the story indicate...What are those lights?

The lights are the *swaroop* of *atma* (soul). The *swaroop* of the soul is the *swaroop* of *jyoti* (light) and to experience where you are, to experience the senses and all that Divine has created, the *swaroop* of soul is insufficient because a soul is beyond all the senses. A soul cannot experience anything, it cannot drink, eat, touch or enjoy; it needs a special suit to do all this — the body. And once you get tied to the body, the physical, you limit yourself and forget that you were unlimited once. You forget the state of bliss you were in and set your goal on something finite, which we call *nashwar*. You even forget your actual *swaroop*.

Does anyone know what the *swaroop* of the soul is? No. You have been born so many times, changed your suits so many times, that you have forgotten your own *swaroop*. Even if you go back in your past life, you only see one of the suits through which you experienced once. No one sees the *swaroop* of *atma;* maybe, just one or two. Because to see that, you will have to detach yourself from the physical — social status, power, money etc. but since you want to increase all of these, it can only happen here, in the physical world. If you think that by going there all this would increase, you are mistaken.

That light is your soul and that suit is your body and you are busy destructing each other's suit, so that you get more. In economics we study that resources are limited and wants are unlimited. If you chase unlimited wants, the resources will exhaust and once that happens then it is over. If you think you can find resources elsewhere, you are mistaken. If you think there is water on moon and you will get it from there, then that is a misconception, there is no water on moon. There is no life anywhere else in this universe. Life exists only here, where we are, only on this planet, though it exists in various dimensions but it exists only here, nowhere else. And as much as you want, life can never be created or destroyed; , just like energy — energy can neither be created nor destroyed.

Look at the foolishness of scientists. On one hand they say energy can neither be created nor destroyed and they accept soul as energy, life as energy, and yet they try to create life in a laboratory. How can you create something when you have accepted that it cannot be created? It is just a transformation from one form to the next to the next. Like energy, even life is permanent — only the forms change, bodies change, relations change, families change, houses change, neighbours change — but you remain what you are. There is no point enhancing what you have because what you have is limited — limited in strength and capacity, you cannot take it to unlimited dimensions and like they say, the more you collect in the physical, the more you spoil your *karmas* because by doing that you are eating into someone else's share in the world of limited resources. If there is a desire for something in the physical, set a benchmark for it — "This is what I want and nothing more than that". When you get that, that point of time itself, you leave; because if you don't leave at that point of time, you will never be able to leave, you will always remain there and this is an unending cycle. The lights went back, but again one of them wanted to come back after a period of time, that is the basic nature, which you have to transgress. Any light, which is able to transgress this basic nature goes back and merges into that big light. It becomes that big light then. And that is the purpose of birth.

You are sent from there to here so that you can get equipped to merge into that big light and not revolve around that; because in that state you cannot merge with it because there is no desire, there is only attraction. It is only in this state, this body which you have, this form which you have, only in this state you have the capacity to merge into that, to go a step beyond the state of those encircling lights.

The merger into that one light is silence. Even those small lights around are not in silence. The day you are able to merge with that big light, that is silence. Silence is not same as thoughtlessness, because when you are stilling your thoughts, you are only coming to a stage where you are encircling that light. Silence is the merger with the source and it can very well happen in this body. Sitting here, you can achieve silence. It is so easy.

Your *swaroop* is not this body. Understand your *swaroop* and understand who or what your near and dear ones are, those sitting around you are not your near and dear ones. To understand that, you will have to go beyond the effect of the five senses; till that happens you will just find yourself in a loop, going round and round. In the end, you will barely be able to breathe and still you will be telling the ones around you, "Call my lawyer. My property should go like this." Even then you will not be able to leave it, you cannot because you are just going round and round under the effect of five senses. Till 30, I can understand, even till 40 I can understand, but after that I do not understand. If you have passed 40 years doing the same things and you want to pass the rest doing the same, then you will continue going in loops, limiting yourself to the physical, that is finite and *nashwar.*

Increase your desire, desire for the ultimate. If you have a limited desire that today I want money, tomorrow something else, and if you are actually with your *Guru* and if your *Guru* has any substance, then you will get it instantly. But then with that you have spent your entitlement. So always when you ask, ask for the unlimited. When you ask for the unlimited, then the *Guru* has the capacity to give you that unlimited. Don't think that the *Guru* does not have the capacity to give you unlimited. Even though he is in the limited, that limit is for him, for you he is unlimited. He can give you the unlimited, how he does it is not for you to think or assess. What you get depends on you entirely, what is it that you are asking for? Ask for the unlimited, and then let's see what happens.

However, people often as me, "How can we ask for the unlimited if our *karmas* don't permit?" That is actually an intelligent question. If you have to go as per your *karmas* then there is no need for a *Guru*. Because when you are limiting yourself with *karmas* then that means you are identifying yourself with what you are individually, because *karmas* are always individual, they are never collective. So when you identify yourself with your own *karmas*, your own body, your own self, then that means you are you, your ego — "I am limiting myself with this" — then there is no scope of a *Guru*. What is the need for a *Guru* then? *Guru* has to take you beyond the bondages and limitations of *karma*, that is, the purpose of a *Guru*.

You are here, in this body, only for a limited number of years. Nobody is in this body for unlimited number of years. Whatever it is that you are busy collecting, you will not be able to enjoy that; it is people who will come after you who will enjoy that. Your children will be doing all that you desire and you will be stopping them from doing that — "What are you doing? Do you know how much effort has gone into it?" But it is their *karma,* not yours. So let them do what they have to, if you are going to stop them, ultimately you are hindering your progress, not theirs. Because they will do what they have to, they will not listen to you. Have you yourself listened to your parents ever? There might be few but the rest... If you yourself have not done it then how can you expect it from them? Why are you wasting your birth and your *karma* by running after them? Be rest assured that you are only wasting it; so many years have passed and the rest will also pass very soon. There is no way, you can stop them so then why not enjoy what you have, why waste that?

Physical growth happens horizontally but spiritual growth is vertical. That means that the experiences of physical growth are limited — that sweet whichever form you may have it in is only a sweet, its taste will remain the same. Similarly, whether you drive a Maruti or a Mercedes, the experience of driving is still the same. It is different if all you want is to make people jealous; if you are driving it then there is not much difference. On the other hand, spiritual growth is vertical and once you rise and look down you will laugh at the things you used to do some time back. But in order to rise, you will first have to leave what you are holding on to. That is the job of a *Guru* how he makes you leave that and makes you rise above that. I can guarantee that the state above your present state is much more pleasurable than this state. But it has to be experienced. Unless you experience it, it is pointless and in order to experience, you have to be in *yog*, there is no easy method that I know of.

Does anyone know what the swaroop of the soul is? No. You have been born so many times, changed your suits so many times, that you have forgotten your own swaroop. Even if you go back in your past life, you only see one of the suits through which you experienced once. No one sees the swaroop of atma.

SERMON 25

YOG AND YUGS

“Nobody gets a big shock straight away. It is always preceded by gentler warnings. In the puranas, there is a mention of the four hands of Lord Vishnu holding pushp, shankh, gada and chakra to warn us.”

25

A *lok* is a dimension of existence. The *lok* that you exist in is determined by your nature and character. Presently, you are in the dimension of *Prithvilok,* from here you may transcend to a higher *lok* or go down, depending upon your nature and character. Today, you have a human body, tomorrow it might be something else, in some other *lok*, because *loks* like everything else in creation are temporary. Getting a human body in this birth does not guarantee a human form in the next birth as well. Your existence in a particular *lok* is bound by time and time is a *swaroop* of *maya*. *Maya* keeps every being tied to time, which is why you think that you still have some time, whether you are 25 or 75…

There is a student of mine whose husband has heart trouble. He is 75 and by 75, something is bound to happen to the heart, especially if you have not been in *yog* throughout your life. As I was coming for the session today, I sensed that something was not right. I called her to check if everything was ok. The moment I asked, her voice sank. Her instant reaction was, 'you mean my husband?' It made me wonder, that a person who has lived for 75 years, and lived those 75 years just for himself, even the slightest thought of him leaving made her nervous and anxious. I am not sure what are all of you thinking. For how long will you go on? Even after 75 years of collecting for yourself, you still have the same fear that you had 10, 20 or 50 years back? Just look at what you have collected in those 75 years… All of it you will have to leave in the next 25 or maybe less, could be the next second. That is the thought that bothers you, that is the cause of your fear. If even after crossing 50, your thought process is that I should collect a little more; that I have 50 more years to go, you are headed in the wrong direction. Tied to this thought process, you will get trapped in the bondage of *maya* and tied to *maya*, your next *yoni* or *lok* would be lower than what it is right now.

Understand it this way. You have five *karmendriyas* and five *gyanendriyas*. If someone gags your mouth, you will have one less power. If your eyes are blindfolded, it would be two less. If your ears are plugged, it would be three less. Next, if your hands and legs are tied, still lesser... If all your *karmendriyas* and *gyanendriyas* are tied, then what will become of you? Will you be a level higher or lower than the present state? Definitely, lower. And the reason why a person comes to a lower level is because he thinks of just himself. He thinks of just himself because he is tied to the bondage of *maya*. The bondage is *maya* leads him to believe that he is here for some more time, so he can enjoy for a little longer. 'What is the hurry?!' You will be surprised to know that 60-65 year olds also tell me that 'It is not our age. It is still not our time to start *yog.'*

The person who starts yog the day the realisation happens, even if he is 18 or 20, only he is deserving of *yog*. The one, who waits because he is not old enough, can never do *yog*. He will keep justifying from morning till evening, blaming people and situations for why he cannot do *yog*. As you justify to yourself the reason for tying yourself in bondage, remember, it is one more sense tied, one less power, one step lower. And that step could be a lower level (*shreni)* in the *Bhulok* (there are three levels in *Bhulok* — servicemen, administrators and rulers) or if you are troubling a lot of people, then you might come down to a lower dimension (*lok* or *yoni*). And this is a reality.

With regular practice of *dhyan* and *Sanatan Kriya* under the *sanidhya* of a *Guru*, you can experience for yourself various *loks*, how they are, the pleasures, pains and fears associated with each *lok*.

Till the *Bhulok,* a being has 10 senses — five *karmendriyas* and five *gyanendriyas*. The more one ties them, the further he goes down and the more one expands them, the further he goes up to higher *loks* beyond the *Bhulok*. The simplest way to expand or develop these senses is doing something for someone else. One cannot develop his senses by giving lectures or showing to the world how much *puja-paath* he does. These things are not for awakening of senses but to earn money and fame. The weaker a person is from inside, the more he wants to tell others that 'I am also somebody, look at me' and he does so by showing off how much he knows or how good he is.

Never forget, creation exists in opposites. If there is fame, the opposite of fame is defamation. Let's take the example of a Supreme Court lawyer. There is a general expectation that he is good and will always win the case. If he makes the slightest of mistakes, even in the least significant of cases, he will get sleepless nights since his reputation is at stake. People will also not see the hundred cases that he won, but magnify the one case in which he faltered. So, the more fame a person has, the more he runs a risk of defamation. The more beautiful a woman is, the smallest of marks on her face makes her that much more ugly. Fame and money, both are directly tied to *maya*. The feeling they give you is just a feeling of falsehood that "I have so much."

The years of your life that have passed, are gone. They are not going to come back in this *yoni* again. Just ask yourself what you earned in the years that have gone — money and fame, or *yog*? You can only earn one of the two at a time. So, if you are desirous of *yog,* take your mind off money and fame. No matter how much money goes away from you, do not bother because there can be nothing better. You can be assured that if you are in *yog,* the money that goes will come back many times more. It leaving you is only a test. God, who is watching you, always thinks of doing good for you and the only way of doing good for you is to minimise your sins as you yourself are too busy taking pleasures to even think of minimizing them. So the other channel God has with him is to open the exit door for your money, which will automatically lighten the baggage that you are carrying. Whenever something happens, which you feel isn't right, that is a clear indication that you have done so much wrong in the past, that it is time to undo all of that.

Nobody gets a big shock straight away. It is always preceded by gentler warnings. In the *puranas*, there is a mention of the four hands of Lord *Vishnu* holding *pushp*, *shankh*, *gada* and *chakra to warn us*. At first, you get a polite nudge by a wise man that what you are doing is wrong and you must change your ways. That is a flower, *pushp*. Ninety-nine percent people do not heed it and mistake it to be a good omen, since they got a 'flower'. Next the *shankh* is sounded to ring a bell in your ears, maybe as a business loss or a minor problem. Most people ignore this as well and think there is still time and continue looking for better proposals and *upays*. After that, is the *gada*, that hits you hard in the form of a serious ailment or catastrophe. Half the population doesn't wake up even after being hit! Finally, *Vishnu ji* has to resort to the last option, the *chakra* — the head is cut, because such existence is of no use. It is better to take another birth because in this birth the vision is veiled by *maya* completely, not letting the person see beyond. This person is like a dysfunctional car, which is best dumped in a garage for recycling. May be the next birth would be better in terms of effect of *maya* on his vision. Those who move towards fame and money, this is how they are warned in stages.

Similarly, those who move towards *yog*, are guided on the path through warnings and indications. *Yog* is a path of self-experience; you do not have to wait for someone to tell you if you are headed the right way. Once you hold the hand of your *Guru*, your own experiences guide and direct you internally. There are indications at every step — how many breaks do you get in *dhyan*, how frequent or rare your experiences have become, is your *dhyan* regular or have you forgotten that you used to do something called *dhyan*, has the *darshans* of *devis* and *devtas* increased or decreased, etc. If you are doing *yog* and if your experiences are decreasing or instability of your mind is increasing or the internal peace is not increasing by the day or you are getting more and more hyper, it means that you are digressing from the path. If your hyper activity is reducing or if your mind is becoming still or your spiritual experiences are increasing, it means that you are moving forward.

The *vedas* describe a cycle of four *yugs* — *Satyug, Tretayug, Dwaparyug* and *Kaliyug.* In *Satyug*, the path of *yog* is the most difficult, as the level of purity is so high that one gets stuck in the beauty of it all and is unable to come out of it. Imagine a fragrant environment with a pleasant breeze, lush green surroundings and clear blue skies; would you want to leave it? So the *shreni* of *Guru* has to be very high in *Satyug,* to pull you out of it. The *Gurus* of *Satyug* are the *saptarishis,* who come straight from *Brahma* to guide and direct you. When the *yug* changes, the progeny of these *rishis* become the *Gurus* of the next *yug*. Whenever you come a step down, a bit of dilution occurs, certain impurities enter and so the *shreni* of *Guru* also reduces slightly. In *Dwaparyug*, anyone can become a *Guru* irrespective of his or her descent or familial occupation. In the *Dwaparyug*, the level of pollution increases to a great extent and it is said that by the end of *Dwaparyug*, Lord *Vishnu* leaves *prithvi (palayan)* since it is no longer worth living. *Adharma* is on the rise and that is why everyone is allowed to become *Guru* because a *Guru* is on the path of *moksha* and does *uddhaar* of others and not himself, which is the need of the *yug*. *Moksha* is relatively simpler in the *Dwaparyug*. All the *shaastras* are available at that time and anyone can become a *Guru* after *adhyayan* of those *shaastras*.

Finally in *Kaliyug*, the *asurs* of *Tretayug* become *Gurus* since they could not get *moksha in Tretayug* due to an *asur yoni*. They are given this last chance, before the *yug* changes, to tread the path of *moksha.* To put in a nutshell, the shortest way to *moksha* is becoming a *Guru*, because a *Guru* is about selfless service. A *Guru* is not about commerce or *maya* or tying you into bondage of *maya* by taking *yog* to a commercial dimension even on the pretext of building hospitals or big *ashrams*. One sees that most *Gurus* today are tied with huge *karmic* baggage because they are unable to let go of their inherent *asuric vritti*. They have got the *shreni* of a *Guru* but have not been able to untie the *asuric vrittis* and that is why the path, which they are treading on, is not the path to *moksha*, but to *Pataal lok*. They are busy amassing wealth *(maya)* and selling the subject of *yog* through false representations. For example, with master-ised looks and a glow-less body, they speak of giving radiance and glowing health to *shishyas,* but of course, in exchange of *maya*.

The rishis and maharishis of *Tretayug* also exist in the *Kaliyug* but not in the *swaroop* of *Guru*, they exist in a *sukshma swaroop* in the Himalayas or the oceans. They cannot take a body because for a body to hold their force, it needs to be extremely pure and such a body cannot exist in the environment of *Kaliyug*. Even *asurs of Satyug* cannot take birth in *Kaliyug* as the environment is not conducive. *Asurs* of *Tretayug* can survive for some time and so they are sent to open your gateways to *moksha*. Quite a few who come into *Guru*'s *shreni* now, are *asurs*. That is why one finds the actions of majority of *Gurus* strange, like giving *shaktipath* en mass, which is unthinkable, as *shakti* can only be transferred to a limited few. The thought of *Gurus* being *asurs* might seem disturbing, but that is the need of the *yug*. If I leave 500 pigs with you, do you need to be civil to handle them? So *asurs of Tretayug* are *Gurus* of this *yug*, they have been given this right and directive to somehow handle this creation and make way for exit of the souls that remain, either to *Swarg* and *loks* above (if they improve their *karmas*) or to *nark* and lower *loks*, to pay for their *paap karmas* by bearing the pain and torture of those *loks*. After bearing that pain, they will be born as lower beings or animals in the next *yug*. Every person reading this text should try his best to become a *Guru.* The path to *moksha* in this *yug* is only by becoming a *Guru* and it's the easiest to become a *Guru.* All you have to do is to be selfless and open your bondages of *maya*. I call it easiest because leaving *maya*/physical assets is an eventual fact, all that you have will be taken away from you and you will leave this world one day with nothing in your hands. All business establishments, all relationships, all properties and assets would leave you or you would leave them, so it is sensible to leave them yourself. At least then what you get in return is a higher dimension/level of existence, which I assure you is much more pleasurable than this. The *yog* of *Satyug* was *gyan*. In *Tretayug*, *dhyan* became the *marg* to *gyan* as *gyan* can come when *dhyan* is achieved. In *Dwaparyug*, it was *karma* and *Krishna* gave the whole *Gita*. If you do good *karmas*, you will be able to do *dhyan* and only if you are able to do *dhyan*, will you get *gyan*. The *yog* of present *yug* is *seva.* When you do *seva* your *karmas* improve automatically, when your *karmas* improve you will become eligible for *dhyan*, and once that happens you will get *gyan* and when you get *gyan,* then you will become eligible for *moksha*. So the only way to get *moksha* in this *yug* is seva and that *bhaav* can be found only in a *Guru*. There is just one path that is left with you in *Kaliyug*. Nothing is going to happen by doing *dhyan* with eyes closed, day dreaming, flying, having fantastic visions, etc. Whosoever is your *Guru* figure, study him and see if you can become like him. And a *Guru is* someone who radiates glow, is not tied by *maya* and does not charge you/sells you *yog*.

It is easiest to get *moksha* in *Kaliyug* as there is no attraction. What is attractive here? Is there any attraction of food or drink or in air, land or water? What is it that you are getting here, for which you want to come back? Observe any aspect of your life — work, relationship, house — you will find that there is no attraction in it. Each one of you is looking for an exit route from whatever you are doing. Just think how easy it is to get *moksha* in this *yug.* And yet, people remain *bhramit* here only. To get a *Guru* in *Kaliyug* is nearly impossible; one needs a strong backing of good *karmas*. It is a pity when those who get a *Guru*, also remain stuck. This, when there is nothing here to stay for, there is nothing besides problems. Just stand on the road for 10 minutes, your face will become black; the inside of your lungs will also turn black by inhaling all the smoke/CNG emissions. If you happen to witness someone's post mortem being done, when they cut the body you will be surprised to see the black sheath on the lungs of even a person who never had a lung problem throughout his life. You may also observe the phlegm that comes out when you cough, it is black. It is your thought process that determines the *yug* in which you take birth. The purer your thoughts are the higher is your entitlement and vice versa. Because what you see around you is your thought only, there is no difference between the two. If you change your thought process, then you will not be able to live in this environment. You will leave this and get *moksha* instantly. This environment is for those people who want to live a little longer and hold on to unreality. Those who think, "We are only 80, let us enjoy a little more."

Maya is *shashwat*. Its effect has been there since the very beginning. Had there been no *maya* people would not have traversed the journey from *Satyug to Kaliyug*. You all are beings of *Satyug.* You have seen that purity also, but you are those beings who could not leave it because it was very difficult to leave it at that time. Then you saw the next *yug*. Then the next and now you are seeing this *yug*. The effect of *maya* is minimal in this *yug*, it was the maximum in *Satyug*. Even *maya* does not need to make an effort to make you stay in *Kaliyug*, it knows that you are its permanent customer. And you cannot leave it even now; it is only a *Guru* who can make you exit the web of *maya*. There is no other way to come out of it. Sitting at home, lighting *diyas* and burning *dhoop-battis*, sitting with eyes closed and having fantastic visions, day dreaming, dancing around robe-clad men who flaunt beautiful flowing beards and hair, will do no good. You have been doing that for so many *yugs* now, you can keep doing it for more. Nothing is going to happen with that. The only route to *moksha* in *Kaliyug* is *seva* and there are two ways to do *seva.* One is the way you feel like. This path will give you *siddhis*, *dhan* (wealth) and *yash* (fame). The other *seva* is that which is told by your *Guru*. If you walk on that path then you get *moksha*.

The volunteers at *Dhyan Ashram* feed dogs. I get reports that at the feeding spots, people throw stones at the dogs and injure them. Recently, a volunteer told me that someone threw hot water on a dog and as a result its skin got burnt and he had to rush it to the hospital. Once a baby pig was walking on road and somebody ran a jeep over him and was laughing after doing so. The people who do such things are not human beings. *Maya* does not need to work hard to send them to *narks*, they are themselves paving the way. Think of how difficult it must be for the *Guru tattva* to interact with such people and lift them despite such a thought process. Only an *asur* can take up this task. No one else can do it. The desire to become a *Guru* is also a self-centred thought. A Yogi or someone who does *yog* is the most self-centred person because his focus is only on his *moksha*. He has seen the reality of this world and is so nervous from within that his focus is set on *moksha*. The one who is ignorant is in bliss as he does not know what lies ahead. I remember, when I was a child, we had gone to *Vaishno Devi*. It was dark and raining and we were climbing up the mountain. All of sudden lightning occurred and we saw that we were standing at the edge of a cliff. We had crossed the entire edge. Had there been light, we would not have dared climb up the way we did. So the one who is ignorant or *agyani* is the happiest person. He has no fear as he doesn't know what lies ahead. His mind is the most distracted and divided. He has to do everything. He has to do *dhyan*. He has to drink also. He has to travel also. He has to indulge also. He keeps doing everything and is happy doing so. The one who is a *gyani* is the most tensed or worried as he knows there is a cliff ahead and if he takes even one wrong step, he will fall. Every day he thinks that one more day has gone. He knows what he is heading towards and what is happening. *Yog Guru* is the most selfish person that can possibly be but he has no option. He sees nothing else but the path of *moksha*.

It is ok to be selfish as you are alone. Nobody else is with you. This is your individual journey, if your partner too is on the path it is just a coincidence. Your journey however, is your own. The problem starts when you think you are with someone... All your problems are because of someone else. Does anyone get troubled by his/her own actions? You always get tensed and worried because of or for someone else. Has any of you been able to make anyone else happy? No matter how much you have tried to make the person next to you happy, has anybody told you that 'you have done a good thing for me?' Nobody is a bigger fool than a person who is trying to make someone else happy as this is not the demand of this *yug*. In this *yug*, you should be scared because you have not seen *narks* yet. You get scared when you fall sick; your heart comes to mouth as you sit in a doctor's clinic anticipating what he has to say. Just think that if anticipation of a pain that lies ahead scares you so much, what will be your state if you have to face it 24/7, as it happens in *narks*? All the enjoyments you are having now, where will they go? Remember, every *bhog* has a *rog* attached with it. The *bhogs* that you are having today will translate into *rog* sooner or later, it is best to start the backward journey, now, on your own, otherwise time will make you take it.

SERMON 26

HUMAN DESIRES AND THE FOUR VEDAS

" *When you connect with Guru, you close the five senses. When the five senses are closed then a sixth sense awakens, which is beyond the five senses but has the samavesh of all five senses in it. That means you are hearing but you are not hearing, you are seeing but you are not seeing, you are having a taste but it is not there and similarly smell and touch are there but they are not there also.* "

26

Agni is the first word of *Rig veda*. It is the only element that cannot be polluted, the only substance that rises up despite the force of gravity. *Agni* rises and holds the capacity to make you rise…

Upon the death of a person, his body is put to fire (*agni*). You might be under the impression that it is done to destroy the body. You will be surprised to know that this is s done instead to liberate the body by the extraordinary quality of *agni*. While the soul leaves the body on the 13th day and gets liberated, the body, which is the five elements, gets liberated (or in other words, merges back into creation) with the help of fire.

The creation is a combination of the five elements and these elements come together to form the body of an individual because of an impurity or *dosha*. *Ayurveda* talks about the *tridoshas* of *vata, pitta* and *kapha*. It is these *doshas* that result in a body, and at any given time one *dosha* predominates the other two. A *dosha* may not push you to do anything or it may push you to do the wrong thing. The *dosha* (imbalance) along with its action tendency (that is, what it prompts you to do or not do) determines your *prakriti* or basic nature. Thus, the traits of a being get determined in the womb itself and do not change throughout the life (unless one is in *yog* and wants to rise upwards) implying that your *prakriti* — *vata, pitta, kapha* — gets determined in the womb only and goes on throughout your life. Your only hope to bring about a balance is *yog*, nothing else can change it. When the *tridoshas* come into a state of balance, the person gets liberated from the body and leaves the body (not death). Otherwise, when the body is cremated, *agni* removes the *doshas* and the body gets liberated. That is the significance of cremation — the body, that is the five elements tied to the *doshas*, gets liberated with the help of fire. No wonder *agni* became the first word of *Rig veda* — the *veda* that contains the *gyan* to elevate a being, what we call *atmic unnati*.

You will be surprised to know that *agni* was not always the first word of *Rig veda*. The *veda* started with the *Gayatri mantra*, given by Sage *Vishvamitra,* a *Kshatriya,* who rose to become a *brahm rishi*. The reason why the order of the *Veda* was changed to feature this *mantra* much later, is because of the conflicts in the society and clashes of ego between the various groups — *kshatriyas*, *Brahmins* and others. The same conflicts and claims of superiority are now causing us to lose our culture. We have forgotten our basics, the *gyan* of the *rishis* and can no longer think beyond the physical aspects — caste, position, status etc. The term *Gayatri* consists of two parts — *'gaya'* from *gayan* indicates that the chant of this *mantra* is not dependant on *vedic uchharan* but on a particular *chhand* and 'tri' or three refers to the three *vedas* (*Rig, Yajur* and *Sam*). The *Gayatri mantra* has the essence of all three *vedas* combined and so has been called the *janani* of all *mantras,* a *Maha Mantra*.

Rig veda comprises of *mantras* for *atmic utthan*, that is, evolving out of the physical and impure body with the power of *agni.* These days many of the *Rig vedic mantras* are chanted in the hope of improving financial condition, relationship, health etc. That, however, is not their purpose. *Yajur veda* covers all the aspects of physical life — politics, arts of war, social networking etc and describes in detail how to lead life in the physical world. *Sam veda* contains the various dance, music and art forms. If you watch a show on television that depicts *Swarglok*, it will be projected as a place where *apsaras* are dancing with *sitar* playing in the background. That pertains to the *Sam veda* only. The artistic and creative people who have their higher *chakras* more developed than the lower *chakras* come in the purview of *Sam veda*.

In earlier times, there were three requirements of a human life — spiritual evolution, material satisfaction and creative indulgence, hence the three *Vedas*. But with the change of *yug*, at the onset of *Tretayug*, the desires of human being tended towards physical pleasures and a physical pleasure (*bhog*) is always accompanied with equivalent pain or disease (*rog).* One must understand here that the basic desire changed from *yog* to *bhog* and *bhog* always leads to *rog*. A vicious circle: *bhog, rog*, *bhog* and *rog*. As the basic desire changed, humans started misinterpreting the *vedas* and the *yugs* also changed. Therefore, a need was felt for a fourth *veda*, the *Atharva veda,* comprising of the healing sciences and *tantric mantras* for fulfilment of worldly desires — health, relationship, power, position, status, appearance etc.

Recently, I had gone to a news channel for an interview. Someone commented on seeing me, "Look he has a big belly, the other *Yog Guru* is so fit. What *yog* he must be knowing?" Such things indicate the extent to which you are embedded into the physical such that your *buddhi* has become *bhrasht*. The more *bhrasht* the *buddhi* becomes, the more you rely on the physical and this has led to the misrepresentation of the *Atharva veda*. I do not have a big belly but a healthy and normal belly and I can assure you that I am fit enough to carry two people on my shoulders and run a mile. People with famished bellies cannot even think of this. This shows how warped the thinking process of today's beings has become. Nowadays you hear of '*tantric mantras*' for causing harm to someone or making someone suffer financially or emotionally... All this is absolute nonsense, there is no such thing mentioned in the *vedas*. Today *tantra* is being confused with occult practices (Voodoo, black magic etc.) that have come from barbaric cultures and were never a part of the *vedic* culture.

The *upanishads* narrate the story of *Agastya Muni* in this regard. When the menace of *rakshasas* increased on Earth, *Agastya Muni* with his penance made the *devs* stronger. The *rakshasas* out of fear, hid in the ocean. *Agastya Muni* then drank all the water from the ocean to make them come out. A war ensued, where some *rakshasas* were killed and the rest fled to *Pataallok*. At that time, there was a *bhavishya vani*, "When the *vedic* culture will fall, that is, when human beings will lose their character, implying that *bhog* and temporary material gains would be the main focus and even divinity would be used for *maya*, at that time, these *asurs* will come out again as the atmosphere will become conducive for them. Then nobody will be able to stop them and they would establish their rule once again." This is what is happening right now since we have lost faith in our culture.

The *Atharva veda* pertains to protection from the negative energies and healing arts. Initially, there was no requirement for *Atharva veda* because there were no *asurs/rakshasas* and there were *Gurus*, under whose cover, the humans left their bodies when they wanted, how they wanted and took up another body. But now there is no *Guru*, so there is no *gyan* and no one knows where he or she is headed. Since one does not know what lies beyond, he gets tied to the physical — property, house, body and relationships, because that is all he knows.

The more of the physical you have, the more you take yourself downward. There is a simple Law of Economics — resources are limited, wants and desires are unlimited. Whenever you take something extra from the creation, you are eating into someone else's share and you do it without the slightest bit of hesitation! In fact, you feel happy to have a bigger house or a new car, not realising that you are losing out on your *karmas*. ***Karma pradhan hai***, there is nothing more powerful than *karma*. You spoil your *karmas* and this depletes your *atmic shakti*. When that happens you are unable to distinguish right from wrong, and see and understand everything *ulta* (upside down).

There are over 2000 emails in my inbox right now and 99 per cent of them pertain to money, relationship, kids, health or career. I often wonder: where has our culture vanished? Nobody wants it, everyone from the ages of 18 to 80 want to tie themselves into more and more knots. Even as I am telling you all this, in your head you are thinking, "After the lecture finishes, I will ask him about this physical problem," because tied to *maya* your polluted body just cannot think beyond the physical. You have not the slightest idea of what lies above this. Just look at each other, how many of you want to see *'Shiv'*? 'See' here does not mean that an image will appear in front of you. 'See' means experience. *Shivoham* does not mean that you are seeing *Shiv* in front of you; it means you are experiencing *Shiv* inside you. It is a different sensation in the body — you get goose bumps, your body becomes absolutely straight, immense strength and power is felt inside the body, what you say starts happening, your thoughts become very powerful, your gaze becomes intense, your touch can heal people, you stop falling sick — all these are indications of 'seeing'. Seeing does not mean seeing with the eyes.

The *uccharan* of *Gayatri mantra* opens your bondages and makes you rise above. And what lies above? Something that is not down here. If you think you will go above and have a bigger bank balance or newer cars... that will surely not happen. When you rise all this heaviness is left behind. You cannot take this with you. So if you want to rise, be prepared to leave all this. Our *rishis* prescribed four *ashrams* — *Brahmacharya*, *Grihastha*, *Vanprastha*, and *Sanyas*. When a being completed his half-life (at that time 50 years was called half-life), he would become a *Vanprastha*. Whatever he had collected, taken from the creation, in the past 50 years, had to be returned back to the creation in the next 50. If you do not return it back to the creation, then it becomes your weight. You must have observed at cremation grounds that some bodies reduce to ash within a few hours and some others keep burning for days. This has a direct link to *karmas* — the more you have collected, the more fun you have had, the more polluted is your body. When a polluted body is put on the funeral pyre, greater effort has to be made by the *agni* to make it go because it is just not ready to go! All the weight one carries through life, he is not willing to leave it even at the funeral pyre. Many such cases stay back as ghosts. The first indication of how much weight you are carrying, how much you have deteriorated is how fast the body turns into ash. The second is, the cow. You must have heard of the phrases — '*Doodh ki nadiyan beh rahi hain*'(Rivers of milk flow) and '*khoon ki nadiyan beh rahi hain*' (Rivers of blood flow). The former indicates prosperity and latter symbolises war/strife. Let us see which of the two descriptions fits today's scenario. Recently, the local police informed us about a shocking reality — certain people pick up stray cows from the street, kill them in the car, sell them in the *mandi* and happily go back home with the money. This is just one example of the kind of atrocities being done on cows these days. How many of you were aware of this? And now that I have told you, how many of you care to do something about it? Hardly anyone! This is what this *yug* is all about; nobody can think anything beyond himself/herself.

The cow is a sign of prosperity, a sign of spiritual evolution. In the earlier *yugs*, it was called '*gaudhan*' and in wars, the victorious side used to take all the cattle with them because the number of cows one had was directly linked to his material and spiritual growth. So the 'river of milk' does not mean drink a lot of milk, it is an indication of prosperity. Those who want to finish this culture are the ones who are involved in slaughtering the cows, whichever community or religion they may belong to. When invasions started happening, the first thing the barbarians did was to kill the cows. They knew that this culture would only be finished when the cow is finished. Today we do not even need invaders to do the job. We have left our cows to feed on garbage dumps and meet painful deaths due to ingestion of plastic. While the invaders could not destroy our culture despite their best efforts, today we are busy bringing our own culture down, by not being concerned about what is happening. When you kill an animal, blood oozes out. So, today we are living in an era of '*khoon ki nadiyan*'.

We cannot call ourselves prosperous anymore; every person is unhappy and troubled, no matter how much he/she has. Prosperity or *aishwarya* does not mean that you have abundance of material wealth, it means that you are happy and peaceful as you have everything you need. In today's times there is hardly anyone who is satisfied with what he has because we have forgotten the basics of *vedic* culture — *karma*, *yagya* (purification) and service to cow. How can you call yourself *vedic* if you do not perform *havans* or take care of the cows? You are busy finding solutions to your problems one after the other, and there is no end to it, because new problems will keep cropping up till the time you do not follow the laws on which this creation rests.

The barbarians (termed *mlechha* in the *vedas*) came from extremely cold or extremely hot (desert) regions, where food was scarce as no cultivation was possible. For them, killing animals to procure food was a basic instinct. It was in this part of the world, where there was prosperity and abundance that one knew about the laws of creation and it was the duty of such a person to make the barbarians aware of these laws. None of you is doing that today. You sit and think that after death you will go to heaven and enjoy, but nothing of that sort is going to happen. If you just start spreading the word about these things, the whole creation will change, otherwise the state is already miserable, and it will only get worse. Unless the barbarian who is in the majority today changes his thought process, there is no hope. He will destroy himself and the creation.

There is a *sadhika* who gets up every morning to do *Surya vandana*. Her neighbours, who are supposedly celebrities, have instructed their guards to create smoke in the morning, just at the time of prayers. Because of the smoke, it is difficult for her to breathe. She asked them to stop, but they just would not budge. These are the indications of *Kaliyug*. This is what the *asurs* do: create havoc wherever there is a *havan*, *yagya*, *Surya vandana* or *yog*; trouble the *rishis* and *munis*; pollute the minds. You have no idea about the amount of smoke you take in everyday from the nearby generators and from the leaves that guards burn to keep themselves warm in winters. When you inhale this air, you are bound to fall sick. And yet, you do not stop them. So you yourself are responsible for your devolution and that of the creation. The time of *asurs* has come again and if you do not wake up soon, there will be nothing left.

Question: How to get peace of mind?

Answer: What have I been saying for the past one hour? Did I not say that at the end of this lecture, you will still be asking me how to get 'this' for yourself... The day you start looking for your neighbour's peace of mind, you will find peace. Just look at the state of affairs, you cannot look beyond yourself, you neither do good *karmas* nor *havans* nor *gauseva*, how do you expect to find peace? Till and unless your environment is *shant,* you cannot be *shant.* I cannot give you arbitrary solutions, like do *Kapal Bhati pranayam*, it does not work that way. The meaning of *yog* is sum total, everything is connected and interdependent. The day you make your first move to create peace in the creation; educate the *mlechhas* and improve the environment that day itself peace will dawn upon you.

Question: I heard something in *dhyan* but could not understand it. What was that?

Answer: A basic human being has five senses — taste, smell, sight, sound and touch. When you do *dhyan* and connect with the *Guru*, you close all five of them. If either of these senses is open, then you go in the direction of that sense. For instance, if you sit in *dhyan* and start thinking of one of your problems, then throughout *dhyan* it keeps coming back again and again. You have 100 other problems, but that same problem keeps coming back again and again. This is called a 'leakage'. The state of *dhyan* comes after *dharana* and *dharana* means that your focus has been established completely towards one. There is no leakage after that. If your *Guru* has any *shakti* then even if your thought leaks a little towards something, you will end up reinforcing that thought and it will manifest. *Guru* is a very powerful *shakti*. When you do *yog* and *dhyan* under the *sanidhya* of your *Guru*, your state is the state of entire creation. Creation is the manifestation of a thought; if a 'leakage' of thought happens, you drift in that direction. I will give you a simple way to know whether you are with your *Guru* or not. Observe what you desire most before you do your *dhyan*, now after you finish your *dhyan* what is the first thing that comes to you. If the beginning was a selfish desire and after *dhyan* a selfless desire, then you are with me (or whoever is your *Guru*).

When you connect with *Guru*, you close the five senses. When the five senses are closed then a sixth sense awakens, which is beyond the five senses but has the *samavesh* of all five senses in it. That means you are hearing but you are not hearing, you are seeing but you are not seeing, you are having a taste but it is not there and similarly smell and touch are there but they are not there also — so the *samavesh* of all five senses is the sixth sense and it is the most active sense.

When at times you have *saiyam* (control) on the five senses during *dhyan* (like you said I do not know where I was), then the sixth sense awakens and shows the *swaroop* of this creation and that *swaroop* is alive, it is a living entity. The *vedas* were not told by anyone verbally, all the *mantras* were revealed to the *rishis* with their eyes closed. They heard the *dhwani* of *mantras* because their focus, their *dharana* was completely on *yog*. Their *dharana* was not on physical things, that now I should get this or that or this should happen.

The senses keep you tied to the physical and do not let you go forward or experience anything. In earlier times, a being used to leave everything for the next generation by the age of 50, and became a *vanprastha* to find the truth. He used to aid in running the creation by doing *yagya* and *hom*. But today it is such a sad state of affairs that a person starts 'living life' and 'having fun' at 50, after collecting a lot of money and position.

Yog means to achieve and then leave it. He who leaves it, after accomplishing what he wanted to is a Yogi. Only such a person can move on, as he has the *dharana* of *yog*, others are just fooling around. You have spent so many births and *yonis*, and you will continue doing that. The experiences of *yog* do not happen that way. Follow what I ask you to do and not what I ask you not to.

Question: How to close the five senses?

Answer: You leave something only when you find something more attractive than that. So you cannot leave the five senses, till you find something more attractive than these. But then this becomes a vicious circle because you will not see something more attractive till the time you do not leave the five senses. This is where the role of *Guru* comes. First and foremost, make a *Guru* and focus your *dhyan* on the *Guru*, when you are able to do that completely, then you will automatically start having experiences and your senses will start coming into *saiyam* or control on their own.

SERMON 27

ON MAKAR SANKRANTI...

“*The only difference between the Divine and a human being is that there is no effect of the positive and negative on the former but both of these have a very strong effect on the latter. It is under the effect of the negative and the positive that a human being gets bhramit and forgets his path and direction. He attaches himself to nashvarta and separates himself from the amar tattva.*”

27

In the process of growing up we have collected a lot of knowledge about things from books and from people around us. Things like why certain days are important, what are gods and goddesses, or what is good or bad, etc. But how many of us really understand these concepts and energies? Very few... because knowledge is for the mind. It is only through experience under the *sanidhya* of a *Guru*, that the *gyan* of things dawns on a being.

Today is *Makar Sankranti*. What is the significance of today?

I had asked a group of seekers the relevance of the day of *Makar Sankranti*. One out of them replied that on the day of *Makar Sankranti*, positive energy starts increasing. When I asked him what he meant by positive energy, he replied that which is to aid the creation, when your mind is attracted towards the right things. Now, *avtars* take birth on the planet for a specific purpose. But then, do they only have positive in them or is there a negative aspect to them as well? Someone replied, only positive, only pure love. If that was so, then why did *Ram* kill *Bali*?

Let us talk about *avtars*. Is an *avtar* a he or she? Some say that an *avtar* is neither he nor she. Then why is *Ram* called *maryada purushottam*? The term *purush* connotes a man. So then is an *avtar* always a he? *Mohini* was a she... and she came twice; once for the *amrit kalash* and at another time for *Bhasmasur*. There are also those who maintain that an *avtar* has both 'he and she'. That is nonsense. When *avtars* take a body, they are normal beings, and in normal beings you don't have he and she, it has to be either. A person with both sexes is not normal, though these days even that is considered normal. But technically it is an abnormality because there are only two purposes to a birth. The first is to experience, which we call *bhog* or *anubhav* and the other is procreation. There is no third purpose, after that you go beyond. If someone misses either of the two purposes, then he/she has to do a lot of *tapa* to go beyond or he/she has to participate in creation, otherwise there is no *moksha*, because his/her experience is not complete. This, however, does not apply to *tapasvis* and *tapasvinis* they can go just like that.

Avtars always take the form of either a man or a woman. Since they have a specific purpose, they need a specific energy inside them to serve that purpose. Every *avtar* has negative and positive inside them. The negative is as strong as the positive, since it is a balance. If you look at the various *avtars* — *Krishna*, *Ram*, *Parshuram*, *Narsingh*, *Varaha*, *Mohini* — none had all positive aspects. Each of them had both aspects because both the aspects exist in the Divine. The only difference between the Divine and a human being is that there is no effect of the positive and negative on the former but both of these have a very strong effect on the latter. It is under the effect of the negative and the positive that a human being gets *bhramit* and forgets his path and direction. He attaches himself to *nashvarta* and separates himself from the *amar tattva*. There is no effect of these on the *avtars* and the Divine.

We should strive to remain unaffected by the positive or negative happening with us because if even the shadow of it falls on us, then we will get carried away and waste our birth. It is because of this *bhram* that the majority keeps wandering in circles looking for solutions to their physical problems. And what is a solution to any problem? Let me tell you, there is nothing called as a 'solution' and *'upay'*, there is only *karma*. If you improve your *karmas,* then there is no need for any *upays.* You do not even need to put your mind to a problem because everything falls into place on its own. The one who leads his life making *karma* as the basis, for him there is nothing, which is unattainable. I am not talking about negative *karmas* here. As soon as a person starts doing good *karmas* the problems start disappearing. Have you experienced this? If not, then better start doing good *karmas* because otherwise you will keep trying to preserve what you have and before you know it, your body will fade, you will leave from here for another *lok*, not necessarily *Swarg*. At that time an account of your *karmas* will be taken and if you have not done anything good, then you will land in hells and bear a lot of pain.

According to the *Ganga Puran,* Lord *Vishnu* left *Prithvi* 5000 years back and gave a time period after which *Ganga* too would disappear from Earth. He said that as *Ganga* would recede, the corruption in the world will start to rise and the world will become more and more *asuric* and *asabhya*. That is precisely what is happening right now. Five thousand years back Lord *Vishnu* decided that this place is no longer worth living and thought it better to leave. The *puranas* also mentions that within 200 to 400 years of receding of *Ganga*, all the other *devi-devtas* would also leave. And when they leave, nothing would remain. Take the case of *Surya*, it is a *dev*, if he goes away, only darkness would remain. That would be the time of *Mahapralay*, what is called the Ice Age. The modern scientists confirm that Ice Age will return and all life-forms will perish with it. That is the indication of the *palayan* of the *Surya dev*. *Palayan* does not mean 'running away', the *Surya dev* would not just disappear or *Vishnu* did not flee from here, *palayan* means that their *shaktis* become *nishkriya* (inactive). When the sky gets covered with dust, the sun will not be seen and so the energy of *Surya* will become *nishkriya*.

Most agree that on the day of *Makar Sankranti (January 13),* the sun starts moving northwards. However, that is not the case anymore. If it were so, then it would mean that all our *shaastras* and their predictions about the coming *yugs* are false... The *yug* is constantly undergoing a change. Technically, *Makar Sankranti* is the day when sun enters the *Makar rashi*. However, the sun started its northward journey much earlier, on 21-22 December. The *sadhaks* who perform *Surya sadhna* observed this phenomenon. How does one explain this?

As *yugs* change, the axis of the Earth tilts. This is called a dimensional change, and it is a clear indication that our *shaastras* are not wrong because the tilt of axis has changed from the times of *Satyug* till the present age of *Kaliyug*. With the recent tsunami, scientists recorded that the axis of Earth tilted a little more. As the axis is tilting more, the *yug* is moving further towards its downfall. The tilt of Earth's axis is indicative of the change of *yug,* which is experienced by us through increasing chaos in the creation. With the change of *yugs,* human *pravritti* is becoming more *asuric, devic shaktis* are receding from the planet. Wherever you see, there is only chaos around you and this chaos will only increase. You will see that within a year kidnappings will occur openly on roads. There is not much time. Now things are changing so fast that it is important to be on alert and to be together. See anywhere around you, without giving bribe you cannot get any work done. You cannot earn money with honesty in today's times; one has to manipulate. And this is the indication of that tilt of earth's axis and all of it is linked to the sun.

Our entire life is linked to two energies – that of sun (*Surya*) and of moon (*Chandra*). *Surya* is the *devta* of *gyan* while *Chandra* is the *devta* of *mann (iccha shakti)*. The *shakti* of both is *Gayatriji*. As you do *Surya sadhna* and *Chandra sadhna*, you experience these energies and their character is revealed to you. For general understanding, it is enough to know that the sun is closely linked to our lives. There is a lapse of 23 days when *uttarayan* really began and what we call as *Makar Sankranti*. This clearly indicates that the astrological sciences of present times are absolutely redundant. According to astrology, the sun has entered the *Makar rashi* today and so *uttarayan* should start today (January 13). But that is not the case as observed by the *sadhaks* who follow the sun. Despite all of this, we run to astrologers to find an *upay* to our problems. What solution will an astrologer give you when he cannot solve his own problems?

The change of *yug* is related to the *Surya dev* and this change is directed towards increase in negativity. That is why every person is steeped in corruption. If you switch on the television today, you will get to see people with their bodies smeared with ash and adorning huge *maalas,* lecturing at the *kumbh mela*. Smearing of ash on the body is indicative of *shat bhaav shunya* — that is, your *bhaav* goes towards *shunya.* If your *bhaav* is *shunya,* then what is the need to give lectures? *Bhasm* is *shunya*. It is smeared on the body, *as poorna gyan* of *shunya* comes from the *bhasm* smeared on the body. I often tell people not to put artificial *bindis* on the forehead because your thought process is triggered by the *Agya chakra*, and if you put artificial things on the *Agya* then your thoughts too will move towards artificiality. Not just the *bindi*, any kind of artificial things you come in contact with — clothes, perfumes, cosmetics — make you more artificial, causing you to lie to yourself and to others.

No astrologer can rid you of your problems. Like we just discussed, the science of astrology is redundant in today's time and its entire basis has changed. In the same way, the basis of natural sciences, or naturopathy, too has changed. It is no longer relevant today, as what grows on earth today is not the same as what it used to be when these sciences were given. As a result its effect on the body is not going to be the same. Naturopathy involves ingesting natural, chemical free foods and living life as per nature's laws. It is not possible today because we have polluted the soil and water to the extent that all the chemicals that go in it make the produce also like a chemical which destructs the body. Similarly, as evening descends which is time for rest, loud music and bright lights are put on, so living in an unnatural world and depending on nature to heal yourself is redundant. It is important to understand that the *yug* we are living in is a very dangerous *yug. Maya* has strangled you in its clutches and you cannot find the way out, you are getting more and more stuck with every passing day. Just look at yourself, from morning to night, you are busy searching for solutions to your problems. No one does service or charity by their own wish (*sweccha)* because such is the effect of the *yug*. In the darkness of this *yug*, you cannot get the *darshan* of the *swaroop* of *param tattva*. It is not possible without a *Guru* who gives you the *prakash* of *gyan*, in which you can see that *swaroop* and that too when you walk the path as told by your *Guru*. Do not 'think' that you are walking on that path, but actually walk it.

I will give you an example about 'thinking' — there is a lady in the Foundation who is a very famous artist and was with some other organisation earlier. For 15 to 16 years she was there and gave large donations to the organisation. Then one day, she met me and had an instant experience. She asked me what it was. I told her that when you do *yog* and form a connection, you instantly get an experience. She told me that she had never had such an experience in the last 15-16 years, even though she was doing everything. I told her to do this and see what happens. Then I asked her what was it that she desired? She told me that she was desirous of *moksha*, she wanted to leave everything and go. I said that it was good that she wanted *moksha* and told her to do certain things. After six months, I asked her if she had any experience. She said "nothing". Then I told her that I was getting to read a lot about her in the papers. Her photographs were everywhere and every television channel was after her. To which she replied, "Yes that has happened. I have progressed a lot in the physical." Upon asking what progress, she replied — "Media is constantly after me. My art is on the top. I have people interviewing me daily. But I have not had any experience of *yog.*"

What do you gather from this narrative?

She said she wanted *yog*, but her desire was not that of *yog*. When she came to me she had said that she was ready to do anything for *yog*, but when I asked her six months hence about what all she had done for *yog*, there was nothing. She said, "I did a show here and I did a show there and all the time I think of you." On service and charity, her lips were sealed. For a person who earns 1.5 to 2 crores a month, her charity was only Rs 5000 per month; that too she had much difficulty in parting with and did it out of obligation. I asked her again, what she had done for *yog*? So then she asked,"Ok, tell me what should I do?" Why should I tell? I do not want to create a fear psychosis inside you...

When you start doing *yog* and if you have a connection with your *Guru,* your primary desire starts getting met with. But if you think the *Guru* is a key, which will fit into every lock then that is a wrong approach. The moment you establish a connection with your *Guru* and walk on the path of *yog*, whatever your primary desire, it starts getting fulfilled, things start happening automatically in your life. That is why I tell you that when you come to meet me, do not talk big things..."We want to leave everything, we want *moksha*." Till you do not have that kind of thought process, do not utter such things, because then actually these things will start going away from you. Your position and power will start leaving you. Because I assume that if someone is saying such a thing to me, he/she must be speaking the truth. This must be their desire. It is applicable for everyone.

The earlier organisation she was in, she was donating 5-10 lakhs monthly, not as charity and service, but out of fear. People in that organisation would say something like, "Oh today I saw a shadow of an evil spirit over you." So she would ask, "So *Guruji* then what should I do?" They would say, "Get this *puja* done." And she would get it done. Then they would say, "Now the effect has lessened a bit — get the *puja* repeated after another two months so that the effect goes away completely." *Pujas* are being used like antibiotics to rid you of an ailment.

Nowadays, majority of the *Gurus* are putting fear into people's mind and thereby binding themselves only more and more into *maya*. "Do this otherwise this will happen, do that otherwise that will happen." And if that fear psychosis is not there, then the same happens as happened with that lady. In one organisation, where she did not have any experience, her problems were increasing and her state worsening, she donated 50-60 lakhs of rupees in six months. But in another organisation, where she was to feed the hungry herself in her own city, she spent only Rs 30,000 in six months. Why? Because we did not create fear within her – "Shadow of an evil over you". Our purpose is *marg darshan*, to show you the way and tell you to walk on that path. If you are unable to walk on it, come to me at the *ashram*, and I will make you walk on that path but your wish should be to walk on that path. Time is slipping away, whatever little time you are left with, while you have the opportunity, utilise it, otherwise you will be left empty-handed. You will not get anything and you will start falling into deeper pits. You have the proof in front of you. All the ancient sciences are failing in today's date because they are no longer applicable.

All good things start on the day of *Makar Sankranti,* when *uttarayan* begins, like the *Kumbh,* which started in Allahabad today. According to us, it should have started on 21/22 December, but if we say that, a crowd of five lakh would gather to argue. Who is going to argue with them that the auspicious date is long gone?

In every *Kumbh,* it is a matter of prestige to be the first to take the dip — there is something called the *Shahi Snan* — that who will take that bath first. Has anyone seen the *Kumbh*? Even if you have not, it is ok; it is of no use to see it also. I had gone there once and saw. What I saw was that as soon as it was time for bath, people made a loud roar as if preparing for a battle and charged towards the water. I wondered what they were trying to do. I was staying at a famous hotel on the side of the road from where the procession went. A lot of foreign media was also staying at that hotel, they had come to cover the event. When they returned after the day's work, they were all battered and bandaged. I asked them, "What happened?" One of them replied, "A *sadhu* hit me." I, then asked, "Why did he hit you?" The reply came — "Because I was taking his photograph. He hit me with the sword that was in his hand." I told them, "That is not the way to take photographs. I will show you how to take them." In the evening, I took my camera and went and stood at the hotel gate. The procession came with people carrying *lathis*, swords, etc in their hands. I took photographs of them, and no one realised that I was clicking. Then I went a little closer, took one, two... I have a strong intuition; the third that I took was a very close shot and one out of the group shot a glance at me. The look in his eyes told me that he was about to attack me, so I shut the camera, ran inside and shut the gate. He could not catch me because of the crowd behind him. I still have that photograph and you can make out how they are charging as if going into a battle... Is this *Kumbh*? It is just their egos that have reached the skies.

Do you know when this system of hitting started? In olden times, when the actual *sadhus* used to go for *snan*, their state of mind used to be such that no one should even see them. They used to go in the night silently to the *ghats* and wait for *brahm-muhurat* and then they would bathe and quietly go back to the mountains. Some miscreants went and tried to trouble them. You see, everyone wants a solution to their problems and the more inaccessible or discrete a person seems to be, the more you run after him thinking what you might get out of him. Now these *sadhus* used to be such that they did not even want to talk to anyone. There was no need for them to talk as they were truthful people and understood that nothing can be achieved by talking. If someone is doing wrong deeds from morning till evening and then comes to them for a solution, what solution could they give them? They thought it to be a waste of time and so did not meet people at all. When these miscreants tried to approach them, one of their *chelas* beat one of them up saying "Why are you troubling *babaji?*" Since then it became a ritual to beat up anyone who saw them. Today we have reached the stage where the very same people who beat up people for clicking them are later seen to be giving interviews on TV channels.

The state of the world at this time is very dangerous. The *tamashas* as per this *yug* have touched the skies and because of that all this is happening. *Makar Sankranti*, (which technically has already passed on 22 December) marks the beginning of auspicious works such as *Kumbh.* It is on this day that *Bhishma Pitamah* left his body. You might have heard that he was lying on a bed of arrows waiting for the end of war, but he was not waiting for that. He left his body the day sun started its northward movement. On this day, the constellations are in such a form that it is conducive for starting anything new and auspicious. The good deeds that you do in this time duration reap manifold *karmic* results. Do not sit and think that you have done a lot of good work and progressed a lot. If you do not do good deeds right now, then your distance with me will start increasing. In the coming one/one-and-a half year, your distance with me will increase with much speed and in six months or a year you will not see me anymore. So to match up with me it is very necessary that all of you keep doing good deeds in your life and all of you should try and become *Gurus*, do *prachaar* of *dharma* and bring your *shreni* to that of a *Guru*. Only then you will attain *moksha.* Because some of the *Gurus* of this *yug* are *asurs*, so doing *marg darshan* after getting a control on that *asuric vritti* is very difficult. We all have *asuric vrittis* at their peak in us because we are all basically *asurs.* There cannot be any *devs* in this *yug* because *devs* cannot last in this environment, they will die in just two days. Go outside and take a long breath and you will get asthma; such is the air quality. Every person here has a lot of negativity in them, due to the *asuric vritti*, but that *vritti* can be changed by doing good deeds. When you start doing that, then you will start having the *darshan* of those energies.

Whatever work the Foundation people are doing, should be done together, only then you will walk that path. Either you join the work that the Foundation people do, go where they are going or call them and make them join your work. The purpose is to do it together, walking on that path. Start doing that and then tell me. When a person's physical parameters are strong then the vibration in the lower *chakras* is more and this should not be so. If you do things together and walk the path then such a problem will not come. Though, other kinds of problems start coming your way as you progress on the path — there is resistance from family members regarding your coming here. How many of you have faced this?

The problem is that nowadays many places make use of evil forces. The common perception then is that whatever they have seen at such places is what must be happening here as well. That is one of the prime reasons. If you see, all our *havans* happen at night and we do not deny that we believe in *tantric* practices. The thing is people do not understand what *Tantra* is and assume that a *havan* at night means, they must be doing something with skulls or something. There is no solution to this problem. Let me give you an example.

There is a student of mine in Hyderabad. She started *yog* and now she has progressed a lot in it. There is a very famous *Gayatri mandir* in Andhra Pradesh where *rishis and munis* come from far and wide and perform *havans*. She has progressed so much, that now only she is performing *havans* at that place. She is a famous socialite and every second day, her picture comes on page 3 with a drink in her hand and yet she is called to the *mandir* to perform *havans* and only she is called. Why? Two years ago, the temple authorities had placed an order for the *murti of Mata*. Till then there was no *sthapna* of a *murti*, only a picture of a *Gayatri sadhak* was placed in the temple, so they thought of getting a *murti*. They had placed the order two years back, but all this while something or the other kept happening and the *sthapna* of *murt*i kept on getting delayed. It was just not happening. Then, after sometime, even they forgot about it.

There is a *Gayatri divas* and so on that day, this lady was performing a *havan* at the temple. The *havan* lasted for over an hour-and-a-half and immediately after that, a truck stopped at the temple, and the driver enquired if they had placed an order for a *murti*... The people of the temple were astonished as they had themselves forgotten. On asking as to why it was being delivered on that day while the order had been placed two years back, the delivery man replied, 'It got completed today so we thought we would deliver it to you." They gave it and went. The temple authorities got that statue installed by that lady herself — it must have happened for the first time in history, that a *murti of Gayatri mata* was installed by a socialite. Her calling was so strong that when this lady remembered *Gayatri mata* during the *havan,* she herself walked up and came to her in the form of that statue. And in her own house, this lady finds nails, amulets, lemons etc — the different *'totkas'* that her family members resort to; to get her out of the Foundation. What can you do?

The more you progress... the more people will try to pull you back. Understand this, there is nothing called family or house or near and dear ones. Everyone is with someone for their own selfish purpose. The more you progress in *yog* the more problems your immediate family will have with you. And if this is happening with you, then it is good news, it means that now you are progressing in *yog*. In today's world the *asuric* energies are very strong. When any positivity comes up somewhere, then all the *asuric* forces get disturbed. When they get disturbed, then they behave in an unreasonable manner — 'don't go', 'what is all this', 'black magic', etc. Those who stop you, fear that you would be doing the same thing as they would do had they been here. What they do not know is that is the precise reason why they are not here. These people do not come into *yog* with a *satvic bhaav*, but because they want a solution to their problems.

Your reasons for coming into *yog* could be of three kinds — *satvic, rajasic and tamsic. Tamsic* is to harm someone, *rajasic* is for financial gain, improving relationships etc, and *satvic* is for evolution. If you are coming to me with a *tamsic bhaav* also, then it is my duty to convert that *tamsic* into *satvic*. That is my job and I know how to do it. But for that it is necessary for you to come to me. But the majority of the people go elsewhere for *tamsic* motives and because they do so, they think that you must also be doing the same over here and their insecurities increase. I get to hear things like 'at home they say that the paint of the house is getting spoilt because of these *havans* that I am doing. It is giving a bad smell.' They say such things because those *asuric vrittis* are strong in them, but you just have to be *sthir* and stick to your path and be focused on your *Guru*, nothing will happen. Let whoever say and do anything and let whatever happen to them, because disturbances will come, it just cannot happen that disturbances will not come and it is a very good sign.

The philosophy of *yog* is that there is no father, mother, brother, sister or son. Each one of you is an individual. The more you attach yourself to someone, the more you tie yourself into *moh-bandhan*, the more you drag yourself down. I have to tell you what the truth is. *Seva* of parents is *sarvocch* (ultimate) and that you should do, but *seva* does not mean attachment. Attachments keep you stuck and do not let you move forward.

Question: Can I touch your feet?

Answer: This is not the time. Let me explain. If you touch me then *vairagya* will come inside you and unfortunately, you don't have the state of *vairagya* yet. So whatever you will get by touching me, you will waste it in attachment. Understand the process. When you touch me there will be a transfer of energy. That energy is for your evolution but your thoughts are physical. So you will run to get your physical work done that energy will go to waste and you will neither be here nor there. A person when in pain or is disturbed — that time he recalls *yog* the most, on the other hand a person who is happy, healthy will never think of *yog*, he doesn't care. So that is why it is not right for you to touch me. That is why I do not allow anyone to touch me. First get the state of *vairagya* inside you, when you feel that now you are focused only towards one side, then you can touch me. There is no ban on touching me, but you can touch me only then, otherwise it will be of no use.

I don't want that anyone should be dragged towards *maya*. Even if it is time for someone to leave their body, I want that they leave their body with full consciousness. You should know where you are going. If you are attached to *maya*, then you will never get the *gyan* and then me being there is absolutely meaningless, there is no use.

Let me repeat one thing for everyone, *yam niyam asan pranayam pratyahar dharana dhyan samadhi,* this is the eight limbed path of *yog*, and we practice this with great difficulty. The first three *siddhis* of *yog* lie in the five *yams* themselves *satya, asteya, aparigrah, ahimsa, brahmcharya*. Of these *brahmcharya* is very important. With practice of *brahmcharya, vairagya* sets in and with *brahmcharya* only that *shakti* comes inside the body. If anyone is practicing *brahmcharya* and doing service and charity and if there is any problem in their body or in their life, then tell me. If you are not doing it then I cannot do anything in that. In life either enjoy physical pleasures or move forward. You cannot do both.

Let me tell you another small story. Has anyone heard of the *Mahakaleshwar Mandir*? It's a *jyotirlinga*, a very powerful place.

People just get up and go to any *teerth sthan*, thinking what they might get out of there. One lady came to me in a very bad condition. She is from the hotel industry. She was very fat and she was facing problems on the work front. Within six months from then, her work life came into a balance, she got back into shape, everything started going smooth because she had started helping people a lot. One day she mailed me. (You need to understand my limitations, I do not have so much capacity as to comment about a *teerth sthan*. I do not want to comment on any *teerth sthan,* I am just telling you a story.) In the mail she told me, that she was going for a holiday to *Nasik* to the *Mahakaleshwar Mandir*. She asked me, "Tell me what I should do when I go there." Immediately, from that mail I understood she is now heading for trouble in the physical world. (Problems coming into your life do not mean that you are regressing, in fact problems should be welcome.) Now the said place is a temple of *Mahakaal.* By going there, you are not going to get *ladoos*... it is a place for *gyan*, a place for *yog.* So I told her that, "Since you have said you are going there, I cannot stop you from going, but do not get any *puja* done there." Since the day she has gone there, her weight has come back to the initial level and she is having problems in the work again. That is, the kind of mess her life was in earlier, it has come back to that state. So she asked me why this happened. I told her, — "I had told you not to get *puja* done." She said, "But that is a *teerth sthan*, should I not go to a *teerth sthan,* is there any stoppage in going to a *teerth sthan*." Now what do you say. You must understand that *teerth sthans* are not shops where you go, give money and buy something and put it in your pocket and bring. These are places of *sadhna* where someone has done *tapasya* for many *yugs.* And the one who did that *tapasya*, after its completion, he would not have asked from God for anything physical, like a big house or good figure. He would have asked for *yog* or *moksha.* If you go to such a place you will get *yog* and *moksha.* Your desires are physical and you have gone to such a place for something else. So understand what you are doing, where you are going. Neither tell me nor ask me about such things because I don't have the capacity to comment about these places.

There is nothing called as a 'solution' and 'upay', there is only karma. If you improve your karmas, then there is no need for any upays. You do not even need to put your mind to a problem because everything falls into place on its own. The one who leads his life making karma as the basis, for him there is nothing, which is unattainable.

GLOSSARY

Aadesh Order

Abha Glow

Abhaav Shortage, Scarcity, Absence

Abhnivesh Fear of death

Abhyas Practice

Adhaar Basis

Adharma Against the principles of *dharma*

Adhyatmic Spiritual

Adhyayan Study

Adi Guru The first *Guru*, Lord *Shiv*

Agni Fire

Agya Energy centre at the centre of eyebrows

Agyani Ignorant

Ahimsa Non-violence in action and thought

Ahuti Oblation

Aishwarya Prosperity

Ajar Imperishable

Akash Ether

Akhand Indivisible

Akriti Form, shape, figure

Amar Immortal

Amrit Divine nectar

Anahad Energy centre at the centre of chest cavity

Anand Bliss

Anant Unending

Anisht Ominous, bad, undesirable, ill

Ansh Part

Anubhav Experience

Anubhuti Perception, apprehension, experience

Anushthan Rite, ceremony

Apana vayu The *prana* that moves navel downwards, regulating the Excretory functions in general

Aparigraha Non collection in thought and deed

Aradhna Worship, propitiation, adoration

Artha Attainment of riches or worldly prosperity, regarded as one of the four ends of human existence

Arti Prayer

Asabhya Uncivilised

Asan A body posture typically associated with the practice of *yog*

Ashram Hermitage

Ashrit Dependent

Ashtang Yog Eight-limbed *yog*

Asmita Ego

Asteya Non stealing in action and thought

Asthir Unstable

Asthirta Instability

Asur/Asuric Negative force

Atma Soul, Spirit

Atmic Spiritual

Avdhoot A realised soul

Avidya Ignorance

Avtar Incarnation

Ayurveda Ancient Indian science of life

Bandhan Tie, boundation

Beej mantras The essence of a *mantra* in the form of sound

Bhaav/ Bhavna	Feeling, emotion
Bhakti	Devotion
Bhasm	Ash
Bhavishya vani	Prophecy
Bhikshu	The path to lowering the ego
Bhog	Pleasure
Bhoot	Lower being, ghost
Bhram	Illusion
Bhramit	Under an illusion
Bhrasht	Corrupt
Bhulok	Dimension of existence of humans
Bhutaal	The lower dimension
Bhuvahlok	The dimension above the *Bhulok*
Bindi	A stick-on put on forehead
Bindu	A *Sanskrit* term meaning "point" or "dot"
Brahm muhurat	Early morning time
Brahma	Creator
Brahmacharya	Celibacy, also, life of a student
Brahmand	Creation as a whole, egg of *Brahma*
Brahmin	Scholar
Buddhi	Intellect
Chakra	Whirling centre of energy perceived with highly developed senses
Chandra	Moon
Charpai	A cot
Cheerharan	An episode from *Mahabharat* where an attempt was made to derobe *Draupadi*, the queen of *Pandavas*
Chhand	Prose
Chhavi	Hue, splendour, brilliance
Chitta	The individual mind
Dakshina	A gift or offering made to the teacher/ priest upon completion of education/ ceremony
Danav	Demon
Darshan	Vision
Dasmaha-vidyas	Advanced practices in *Tantra*
Dev/Devta	Celestial beings, gods
Devi	Goddess
Devic shakti	Positive force
Dhan	Wealth
Dharana	One pointed focus
Dharma	The right path
Dhoopbatti	Incense stick
Dhwani	Sound
Dhyan	Internalised awareness at one point of the entire creation, often misunderstood as concentration
Diwali	Festival of lights
Diya	Lamp
Door-drishiti	Far sightedness, clairvoyance
Dosha	Literally means faults/contaminants, in *Ayurveda* refers to the 3 humors of the human body
Drishti	Sight
Droh	Deception, breach of trust, treachery
Dwaparyug	The third *yug* in which only two legs of *dharma* remain as against four in *Satyug*
Dwar	Gateway
Ek	One

Ekant	Solitude
Gada	Mace
Gaumukh	Source of *Ganga*
Gauseva	Service to the cow
Gayatri	Mother Goddess
Ghat	River bank
Ghiya	Bottle gourd
Ghor	Grave
Gita	Book of knowledge and code of conduct
Golgappas	Indian savoury dish
Granth	Scripture
Granthi	Etheric knot
Grihastha	Householder, Second stage of a human life
Gulab jamun	Indian sweet
Guru	Energy without which evolution is impossible
Guru kripa	Grace of *Guru*
Gurudwaras	*Sikh* place of worship
Gyan	Knowledge experiences
Gyanendriyas	Sense organs
Gyani	Realised soul
Havan	An interaction with the gods through the medium of fire
Hinsa	Violence in thought or action
Holi	Festival of colours
Iccha mrityu	Death by will
Iccha shakti	Will power
Indri/ indriyas	Senses of perception
Isht dev	A form of Divine consciousness to which you devote yourself
Ishwar pranidhan	Submission to Divine Will
Jaap	Repetitive chanting of *mantras*
Jagriti	Awakening
Jal	Water
Jallandhar bandh	Chin lock
Janalok	Higher dimension
Janam	Birth
Janani	Mother
Jeev-jantus	Living beings
Jeevatma	The soul that has manifested itself in a form
Ji	A suffix added to the name or title of a person as a mark of respect
Jyoti	Light
Jyotirlinga	Specific locations on earth with high concentration of energy
Kailash Mansarovar	The manifested earthly abode of Lord *Shiv*
Kaliyug	The last phase of creation marked by rise in *adharma*
Kama	Carnal desire; desire for sensual gratification considered as one of the four ends of human life
Kapalbhati	A hyper *pranayam*
Kapha	The water humor, according to *Ayurveda*
Karma	Action in thought or deed
Karmendriyas	Motor organs
Karya	Work

Karyakshetra	Field of work
Kathas	Tales and stories
Katora	Capacity, Vessel
Kevalya	Detachment of soul from matter, final emancipation
Kinnar	Neuter
Krishna	Incarnation of Lord *Vishnu*
Kriya	Practice
Kriyasheel	Active
Kshamta	Capacity
Kshatriya	Warrior, administrator
Kumbh mela	A spiritual assembly held every four years at the locations where divine nectar fell from the *kumbh* (pot) in the contest between *devs* and *asurs* (*Samudra manthan*)
Kumbhak	Natural cessation of breath
Kundalini	Force of the Mother Goddess
Ladoo	Indian sweet
Lakshan	Sign, Trait
Langar	Charity meal
Lathi	Wooden stick
Lok	Dimensions of existence
Maala	Rosary
Mahabharat	An epic written around four thousand years back
Mahakaal	A form of Lord *Shiv*
Mahalok	Higher dimension
Mahapralay	The great flood marking the end of one cycle of four *yugs*
Mahapranas	The five major *pranas* that govern various body functions
Maharishi	A higher dimension of a *rishi*
Mahatma	Evolved soul
Mahayugs	One cycle of four *yugs- Satyug, Dwaparyug, Tretayug and Kaliyug, vedic* measure of time
Mahesh	Lord *Shiv*
Mahima	Greatness
Makar Sankranti	The day when sun enters the zodiac of Capricorn
Manav	Man
Mandi	Market
Mandir	Temple
Manipoorak	Energy centre at the level of navel
Mann	Will, wish, desire
Mantra	Codified energy in the form of sound
Marg darshan	Guiding on the right path
Maryada	The content or outline of intrinsic moral law
Masala	Spice
Masjid	Mosque
Mata	Mother
Maya	Prime *shakti* of Lord *Vishnu* that binds us to the physical world
Meru	Central bead of the *maala*
Moh	Attraction
Moksha	Salvation
Mool bandh	Perineum lock
Mooladhar	Energy centre at the perineum, base of spine

Moolsthan	Location of *Mooladhar*
Mrityu	Death
Mudra	Posture in yoga to manipulate *prana*
Mukt	Liberated
Muni	Ascetic
Murti	Idol
Naag	A generic term for the serpent family
Nadi	Channel in the etheric body
Namaz	*Islamic* prayer
Nark	Hell
Nashwar	Perishable, transitory, transient
Nimn	Low
Niradar	Disrespect
Nirantar	Continuous, constant
Nishkaam	Without attachment
Nishkriya	Inactive
Niyam	Discipline
Ojas	Radiance related to celibacy
Oorja	Energy
Paap	Sin
Paath	Lesson
Palayan	Retreat
Pandit	A learned person
Param shakti	Supreme energy
Paramatma	Supreme Consciousness
Parampara	Tradition
Paramtattva	Supreme element
Partattva	Element beyond the five elements
Parvati	*Mata Shakti*, consort of Lord *Shiv*
Parvishay	Ultimate subject
Pataal	Lower dimension
Patanjali Yogsutras	Treatise on *yog*, given by *Rishi Patanjali*
Pishach	Lower being
Pitta	Fire element in the body, one of the three humors of body according to *Ayurveda*
Poorna	Complete
Poorva nirdharit	Predetermined
Prachaar	Publicity
Pradakshina	Circumambulation
Pradhan	Foremost
Prakash	Light
Prakriti	Nature
Prana	Pure energy
Pranayam	Salutation to the *prana*
Pratyahar	Withdrawal of the senses
Pravritti	Individual traits and nature
Prayog	Practice
Pret	Lower being
Prithvi	Earth
Puja	Worship
Punya	Virtuous/good deed
Puranas	Ancient text
Purush	The soul
Purushottam	The greatest among men
Pushp	Flower
Rajas	The second of the three constituent

	qualities of all material substances, the cause for great activity
Rakshas	Demon
Ram	Incarnation of Lord *Vishnu*; a power *mantra*
Rasataal	The lower dimension
Rashi	Zodiac
Rig veda	The first *veda*
Rishi	Sage
Rishi Patanjali	Incarnation of *Sheshnag*
Rog	Pain/disease
Roop	Form/appearance
Roti	Indian bread
Sadhak	Practitioner of spiritual sciences
Sadhna	Spiritual practice
Sadhu	Someone who is in search of *siddhis* (divine powers) through the path of penance
Sadhya	Object of *sadhna*
Sadmarg	Correct path
Sahastrar chakra	An energy centre developed only in evolved beings
Saiyam	Control
Sakshat	In a bodily form; in front of your eyes
Sakshatkar	Realisation, perception
Sam veda	The third of the four *vedas*
Samadhi	One with divinity, complete knowledge of creation and creator
Samana vayu	The balancing *vayu* in the body
Samavesh	Sum total
Samooh	Group
Samvad	Dialogue
Sanatan Kriya	*Ashtang Yog* in its unadulterated form assilimilated into a six-step practice
Sanchalak	Controller
Sanchalan	Control
Sandhya	Powerful time of the day when transition of energy happens
Sanidhya	Cover of *Guru*
Sankalp	Vow
Santosh	Contentment, satisfaction
Sanyas	Renunciation, the fourth stage of human life.
Sanyasi	A renunciate
Saptarishis	The seven sages
Sarvocch	Highest
Satvic	Dominant in *sattva*; lightest
Satya	Truth
Satyalok	The dimension of absolute truth
Satyug	The first *yug* when dharma is at its peak
Saundarya Lahiri	A famous literary work by *Adi Shankaracharya*
Seva	Service
Shaastras	Scriptures
Shahi snan	Royal bath
Shakti	Consort of Lord *Shiv*, responsible for transformation
Shakti	Pure energy responsible for transformation, force, power
Shaktipath	Transference of energy from the *Guru* to *shishya*

Shaktipeeth	The specific location on Earth with high concentration of energy
Shamshan	Cremation ground
Shankh	Conch
Shant	Peaceful, stable
Shareer	Body
Shashank	Rabbit
Shashwat	Eternal
Shastra	Weapon
Shauch	Cleanliness
Shirshasan	Head stand
Shishya	A seeker, who has the ability to evolve
Shiv	Transformer
Shiv samhita	Ancient Indian text
Shivir	Camp
Shivratri	One of the four most powerful nights in the year for a spiritual aspirant
Shloka	*Sanskrit* verse
Shreni	Level, status, rank
Shunya	Nothingness, which encompasses completeness
Siddhasan	Accomplished pose for meditation
Siddhi	Spiritual power
Smaran	To remember
Snan	Bath
Sthapna	Establishment
Sthir/ Sthirta	Still/ stillness
Sthit	Situated
Sthiti	State, situation, condition
Sthool	Physical
Stotra	A hymn
Sukra	The essential body fluid that provides lubrication in the body
Sukshma	Subtle
Supatra	A deserving candidate
Sur	Positive forces
Surya	Sun
Sushumna nadi	One of the main channels in the etheric body through which the *Kundalini* rises
Svahlok	The third dimension, the level of existence of *devs* , also known as *Bhoglok*
Swadhisthan chakra	Energy centre at the level of reproductive organs
Swadhyay	Self study
Swami	A title given as a mark of respect
Swarglok	**See** Svahlok
Swaroop	True form
Tamas/ Tamsic	Sleep; lethargy; darkness (of the inner world)
Tamasha	Drama
Tantra	Ancient science of expansion and liberation
Tapa/Tapas	Heating of the body for self-purification
Tapalok	Dimension of *tapasvis*
Tapasvi	One practicing penance (masculine)
Tapasvini	One practicing penance (feminine)
Tattva	Element
Tattva Shuddhi	Elemental Purification
Teerth sthan	Place of pilgrimage
Tej	Glow

Tejomaya	Radiant
Totka	Ritual practice to ward off evil or to attain a specific goal
Tretayug	The second *yug* in which three legs of dharma remain as against four in *Satyug*
Tridev	Trinity
Tridosha	The three humors – *vata*, *pitta*, *kapha*
Uccharan	Pronunciation
Udana vayu	Upward rising *vayu* in the upper parts of the body
Uddhaar	Upliftment
Udyan bandh	Abdominal lock
Upanishad	Ancient text
Upasana	Worship
Upay	Solution
Uttarayan	Northward movement of the sun
Vaak shakti	Ability to manifest the spoken into the physical
Vaham	Superstition
Vaibhav	Affluence
Vairagi	A person in a state of complete detachment
Vairagya	Detachment
Vakya	Sentence/statement
Vani	Speech, voice, sound
Vanprastha	Hermit, the third stage of human life
Vardan	Boon
Vasna	Wish, desire, inclination, expectation
Vata	Air element in the body, one of the three humors (*doshas*)
Vayana vayu	The reserve force in the body
Vayu	Air element
Vedas	Supreme *gyan*
Vidya	*Gyan*, knowledge, science, knowledge-technique
Vikriti	Against nature
Vishnu	Preserver
Vishuddhi chakra	Energy centre located in Adam's apple area
Vritti	Action tendency
Yagya	Fire sacrifice
Yajur veda	The second of the four *vedas*
Yaksh	The guardians of the *devs*
Yam	Code of conduct as given in *Patanjali Yogsutras*
Yantras	Energy codified in a diagram
Yash	Fame
Yodhas	Warriors
Yog	A union with the self
Yogi	Someone who is in union with creation
Yoni	Dimension of existence
Yug	*Vedic* measure of time

SOME CHARACTERS AND PLACES

Adi Shankaracharya – A renowned philosopher, he consolidated the doctrine of *Advaita Vedanta*. He advocated leading a monastic way of life as stated in the *upanishads* and *Brahma Sutra*.

Agastya Muni – Born to Gods, *Mitra* and *Varuna*, he was a revered sage in the *vedic* period, who is also the author of the *Agastya Samhita*.

Anusuiya – A pious lady, she was the chaste wife of Sage *Atri* and mother of Sage *Dattatreya*, Sage *Duryasa* and *Chandraatri*.

Arjun – The third of *pandav* brothers, the greatest archer, who received the *gyan* of *Gita* from Lord Krishna Himself in the great war of *Mahabharat*.

Asur Mali – Mali was the son of the powerful *rakshas Sukesa*, an ardent devotee of Lord *Shiv*.

Bali – In *Ramayan*, the *vanara Bali*, king of *Kishkindha*, a son of *Indra* and the elder brother of *Sugriva*, was killed by Ram, an *avtar* of Lord *Vishnu*.

Bhasmasur – A devotee of Lord *Shiv*, *Bhasmasur* was an *asur* who was granted the power to burn and turn anyone into ash if he touched their head with his hands.

Bhattacharya – *Kumarila Bhatta*, a philosopher and *Mimamsa* scholar from Assam, India. He was a staunch believer of supreme validity of *vedas* and is famous for many of his seminal theses on *Mimamsa*, such as *Mimamsasloka-varttika*.

Bhishma – He was the eighth son of the *Kuru* King *Shantanu* and grand uncle to both *Pandavas* and *Kauravas*.

Dattatreya – An embodiment of the trinity - *Brahma*, *Vishnu* and *Shiv* in a human form. The name when broken down, means: '*Datta*' (meaning given) and '*Atreya*' referring to the sage *Atri*, his physical father. *Dattatreya* is credited as the author of the *Tripura Rahasya* given to *Parshurama*, a treatise on *Advaita Vedanta*.

Draupadi – In the *Mahabharat*, *Draupadi* is the daughter of King *Drupada* of *Panchala* and wife of the five *Pandavas*.

Duryodhan – The chief antagonist in the *Mahabharat*, he was the first born of the hundred sons born to King *Dhritarashtra* and Queen *Gandhari*.

Gandhari – Mother to a hundred sons (*Kauravas*) and one daughter, she was the incarnation of the Goddess of Intelligence, *Mati*. She was married to King *Dhritarashtra* who was blind by birth and decided to share the pain of her husband by blindfolding herself throughout her married life.

Guru Gobind Singh – A warrior, poet and philosopher, he was the tenth of the ten *Sikh Gurus*.

Hanuman – The energy corresponding to the *Rudra* aspect of Lord *Shiv*, manifested on earth at the time of *Ramayan* as an ardent devotee of Lord *Ram*.

Janmajeya – *Kuru* king, who succeeded his father, *Parikshit*, to the throne of *Hastinapur*. He was the grandson of *Abhimanyu* and the great-grandson of *Arjun*, the valiant warrior hero of the *Mahabharat*.

***Mahakaleshwar* Temple** – Located in the city of *Ujjain*, in Madhya Pradesh, it is one of the twelve *Jyotirlingas*, said to be sacred abodes of Lord *Shiv*.

Meera – Or Meera Bai, was a *Rajput* princess, popular mystic poet and devotee of Lord *Krishna*.

Meghnath – Son of the king of *Lanka*, Ravan.

Mohini – The enchantress, she is the only female *avtar* of Lord *Vishnu*.

Narsingh – An incarnation of Lord *Vishnu*, half

man- half lion, who killed the demon king *Hiranyakashyap*.

Panj Pyare **–** Name given to the five *Sikh* men by *Guru Gobind Singh* at *Anandpur Sahib* in1699, after they offered their lives for the cause of *Guru*.

Parikshit – *Kuru* king, who succeeded *Yudhishtir* to the throne of *Hastinapur* in the great epic *Mahabharat*.

Parshuram **–** A warrior-*rishi,* pupil of Lord *Shiv*, he is the sixth *avtar* of Lord *Vishnu*.

Prahlad **–** Born to the evil King *Hiranyakashyap,* he has been mentioned in the *puranas* as a devout devotee of Lord *Vishnu*.

Radha **–** Incarnation of Goddess *Lakshmi*, she is Lord *Krishna's* beloved and is also revered as the Supreme Goddess.

Ramakrishna Paramhansa **–** A famous saint in the 19th century, his school of thought led to the founding of Ramakrishna Mission by his disciple *Swami Vivekananda*.

Ramana Maharishi **–** Born in 1879 in South India, he was known as one of the outstanding Indian *Gurus* of modern times.

Ravan **–** The demon king of Lanka, given the boon of ten heads by *Brahma*. Prime devotee of Lord *Shiv*, *Ravan* abducted Goddess *Sita*, wife of Lord *Ram,* in the *Ramayan*.

Rishi Vishwamitra **–** A valiant warrior king in ancient India, he is also one of the most respected sages who has been mentioned in the *Puranas* to be one of 24 *rishis* who understood and wielded the power of the *Gayatri Mantra*.

Sandeepan Rishi **–** *Rishi* of Ujjain, Madhya Pradesh, India. *Guru* of Lord *Krishna*. While staying as students at the residence of *Sandeepan Rishi*, the two brothers—*Krishna* and *Balrama*—and their friend, *Sudama*, mastered every single lesson, although only having been instructed in each once.

Satyanand Paramhansa **–** Disciple of *Swami Shivananda Saraswati* who founded the Bihar School of Yoga at *Munger,* Bihar, India and authored many volumes on *yog*.

Shivanand **–** An accomplished *yogi* and Guru of *Satyanand Paramhansa*.

Shravan Kumar **–** In *Ramayan he was* known for extreme devotion to his blind and aged parents, and who succumbed to the wound caused by an arrow hit by King *Dasaratha*.

Takshak – the *naga* king, who avenged the wrongs committed by *Pandavas* on his race, by poisoning and slaying their grandson, *Parikshit*.

***Vaishno Devi* –** She is the manifestation of the Mother Goddess. *Vaishno Devi* Shrine is located at the *Trikuta* Mountains, at an altitude of 5300 feet, within the Indian state of Jammu and Kashmir.

***Vaishya, Shudra, Kshatriya and Brahmin* –** Division of society into four groups (*varnas)* depending the roles taken up by the members voluntarily- *Brahmin* (priest involved in intellectual activities), *Kshatriya* (king or warrior involved in administration, defense and warfare), *Vaishya* (merchant or farmer involved in economics and animal rearing), *Shudra* (artisans, agriculturists and those engaged in services).

***Varaha* –** An incarnation of Lord *Vishnu* in the form of a boar, when the demon *Hiranyaksha* stole the earth (personified as the Goddess *Bhudevi*) and hid her in the primordial waters, Lord *Vishnu* appeared as *Varaha* to rescue her. *Varaha* slew the demon and retrieved the Earth from the ocean, lifting it on his tusks, and restored *Bhudevi* to her place in the universe.

***Yudhishtir* –** the eldest of *pandav* brothers, king of *Indraprastha*, son of *dharmraj*, well known for his just and moral nature.

ABOUT THE AUTHOR

Yogi Ashwini is adept in the ancient sciences of *Yog*, *Tantra*, Spiritual Healing, *Mantra* Chanting, Science of *Havans*, Past-Life Visitation, *Vedic* Martial Arts and the Art of Mace. He speaks many languages fluently, and is widely travelled. With an Honours degree in Economics, a Master's in Management and a successful business, he is the author of many global best-sellers on ancient *vedic* sciences, and an eminent writer for leading newspapers, journals and magazines internationally. He is an acclaimed speaker having been invited to prestigious forums such as Oxford University, UK and Indian Institute of Management, Bangalore and popular talk shows to share his thoughts and opinions on the sciences of nature and being. He is also the honorary editor of the monthly spiritual magazine *'The Inner World'* and the Guiding Light of Dhyan Foundation.

After studying the being for decades, spending years in silence and having interacted with the Himalayan masters, *Yogi Ashwini* propounded the *Sanatan Kriya*, an assimilation of the eight limbs of *Ashtang Yog*, as given by *Sage Patanjali* 4500 years back, without any dilutions and modifications, documented in the book *'Sanatan Kriya: Essence of Yog'* which is a practical step-by-step guide to the journey beyond and comes with a CD.. He unravels the deep and sublime aspects of ancient Indian sciences in a scientific and logical manner in the book, *'Thoughts...of the Inner World'*, in a simple language for the understanding of a layman. *'Sanatan Kriya - 51 Miracles and a Haunting'* documents the experiences of *sadhaks* as narrated by them, with medical records as provided by them. His two decades of pioneering research on anti-ageing, published in the book *'Sanatan Kriya: The Ageless Dimension'*, has found validation in recent studies by certain Western Universities. The book is acclaimed as a thesis on anti-ageing by leading doctors across the country.

Having dispelled many popular myths about *yog* and having changed the lives of countless people from all walks of life, *Yogi Ashwini* is on a mission: to make people experience the real power of *yog*, in accordance with the *Guru-shishya parampara*.

The master believes that every being is unique and it is an individual journey and therefore *yog* cannot be taught as a mass exercise. He maintains one-to-one interaction with all his students worldwide and accepts nothing from his *shishyas*. Thousands have benefited physically, emotionally, mentally and spiritually from the practice of *Sanatan Kriya*, which is taught across the globe free of cost.

Yogi Ashwini insists upon charity and service as the root of the *vedic* sciences and culture. In fact, he dedicates most part of his life to service of mankind – running schools for the underprivileged (*Anand Vidyalayas*), protecting wildlife and looking after injured animals ('Save a Cow' and 'Feed a Dog'), countrywide daily food distribution camps (*Langars*), sponsoring higher education of the poor and the blind, generating employment for the under-privileged, providing medical help to humans and animals alike, to name a few.

For more, visit www.dhyanfoundation.com

Please Note: No claims of causing any miracles to happen or of miracle cures have been made by the author or the publisher.

MORE BOOKS BY THE AUTHOR

SANATAN KRIYA : ESSENCE OF YOG

ISBN : 978-81-904506-0-7

THOUGHTS...OF THE INNER WORLD

ISBN : 978-81-904506-1-4

SANATAN KRIYA: 51 MIRACLES AND A HAUNTING

ISBN : 978-81-904506-4-5

SANATAN KRIYA: THE AGELESS DIMENSION

ISBN : 978-81-904506-6-9

Other Dhyan Foundation Publications:

Doomsday Y? Warning of the Vedic Rishis to Mankind

ISBN : 978-81-904506-8-3

The Inner World

A monthly spiritual glossy newspaper that propagates healthy, natural way of living, covering topics like *Yog, Ayurveda,* Health and Beauty, and other spiritual sciences. For more visit, www.theinnerworld.org